OXFORD MONOGRAPHS ON MUSIC

The Sound of Medieval Song

The Sound of Medieval Song

Ornamentation and Vocal Style
according to the Treatises

TIMOTHY J. McGEE

Latin translations by
RANDALL A. ROSENFELD

CLARENDON PRESS · OXFORD
1998

Oxford University Press, Great Clarendon Street, Oxford OX 2 6DP

Oxford New York

Athens Auckland Bangkok Bogota Bombay Buenos Aires
Calcutta Cape Town Dar es Salaam Delhi Florence Hong Kong Istanbul
Karachi Kuala Lumpur Madras Madrid Melbourne Mexico City
Nairobi Paris Singapore Taipei Tokyo Toronto Warsaw

and associated companies in
Berlin Ibadan

Oxford is a trade mark of Oxford University Press

Published in the United States
by Oxford University Press Inc., New York

British Library Cataloguing in Publication Data
Data available

Library of Congress Cataloging in Publication Data
Data available

ISBN 0–19–816619–2

1 3 5 7 9 10 8 6 4 2

Typeset by Cambrian Typesetters, Frimley, Surrey
Printed in Great Britain
on acid-free paper by
Biddles Ltd.,
Guildford & King's Lynn

This book is dedicated to

Eugene Joseph Leahy

Preface

THE motivation behind my pursuit of this topic and its eventual shape came from several different quarters and grew over a period of approximately twenty years. As a performer of early music in the 1970s I was aware of the importance of adding ornamentation to all early music, but outside Ernst Ferand's *Die Improvisation in der Musik*, and a few minor studies, no information was available. Finally, I came across Carol MacClintock's translation of a portion of Jerome of Moravia's *De musica*, and was intrigued by what I found there. MacClintock's translation only partially cleared up the confusing statements by Jerome, but at least that was a good starting-place for the information I needed. Later I attempted to interpret Jerome's instructions and relate them to practical suggestions, and added this to my performance instructions in *Medieval Instrumental Dances*. At that point Roland Jackson encouraged me to explore Jerome more fully as well as other medieval theoretical writings, with a view to publication in his journal *Performance Practice Review*. By coincidence, my colleague Andrew Hughes was also in need of some of Jerome's information, and so the two of us enlisted the aid of Ann Kuzdale, at that time a doctoral student in medieval history, who had a good grasp of medieval Latin. The three of us set out to work on a translation of Jerome with commentary. (The resultant monograph is forthcoming.)

In the 1992 school year it became apparent that there was enough material to make an interesting graduate seminar, and the students in that class were very helpful in bringing new sources to my attention and suggesting interpretations of many of the puzzling passages. A paper on the subject, read at the annual meeting of the American Musicological Society in Pittsburgh in 1992, brought forth suggestions and questions from various members of the audience, which again assisted my investigation.

As the work progressed it became apparent that I could not restrict my examination so narrowly to the ornaments themselves. Some of the ornaments described by the theorists went past the mere addition of notes: they suggested vocal nuances and sound production that is no longer in practice and an origin for the ornaments that was a part of the vocal style itself. In order to put the information on ornaments in its proper perspective *vis-à-vis* the sound that would result from their employment, it would be necessary to widen my study to include instructions about articulation, expression, and vocal practices, and ultimately to concern myself with the actual vocal sounds. A paper on that subject delivered at the British Medieval and Renaissance Music Conference in Glasgow in 1994 resulted in additional helpful comments and suggested new sources of information and paths to explore.

It was never my intention for this study to be exhaustive in terms of all theoretical writings. Even if such an objective would now be in reach, given the wonders of modern data processing, the results would not necessarily be a substantial improvement. There is no doubt that in the future others will find a phrase here or a paragraph there that will clarify or magnify what is reported in this study, but for the most part I believe that what I have found is both the bulk of the information available and the essence of the idea of medieval ornamentation and singing style. In gathering this material I have read through well over 150 treatises, and included excerpts from forty-six of them. Many more could have been included, if duplication would have added to the understanding of any topic, but when blessed with more than one statement on a particular subject I have chosen to present what appears to me to be the clearest.

As a final remark I should like to point out that, although I have included some practical examples in order to support and amplify the theoretical statements, this book is not intended to be a manual of practical application. What is intended here is a scholarly study of the available information about how medieval music actually sounded. The primary goal of this book is the presentation to the scholarly world of an aspect of medieval music that is often ignored because it cannot be seen on the page. Although some scholars of medieval music admit that ornamentation was applied to the music, neither the details of the ornamentation nor the extent to which it was employed have been understood, and the idea that medieval vocal style was radically different from modern Western practices has been only the speculation of a few. The result is that the music is often studied and taught as if all that was heard—or intended to be heard—was what was on the page. It is my hope that as a result of this exposition, the study of medieval music will take on a more lively and flexible aspect.

I do not deny that serious practical implications follow from this material. There is no doubt that as a result of the information presented here we must adjust our idea of how medieval music should be performed. Although several excellent ensembles have been ornamenting medieval music for some time, following some of the theoretical information included here, most have not. The modern classically trained voice cannot be used as the model for vocal sound, and the practice of performing exactly what is on the page—no matter how beautifully it is done—is simply incorrect as a reconstruction of the sounds of the past. Modern ensembles wishing to recreate medieval music as closely as possible to the expectations of the Middle Ages must now learn a new vocal style and revise their performance practices. For performers anxious to translate the information given here into practice, I intend to publish a separate volume directed at the practical level.

The original Latin for all quoted passages appears in the Appendix; missing words have been added in angle brackets. I have placed the theorists in alphabetical order by first name, and numbered the translations to correspond with the editions of the Latin texts. For the convenience of the reader, these excerpts are necessarily printed here in the order in which they appear in the treatises. Line, paragraph, or page numbers are supplied with the Latin excerpts in order to facilitate cross-reference with the modern edition of the treatises. I have also supplied sources of modern editions of the works, and any available published English translations. At the end of each Latin passage will be found the page in this book where the translation appears.

All translations used in this book, with a single exception, have been done by Randall A. Rosenfeld, working directly from the published editions of the Latin. Clarificatory material appearing in square brackets is editorial.

T.J.M.

Acknowledgements

It is my pleasure as well as my duty to acknowledge those who have assisted me in this project. My largest debt is to Ann Kuzdale who provided me with draft translations of more than half of the quotes used here, and who guided me to several sources I would not have found.

My thanks are also due to Katherine Hill, who at my request studied Eastern Mediterranean vocal technique so that we could experiment with vocal style. Her innate musical sense has helped me to understand the subject on a practical level.

I gratefully acknowledge assistance of various kinds from the following: Charles Atkinson, Andrea Budgey, Paul Boncella, Thomas Brothers, Judith Cohen, Thomas Connolly, James Grier, Andrew Hughes, Roland Jackson, Rosanne King, Andrea Retteghy McGee, Darach McGee, Robert Nosow, Brian Power, George Rigg, Randall Rosenfeld, Ingrid Rowland, Norma Vascotto, The University of Toronto, and The Villa I Tatti.

Bonnie J. Blackburn served capably as copy-editor but her contribution went far beyond that; I am indebted to her and to Leofranc Holford-Strevens for their assistance in improving the quality of this book in a number of ways.

The following have granted permission to reproducee published material and photographs of manuscripts: Bryan Gillingham; James Grier; Charles W. Warren; Hänssler-Verlag; the Master and Fellows of Corpus Christie College, Cambridge; Bibliothèque Municipale, Laon; Stiftsbibliothek, Benediktiner-kloster, Einsiedeln; Department of Manuscripts, The British Library; The Italian Ministero per i Beni Culturali ed Ambientali; Bibliothèque Nationale de France; The University of Chicago Press; Oxford University Press; *The New Grove Dictionary of Music and Musicians*, edited by Stanley Sadie, in twenty volumes, 1980, Macmillan Publishers Limited, London.

Contents

List of Illustrations

(between pp. 108 and 109)

Maps

List of Tables

List of Musical Examples

Abbreviations

BNF	Bibliothèque Nationale de France
CMM	Corpus mensurabilis musicae
Coussemaker, *Scriptores*	Edmund de Coussemaker, *Scriptores de musica medii aevi*, 4 vols. (Paris, 1864; repr. Hildesheim, 1963)
CSM	Corpus scriptorum de musica
EG	*Études grégoriennes*
Gerbert, *Scriptores*	Martin Gerbert, *Scriptores ecclesiastici de musica sacra potissimum*, 3 vols. (St Blasien, 1784; repr. Hildesheim, 1963).
JAMS	*Journal of the American Musicological Society*
LU	*The Liber Usualis* (Tournai, 1934)
MD	*Musica disciplina*
MGG	*Die Musik in Geschichte und Gegenwart*, 17 vols. (Kassel and Basle, 1949–86).
MQ	*Musical Quarterly*
MSD	Musicological Studies and Documents
New Grove	*The New Grove Dictionary of Music and Musicians*, ed. Stanley Sadie, 20 vols. (London, 1980)

Introduction

ALL musicians understand that for much of the repertory there is a substantial difference between music as it appears on a page and as it sounds in performance.[1] Regardless of how detailed the notation, in all repertories there is always something a performer must add in order to bring a composition to life, the amount and the nature of the additions varying according to the repertory. For the music of the Middle Ages the gap between the written form and the performed version is substantial. The problem of conceptualizing the sound of medieval music is compounded for the modern scholar by three elements: the early notation system that is still only partially understood; a complex and involved tradition of extemporized ornamentation; and a vocal style that is basically different from the one currently employed for art music.

My original intention was to write only about ornamentation, but it became clear very early on that it was not possible to discuss the ornaments without an understanding of the vocal sound and style of the period. Indeed, for the most part the two subjects are inseparable, and therefore I shall begin my study with instructions for singing. As will be seen in the following chapters, what we today would call 'ornaments' were in reality an integral part of the medieval concept of musical line. They were a part of the vocal technique and are indistinguishable from the other sounds when the music is performed with the appropriate vocal quality: the entire early vocal style *itself* is ornamental. As a result, medieval music takes on a sound image substantially different from Western art music of later centuries. To understand what follows, therefore, the reader should think of the two elements—vocal technique and ornamentation—as basically the same. All discussions of ornaments below imply performance with the vocal style and technique discussed in Chapter 2.

There is little question that ornamentation was a part of musical performance of the Middle Ages. But although most musicologists agree on this rather general statement, there has been little understanding of the extent or the nature of much of that ornamentation. The subject has received some attention from scholars over the years both directly and indirectly, but most discussions are

---

[1] For a thoughtful and perceptive discussion of this point see Thomas Binkley, 'The Work is not the Performance', in Tess Knighton and David Fallows (eds.), *Companion to Medieval and Renaissance Music* (New York, 1992), 36–43.

limited to relatively short time periods or to specific ornaments or ornamental practices.[2] Whereas the current scholarly material on Baroque ornamentation is highly refined, and that on the Renaissance is at least available in overview with a few specific studies, for the late Middle Ages there really is no secondary source available for an overall glimpse of the subject or even a study of many of the areas. The present work is intended to introduce the breadth of the subject through an analysis of many of the details to be found in the theoretical sources from the period.

The medieval attitude towards musical composition that allowed some of the details to remain flexible can be seen in the existence of variant readings of many works from that era; notes could be added, subtracted, or changed, and rhythms could be adjusted or varied. The statements by theorists, many of them collected here, affirm this attitude. As an illustration of this aspect of medieval music, Ex. 1.1 shows the basic lines of the *Quem quaeritis* Easter Resurrection dialogue from three twelfth-century sources. There is sufficient similarity in the melodic curves to indicate that all three are versions of a basic common melody, although they differ from one another in small details.[3] Another possible interpretation of these variants is that they could be the result of errors in transmission—and that is certainly a possibility—but given the quantity of chants with variant readings from manuscript to manuscript, a conclusion more in keeping with the spirit of the late Middle Ages is that, in the transmission of a chant from one locale to another, exact replication was not considered to be important.[4]

This kind of variation, evident in the written versions of chant and other repertories, would be further extended in actual performance by the addition of

---

[2] For example, ornamentation is discussed as an adjunct subject in Ernst T. Ferand, *Die Improvisation in der Musik* (Zurich, 1938). Barbara Thornton, 'Vokale und Gesangstechnik: Das Stimmideal der Aquitanischen Polyphonie', *Basler Jahrbuch für historische Musikpraxis*, 4 (1980), 133–50, studies vocal quality and vowel sounds necessary for singing the Aquitanian repertory. The study by Howard Mayer Brown, 'Improvised Ornamentation in the Fifteenth-Century Chanson', *Quadrivium*, 12 (1971), 235–58, is limited to only one century. And those by Charles W. Warren, 'Punctus organi and Cantus Coronatus in the Music of Dufay', in Allan W. Atlas (ed.), *Dufay Quincentenary Conference* (Brooklyn, 1976), 128–43; John Harutunian, 'A Comparison of the Oriscus in the Introits of the Manuscript Vatican Latin 5319 with its "Translations" in Those of the Manuscript Archivio di San Pietro F.22' (MA thesis, University of Pennsylvania, 1976); and Andreas Haug, 'Zur Interpretation der Liqueszenzneumen', *Archiv für Musikwissenschaft*, 50 (1993), 85–100, each discuss only a single ornament or ornament type. For an overview of the subject see Ernest T. Ferand, 'A History of Music Seen in the Light of Ornamentation', *International Musicological Society: Report of the Eighth Congress, New York 1961* (Kassel, 1961), i. 463–69.

[3] Approximately 500 manuscripts from all parts of Europe include the Easter dialogue; over eighty of these date from earlier than the year 1200, and all show minor variants similar to those in Ex. 1.1, from Utrecht, Saint-Maur, and Piacenza. For analysis of the variant transmissions see Timothy J. McGee, 'The Liturgical Origins and Early History of the *Quem Quaeritis* Dialogue' (Ph.D. diss., University of Pittsburgh, 1974), ch. 7.

[4] Theoretical statements supporting this general view and proposing reform are discussed in Ch. 6.

Ex. 1.1. Three versions of the *Quem quaeritis* Easter dialogue: (*a*) Utrecht, Rijksuniversiteit, MS 406 (from Utrecht); (*b*) Paris, BNF, lat. 12044 (from Saint-Maur); (*c*) Piacenza, Biblioteca Capitolare, MS 65 (from Piacenza)

spontaneous vocal ornaments, resulting in a unique version of the composition on each occasion. As will be demonstrated in the following chapters, the amount of leeway granted to (or taken by) a performer was such that the written versions of medieval music give only a pale impression of what was actually performed or heard. The inevitable conclusion is that the role of ornamentation in the Middle Ages was at least as strong as in the following periods; one might even argue that, because of the association of ornamentation with vocal technique, and the linear rather than vertical orientation of this repertory, it was far more essential.

It is incorrect to view the surviving written versions of much of the medieval repertory as dogmatic texts that were intended to be reproduced exactly as written. In performance each composition became a living creation precisely because the performer took on some of the role of a composer, adjusting each composition in a personal way. Many of the compositions preserved in manuscripts are either outlines to be filled in by the performer or records of an ornamental elaboration invented by a particular performer. Both types of texts could serve as guidelines for the next performance, but they were intended to be embellished and adjusted according to the talent of each singer.[5] I refer here mostly to soloists and solo music, but even for choral performance some of this is relevant—in teaching chants to the choir the *magister cantorum* would have added to and adjusted the melodies to some degree.

The first question that must be asked by anyone attempting to write a book such as this is that posed by an insightful anonymous reader in reaction to my original book proposal: 'What is ornamentation? Is it decoration of something already complete, is it part of the composition process, is it a feature of performance practice, is it a licence or a requirement?' The reader went on to point out that the concept of ornamentation of a fundamental structure was basic to the way in which medieval musicians thought about music.

My reply to the question is that ornamentation, as I address it here, is all of those things precisely *because* it was part of the basic medieval concept of music. Ornamentation was both the duty and privilege of every composer and soloist; it was the way in which a composer approached his art and the performer executed what was given; it was embodied in the vocal style of the period and undoubtedly in the instrumental style as well. If this seems to be a very broad definition, it is meant to be so as the only way I can reconcile the various freedoms and requirements of medieval music as explained in the many treatises.

---

[5] The theory that elaborate melodies are ornamentations of simpler versions that evolved through a process of oral transmission until finally being written down is discussed and criticized in Peter Jeffrey, *Re-Envisioning Past Musical Cultures: Ethnomusicology in the Study of Gregorian Chant* (Chicago, 1992), esp. 98–115.

At one point in my investigation of the subject I attempted to keep separate the theoretical remarks clearly aimed at composers from those addressed to performers, and I spent some time trying to classify the various treatises or sections on that basis. Eventually, however, it became clear that (as my reader noted) to the medieval mind there was no real separation between the basic goals of the two activities—composition and performance—and that the instructions were often similar for both audiences because they were intended to produce similar results: embellishment of a basic framework. Anonymous II, while discussing discant, speaks of composing and performing by improvisation as if they were not separate ideas (311).[6] This inherent relationship between composer and performer/composing and performing is behind Johannes Tinctoris' remark in his treatise *Liber de arte contrapuncti* (107), which demonstrates many similarities between written and improvised composition. Tinctoris points out that the difference between *res facta* counterpoint and counterpoint 'without qualification' was whether it was written or improvised. The general technique was much the same for both types although a significant difference did exist: for composed music all parts must obey the laws of concord, whereas for improvised counterpoint each part has to be consonant only with the tenor.[7]

Anon. II, 311. Here follows the discussion of discant. Since hidden knowledge benefits no one and quickly passes away, but when shared it is of much benefit and is greatly augmented, for that reason I intend to elucidate for our special friends, according to my ability, the art of knowing how to compose and perform improvised discant, which for a long time was a secret among certain experienced musicians.

Johannes Tinctoris, 107. Counterpoint, both simple and diminished, is made in two ways, that is, either in writing or in the mind. Counterpoint that is written out is usually called *res facta*. On the other hand, that which we achieve entirely in the mind we call counterpoint without qualification, and those who perform it are commonly said to sing on the book (*super librum*).

On first reflection it might seem difficult to apply the same concept to both activities; in fact they may even appear to be at odds with one another. One can easily imagine a composer applying some of the various techniques discussed below in order to elaborate a basic framework. But once that is done, would not

---

[6] This situation is discussed at length in Daniel Leech-Wilkinson, 'Written and Improvised Polyphony', in *Polyphonies de tradition orale: Actes du colloque de Royaumont—1990* (Paris, 1993), 171–82.

[7] It is not intended here to dismiss lightly this significant detail of composition. My point is that the basic goal, filling in a polyphonic outline, remained the same in both types of composition. For a detailed discussion of compositional practices including *res facta*, see Margaret Bent, '*Resfacta* and *Cantare Super Librum*', *JAMS* 36 (1983), 371–91; and Bonnie J. Blackburn, 'On Compositional Process in the Fifteenth Century', *JAMS* 40 (1987), 210–84.

Iam Chri-stus astra a-scen-de-rat, Re - ver-sus un-de ve-ne-rat,

Pa-tris fru - en-dum mu-ne - re San-ctum da-tu - rus Spi-ri-tum.

Ex. 1.2. *Jam Christus astra ascenderat*, Matins hymn for Whit Sunday in mode 1, verse 1 (*LU* 866)

a performer's ornamentation be an embellishment of something already embell-ished? Again I answer yes. Ornamentation took place on two levels: composers elaborated basic outlines, and performers (in many cases, the same person as the composer) added additional levels of embellishment to that, proceeding accord-ing to many of the same principles, although, as we shall see below, ornamenta-tion by the performer includes many more kinds of additions. Perhaps the issue will become somewhat clearer if I depart from large generalities and illustrate my idea with specific types of cases.

CASE 1. A composer decides to create a simple syllabic composition. The initial idea takes shape according to a basic musical outline—either a modal pattern (monophony), or modal pattern plus pre-existent material (polyphony). The composer will create a melodic shape that conforms to the dictates of the modal outlines (and in polyphony is guided also by the pre-existent tenor that was chosen for its adherence to those principles). That is to say that certain structural elements of his melody are determined by the mode itself (cadences, range, recit-ing tones, etc.), and in making a new melody the composer's creativity is restricted by requirements of the modal outline.[8] In Ex. 1.2 an asterisk marks the notes dictated by the requirements of the mode. Those notes not marked indi-cate the area of freedom left to the composer, although even within this freedom the range of the chosen mode must be observed (in this case, to keep the melody within the range of mode 1, the composer could not exceed the limits of *c* to *d'* for any significant period). The act of composition, therefore, can be thought of as an elaboration or a filling-in of the modal outline.

CASE 2. A performer is faced with this syllabic composition. The basic melodic line has been established by the composer, and the performer adds embellish-

---

[8] The extent to which modal principles governed early polyphony is still under discussion. See the recent contributions in Ursula Günther, Ludwig Finscher, and Jeffrey Dean (eds.), *Modality in the Music of the Fourteenth and Fifteenth Centuries/Modalität in der Musik des 14. und 15. Jahrhunderts* (Neuhausen–Stuttgart, 1996).

ments that include elaborating around the written notes and filling in the written intervals.

CASE 3. A composer decides to write an elaborate, melismatic composition, either monophonic or polyphonic (or to elaborate on the syllabic work done in Case 1). The elaboration of each of the notes takes the shape of those in Case 2—diminutions and filling in and around the notes of the metric structure, using notes of lesser value. Ex. 1.3 is a melismatic composition followed by two hypothetical levels of reduction: (*b*) is my suggestion of what a basic, syllabic version of this same melody might look like, further reduced to the modal requirements (the '***' marks).

CASE 4. A performer is to present a composition that has already been elaborated melismatically by the composer (Case 3). In this case most of the performer's additions would probably be of the type of ornament we call `graces' and vocal and pitch inflection.

The cases presented above are intentionally simple in order to illustrate my point, and except for a few rather specific types of musical forms, most medieval compositions include a mixture of various types of syllabic and melismatic writing. But the basic approaches to be taken by composer and performer are as above, to be applied according to the elements presented in any particular situation. To augment the statement of my perceptive reader: the concepts of elaboration and ornamentation were basic both to composition and performance;

Ex. 1.3. *Deriventur fontes tui foras*, Gradual for 20 July in mode 2 (*LU* 1562) with a hypothetical syllabic outline (* indicates modal requirements)

they were the way in which the composer created and the performer communicated.[9] At the level of actual practice, of course, the two activities took on somewhat different details, with the composer being far more involved in the specifics of modal and harmonic practices and having the much larger picture of the entire composition in mind. For the performer, a knowledge of the basic elements and rules of mode and harmony was also desirable (although it would seem that many simply learned by imitation; see the Arnulf excerpts in Ch. 2); this would be especially true in the cases where performers extemporized monophony and polyphony. But when dealing with music already composed, the performer worked on a much smaller scale, and the details of that activity involved the application not only of additional notes, but more basically of sound elements such as tone and pitch inflection—performance details that do not directly concern the composer.

Statements about the embellishment of music are included in the works of a number of theorists of the late Middle Ages, with remarks varying from a mere mention to some rather specific instructions on what to do and how to apply it. There is no standard vocabulary, either to describe the practices or to name the ornaments, a factor that sometimes causes confusion, although the general intention is usually not difficult to understand. The writers make it clear that embellishments of a variety of kinds are applied to both monophonic and polyphonic music in much the same manner. As a way of introducing the subject, as well as pointing out the inseparability of compositional and performance instructions, I quote a few paragraphs from Johannes de Garlandia.[10] In the first short paragraph (96:22) he touches on the techniques of augmentation, diminution, and pitch inflection as ways of enhancing a melody. In the last phrase he appears to be referring to the use of expression in the voice, over and above the addition of notes:

Johannes de Garlandia, 96:22. Ennoblement of a sound is the expansion or diminution of it by means of pride;[11] by expansion so that it may be perceived more easily; in magnitude so that it may be heard better; with invention (*fictione*)[12] so that it may be more attractive; and in performance so that the spirits may be refreshed.

Further on, during a discussion of how to add a quadruplum, he again advocates embellishing music (97:16), this time using the word 'colour' (*color*) to

---

[9] The two techniques—elaboration and ornamentation—are often inseparable and indistinguishable in the process described here.

[10] In his commentary on the treatise, Erich Reimer doubts that Garlandia wrote chapters 14–16—the source of all 'Garlandia' excerpts quoted in this book. For convenience, however, I shall refer to the author of these passages as Garlandia, since that is the only association known for the material.

[11] The last phrase, 'per modum superbiae', seems to refer generally to 'altering the melody'.

[12] The Latin word *fictione* could be translated as *musica ficta*, but during Garlandia's time that concept would more likely have been referred to as *falsa musica*. I am grateful to Thomas Brothers for this observation.

mean the addition of melodic embellishments. He says that adding 'colour' makes music more pleasing and more memorable.[13] He also allows for the inter-polation of musical quotations in the form of phrases from compositions, both vocal and instrumental, already known to the listener:

Johannes de Garlandia, 97:16. The third rule is to put colours in place of unfamiliar proportionate sounds [i.e. melodic phrases], for the more you colour it, the more the sound will be familiar, and if it is familiar, it will be pleasing. Or in place of any colour in the region put a familiar cantilena, phrase (*copula*), or section (*punctum*) or a des-cending or ascending instrumental phrase of some instrument, or a phrase from a *lai*.

From another statement Garlandia makes about 'colour', it is apparent that he has a very broad view of what that word represents (95:10). In his frame of refer-ence 'colour' is anything that is added to a composition to enhance it, including harmonic variation and repetition of a phrase as well as the addition of melodic embellishments and sound variation:

Johannes de Garlandia, 95:10. Colour is the beauty of sound or the object of hearing through which the ear receives pleasure. It is created in several ways: through well-ordered sound [i.e. selection of intervals]; through the embellishment of the sound; or by repetition of the same or a different melody (*vox*).

Elias Salomonis also touches on the ornamentation of polyphony in such a way that it would seem to have been a rather common practice. In the instruc-tions for four-part improvisation over a plainsong he encourages the rector first to assign each singer his part, and then to provide an ongoing critique, whisper-ing corrections into the ear of each singer, such as that they are singing too many notes.[14]

Arnulf of St-Ghislain mentions embellishment as one of the attributes of a skilled and knowledgeable singer (his fourth category, 16:56), using the word 'colour', and making it clear that an ability to embellish also extends to polyphony (as does Garlandia in 97:16, above):

Arnulf, 16:56. The fourth in order, but the first in dignity, shines clearly in those whom a natural impulse supported by a sweet voice cause to sing (figuratively speaking) like nightingales; however, they are by nature much better than nightingales, and deserve no less praise than larks. These are men in whom the noble acquisition of the art of singing directs the natural instrument of the voice according to rule in mode, measure, number, and colour, and which by making various combinations of consonances with a wonder-ful melody, and with a varied diversity of modes, brings new refreshment to the soul of

---

[13] On the word *color* and its use and meanings in theoretical writings see Gilbert Reaney, 'Color', *MGG*, iii. 1566–78. The term itself comes from rhetoric and has a wide array of applications. I inter-pret it here as 'embellishment' in both its narrow sense of added ornaments, and in the broader sense of considering any interpretive device to be an embellishment.

[14] See quotation and discussion in Joseph Dyer, 'A Thirteenth-Century Choirmaster: The *Scientia Artis Musicae* of Elias Salomon', *MQ* 66 (1980), 83–111 at 96.

the listener. [Such a singer] even, by the grace of superior performance, restores all uncouth and improperly composed works of music to a better shape, as if recoining them on the anvil of the throat. Who is there, indeed, who cannot marvel to see with what expertise in a performance some musical relationship, dissonant at first hearing, sweetens by means of their skilful performance and is brought back to the pleasantness of consonance?

The word 'colour' therefore is sometimes used by the theorists to denote melodic embellishment; it can refer to the improvised singers' art, as seen in Arnulf above, or to composed embellishment, as in the praise of Perotin by Anonymous IV:

Anon. IV, 46:12. Master Perotin himself made the best quadrupla, like *Viderunt* and *Sederunt*, with a wealth of colours of the harmonic art.

Another word for embellishment, found in several of the theoretical sources, is 'flower', as in the statement by Petrus dictus Palma ociosa where it is clear that for him, at least one of the meanings of 'flower' is what we would call diminution: many notes used in the place of one. He states directly that this applies to polyphony (discant):

Petrus dictus Palma ociosa. They speak of the flowers (*flores*) of mensural music when many sounds, or notes (which is the same thing), variously ornamented according to the quality of each one, are placed in one voice in due proportion against a single sound or a simple note of only the same duration [in another voice]. Although some say and affirm, however, that the flowers of musical science are numberless depending on the various methods of discant, and that it is not possible to have certainty about things numberless, for wishing for this reason to compose a technical treatise concerning such flowers. Nevertheless, in order that youths and others desiring to progress in the said science but possessing no technical treatise concerning it may not become lukewarm or negligent in learning more, I, as far as the capacity of my feeble intellect allows, have compiled twelve modes or manners of mensural discant embellished with flowers.

'Flower' and 'colour' are the words most often found, but their use in the various treatises is often very general and somewhat inconsistent. Distinctions that are used in this study, therefore, are in most cases my invention or adaptation for purpose of clarity in discussion and in order to assist the reader to conceptualize the individual item in modern terms. Following Howard Brown's lead I have adopted the words 'graces' and 'passaggi' to describe the basic categories of embellishments because of their familiarity to the modern reader, although neither term was used in this sense in the Middle Ages.[15]

The embellishments advocated and described by the theorists are quite sophisticated. In addition to what we would refer to today as 'graces' and

---

[15] Howard Mayer Brown, *Embellishing 16th-Century Music* (Early Music Series, 1; London, 1977), 1.

'passaggi', a number of other ornaments are discussed: several types of vibrato and tremolo, trills of various sizes and speeds, appoggiaturas, several types of voice inflection, the use of intervals other than the standard tone and semitone, and combinations of all these.

The subject of vocal style in the Middle Ages has received even less attention than ornamentation. The few statements that can be found in modern scholarship are either based on observations of singers in medieval art, or attempts to interpret a few singing instructions in terms of modern practices.[16]

There are many differences between the vocal style of the earlier centuries and that which has evolved in the last two hundred years as the Western classical style, a point that will become apparent in the discussions of sound and technique throughout all the following chapters. In addition to the theoretical statements about singing, evidence concerning medieval vocal practices will be extracted from the techniques required to execute the ornaments themselves. The sliding sound of a liquescent, the 'abandonment' of the final pitch of a pes, the pulsing sounds of the quilisma and oriscus, and use of quarter-tones in trills, vibrato, and filled intervals are all foreign to modern classical Western practices but were in common use during the Middle Ages, and were important basic ingredients in what may be termed 'the medieval vocal sound'.

To obtain an accurate view of the actual sound of medieval music we must imagine it as it would have been performed, sung in a vocal style in which a dazzling and colourful array of embellishments and vocal inflections were basic not only to its sound in performance, but to the medieval concept of music.

THE THEORISTS AND THEIR EVIDENCE

Before concentrating on the details of vocal style and ornamentation it is important to understand the repertorial, geographical, and temporal boundaries of the information presented here, and the limitations of how this material can be applied. We must be careful to understand to what music these statements apply, and during what period of the many centuries encompassed by the term Middle Ages they are applicable. There are many aspects of the subject that are not clear, at least in terms of the details, and some of the limitations of the sources at first would appear to be serious obstacles.

Much of the source material for this book is taken from theoretical treatises, and although the forty-five theorists quoted here are more than one might have imagined to have provided practical performance information, that number is

---

[16] There is no doubt that the problem is a difficult one, but the rather extreme position stated recently by Lance Brunner may be a bit exaggerated: 'If the quest for authentic interpretations of rhythm and ornaments is perilous and uncertain, the attempt to discover authentic voice production is hopeless'. Brunner, 'The Performance of Plainchant: Some Preliminary Observations of the New Era', *Early Music*, 10 (1982), 317–28 at 324–5.

very broadly spread in terms of both date and geography. As Table 1.1 illustrates, the theoretical sources encompass the dates *c*.600 to *c*.1490, and the areas of (in modern terms) Austria, Belgium, England, France, Germany, Italy, the Netherlands, Spain, and Switzerland.[17] There is no doubt that during those nine centuries the practices of singing and ornamenting evolved,[18] and further, during any one period the practices would not have been the same in all areas of Europe.

The time period involved here witnessed the invention and development of polyphony, a type of composition that by its very nature changed the focus of composition from a single line to the interaction of two or more lines. It is not difficult to imagine that this new compositional type would have had an impact on the vocal style and ornaments that had been developed to enhance mono-phonic music. The vocal style described here as appropriate for medieval orna-mentation must have changed (evolved) over the centuries, eventually to become the 'bel canto' of the seventeenth century. It is probable that the changes were quite gradual, and we might speculate that the kind of vocal sound and style used in the fifteenth century was well along the road to change from that used in the ninth. As will be seen in the following chapters, much of the orna-mentation was intimately connected with the vocal style, and therefore some aspects of ornamentation necessarily would have changed with the evolving singing techniques.

During all centuries people in different geographical areas observed different customs, including those involving music. It is obvious, for example, that during any century a performance in Spain would have been stylistically different from one in northern France or Austria. Modern scholarship in performance practices of the Baroque era has established clearly differentiated regional styles of perfor-mance, and we can imagine (although not very clearly) that those differences that were evident in the seventeenth century had descended from regional differences already present in earlier centuries.[19]

In introducing the very fact of ornamentation above I drew on statements from five theorists encompassing the dates 1274 to *c*.1400 and from the areas of England, France, and Italy. As can be seen in Table 1.1, this time period represents the largest concentration of theoretical statements on the subject, and therefore

---

[17] The geographical areas assigned to the theorists and treatises are not all equally accurate. When the place of writing is known, that is indicated rather than the author's place of origin (e.g. Jerome of Moravia, writing in France). On the other hand, although the Arnulf of St Ghislain is probably from Hainaut, in the southwest corner of Belgium, nothing is known of his training or his location when writing the treatise.

[18] My use of the word 'evolve' in this book refers only to a gradual process of change. No value is implied.

[19] To date there has been little work done in regional stylistic differences for the music of the Renaissance, making much more difficult the task of establishing those differences in earlier centuries and attempting to trace them through to the seventeenth century.

TABLE 1.1. *Distribution of theoretical treatises*

England	France	Italy	Other
			Isidore (Spain, *c.*600)
		John Deacon (9th c.)	
	Aurelian (850)		
			Hucbald (Flanders, 893)
			Notker (St Gall, *c.*900)
			Regino (Germany, 900)
			Anon. I (G) (Austria, 10th/12th c.)
	Adhémar (11th c.)	Guido (1028)	Aribo (So. Germany, 1078)
			Commentarius (Liège, 1100)
			Jo. Affligemensis (So. Germany, 1100)
			Rudolf (Liège, 1120)
Ailred (*c.*1150)	Bernard (*c.*1140)		
——————— John of Salisbury (*c.*1170) ———————			
			Instituta (St Gall, 1200)
			Summa (So. Germany, 1200)
Statuta (1250)			
	Franco (1280)	Elias (1274)	
Metrologus (13th c.)	Anon. II (13th c.)		
Anon. IV (1300)	*Ars musicae* (1300)		
Quatuor principalia (1300–50)	St Emmeram (1300)		
Walter (1300)	Jerome (1300)		
Anon. I (C) (14th c.)	Garlandia (1300)		
	Grocheio (1300)		
	Lambertus (1300)		
	de Muris (1323)	Marchettus (1318)	
	Petrus (1336)		Jacobus (Liège, 1330)
——————— Boen (1355 Oxford, Paris, Netherlands) ———————			
Breviarium (1400)			Arnulf (Hainaut, 1400)
		Giorgio (1434)	Canon (Basle, 1435)
	Tinctoris (1477)		
		Guglielmus (1490)	
		Bonaventura (1497)	

in the following chapters the bulk of the statements will be drawn from this period. Although these treatises can be used to establish the ornamental practices in England and France for that period with some degree of accuracy, because of the paucity of writings from other areas and earlier centuries, the degree to which these conclusions can be broadly applied will require other evidence and considerable discussion.

It is not possible at this time to date or place with accuracy the information found in the theoretical treatises from any era. Classification of the treatises according to time and the geographical location of their places of origin or that of their authors, as in Table 1.1, only appears to establish relationships among them. Even if we knew the author and provenance of each of the treatises, we would be some distance from understanding the relevance of their contents. The way in which treatises are or may be related to one another is quite complex, involving what any one theorist has deemed important to include, the tradition of passing on this kind of information, the musical and liturgical traditions of the different monastic orders, and the intended audience or use of the treatise. Since it was the accepted practice in writing a treatise to quote liberally from earlier writings, in order to date the information in any treatise, besides knowing the date of its authorship we must establish from whom the author copied, what has been revised, and what is new. Thus contemporaneous treatises may differ in that one includes only old material while another transmits more recent developments. Writings of this type often travelled within the confines of individual monastic orders, making it possible that treatises separated by long distances may actually be united through a similar monastic tradition, while those from the same area but belonging to different monastic houses may be the product of dissimilar traditions. Some treatises contain material of a highly complex and sometimes abstract and philosophical nature, perhaps intended for very advanced students. Others are written on a more elementary level.

These details must be known about each of the treatises before an analysis of the information contained in them can be refined, but we are a long way from that stage of scholarship. Many of the treatises used here have not yet been fully studied, and thus for the time being we must work around the lack of accurate knowledge of their place and tradition of origin.

After all these caveats the reader may now wonder of what use the following information can be. My point in stating the above has been to acknowledge the limitation of this study in pinpointing certain details of vocal and ornamental style along the temporal and geographical boundaries as stated. But that does not prevent me from presenting a sharp image of the subject. I have exposed the above reservations not as a disclaimer, but to make the reader aware of *certain kinds of limitations* of this study. At the same time I am confident that all the information here is correct and that it paints a good general picture of medieval vocal sound. What I cannot claim is that the picture is completely in focus for all places during all centuries of the Middle Ages.

I say 'certain kinds of limitations' because for much of the topic the lack of detail in the theoretical treatises is not as serious as it may seem. Surprisingly, the broad aspects of the subject appear to have remained constant throughout the period, as witnessed by the similarity of theoretical statements from all centuries and locations. Fortunately, there are other sources of information to supplement

that found in the writings. Thus, in spite of what at first may seem to be important lacunae in the theoretical treatises, other bits of information, much of it
musical, can be used to fill many of the gaps and to assist in sorting and refining
the data.

Acknowledging that there are limitations, my method of investigation will be
first to describe the vocal and ornamental practices rather broadly by pooling all
the information in order to establish the breadth of the subject. At the same
time, as we proceed it will also be possible to identify certain local practices and
demonstrate aspects of evolving techniques. The end result should be a strong
basic understanding of the style of singing and ornamentation in the Middle
Ages and how it changed over the centuries, and a more general impression of
the stylistic differences from one area to another.

As to the question of repertory, the evidence is that both the vocal and the
ornamentation practices described here were applied broadly to all types of
music, both sacred and secular, although in different degrees. Most of the treatises address sacred music; many of them mention ecclesiastical chant exclusively. But there are sufficient references and comparisons of monophonic chant
to polyphony and sacred music to secular to establish the fact that there was a
single basic approach. The subject of how these techniques might have been
applied to the various repertories of music will be taken up again after we have
viewed all the instructions.

2

Vocal Style and Technique

Giorgio Anselmi, III:4. Because the human voice is melodious, wherever it is inherently talented and trained by art it is equalled by no musical instrument, surpassing them all in a wonderful manner so that no sound can be compared with it in caressing human ears, in calming the passions of the body and the weariness of the soul, with such measure, evenness, regularity, and so sweet a sonority does the trained singer produce melodious notes (though men of this type are very few), for he surpasses the voices of all living beings and the sounds of instruments by means of the inflection and measure of his voice; for he knows how to harden or soften the strength of that same voice, and to transform any song into any genre by art, according to his judgement.

Giorgio Anselmi's praise of the voice, written in 1432, resembles similar tributes down through the centuries, including the present. But while such consistent characterization of the voice might suggest that little has changed in terms of vocal sound during that period, nothing could be further from the truth. What has remained constant is the attraction of the well-trained voice, but as will be demonstrated in the following chapters, the actual sound made by the voice has changed drastically over the centuries, and the sound that was valued so highly in the time of Giorgio and earlier was one that was highly ornate. By studying the ornaments that were an integral part of the singing style of the Middle Ages along with an analysis of the various commentaries on singing and singers, we shall be able to come to some understanding of the nature of the particular vocal sound that inspired Giorgio's remarks.

The ornaments described in the treatises and found in the manuscripts require specific vocal techniques, many of which are not a part of classical Western training (although they are required of a singer of twentieth-century repertory and also are present in the vocal practices of the Middle East). Once it is understood what techniques were employed by singers and what was considered to be good vocal delivery, the instructions for ornamentation of the repertory will be seen to be simply an extension of an already existing concept of singing. We can begin by reviewing performance instructions and commentaries on voice placement, vocal colour, articulation, expression, and interpretation found in some of the theoretical sources.

GENERAL SINGING INSTRUCTIONS

The comments about singing style found in the treatises are both positive and negative; when assembled, they can assist with an understanding of what was considered good singing practice and what was frowned upon. The most interesting to read are the invectives that usually are directed towards unschooled singers or those in an adjoining geographical region. Although this type of remark often appears to be the product of ill temper, pedantic snobbery, or simple prejudice, even then it is possible for us to receive an impression of what was considered good and bad performance. Some of the most entertaining of this type of diatribe are those by John the Deacon, Adhémar de Chabannes, and Elias Salomonis.[1]

The criticism by Adhémar is from the eleventh century and has to do with the inability of French singers to adopt Roman chant practices. (Chabannes is in present-day south-west France near Limoges. Adhémar would have thought of the people farther north—near Paris—as 'the French'). He criticizes them for lacking the vocal agility and techniques necessary to reproduce certain of the subtle vocal nuances in Roman chant, faults noticed over two hundred years earlier by the ninth-century Roman writer John the Deacon, who lumped together the French, Swiss, and Germans—people on the other side of the Alps. In the light of these views of 'Alpine' singing it is therefore interesting to note a similar type of broadside hurled at the singers of Lombardy in the late thirteenth century by Elias, a native of south-western France who was attached to the papal chapel, and who incorporates his caricature of north Italian voices into a description of technical details of the modal system and four-part improvised organum.

Adhémar de Chabannes. All the singers of France have learnt the Italian style (lit. Roman note) that they now call 'French', but the French cannot express perfectly the tremulous or sinuous notes, or those that are to be elided or separated. Rather than expressing these sounds, they subdivide the notes in their throats with a barbarous voice.

John the Deacon. For the Alpine people, roaring loudly with their thunderous voices, cannot bring forth the proper sweetness of the melody, because the savage barbarity of their drunken throats, while endeavouring with inflections and repercussions and diphthongs of diaphonies to utter a gentle strain, through its natural noisiness proffers only unmodulated sounds like unto farm carts clumsily creaking up a rutted hill: with the result that the sound, instead of softening the heart of the hearer as it was meant to do, serves only to disturb it with exasperation and noise.

---

[1] For a number of additional quotations about singing from early writers see Franz Müller-Heuser, *Vox Humana: Ein Beitrag zur Untersuchung der Stimmästhetik des Mittelalters* (Kölner Beiträge zur Musikforschung, 26; Regensburg, 1963).

Elias Salomonis, 60. Why are voice parts not separated by the same number of notes [i.e. identical intervals]? I answer: this is because of the consonance of voices, for neither the character of artificial or of natural song allows this, and if it were to happen, it would produce an ugly sound. It is, therefore, reflected in the neumes (*in figura*) in an artful and well-organized fashion, and it is correct; otherwise it would not. It should be recognized that the music of the laity is impressed on them by nature, as is the case in most things, and the music of wooden instruments strives after that same thing. This is, however, not the case with the song of the Lombards, who howl like wolves. All this is clearly evident, for if one layman should hear another sing in the first a low note, he would leap straight to the third [voice, i.e. an octave away], but certainly not to the second [voice, i.e. a fifth above]; or conversely [he will jump] from the third to the first, but never to the second [a fourth below].[2]

In the earliest of these three statements, that by John, the desire is for a voice to be flexible enough to articulate 'repercussions' cleanly and without overemphasis, to be capable of modulating in order to execute vocal inflections, and to have the control to add expression to melodies. Adhémar also seems to be concerned with the development of a flexible articulation. We can equate his term 'tremulous' with John's 'repercussions', and his concern for 'sinuous notes' with John's call for 'inflections' and expression. Adhéamar's preference for projecting the voice rather than placing it in the throat matches later statements about vocal production (see the Canonical Rule, below).

Criteria and instructions more positively stated come from the abbey of St Gall *c.*1200, by way of the anonymous writer of the *Instituta Patrum de modo psallendi* (8), and 200 years later in the informative treatise by the Belgian theorist Arnulf of St-Ghislain (15:4), both of whom have strong opinions about untrained singers. The writer of the *Instituta* directs some of his comments towards members of the religious orders who should not be allowed to sing in the choir, including among other unacceptable traits the possession of a voice more suited to the peasants in the nearby Alps. Here, as with the writers of the earlier remarks, the group singled out for the insults is a nearby foreign neighbour whose untrained vocal style is unwelcome in the more refined church repertory. His most informative statement for our purposes is that a good singing voice for ecclesiastical music must be trained to have the flexibility necessary to perform the nuances demanded by the neumes, and that not everyone is capable of developing it; the concepts of 'vocal flexibility of a voice for

---

[2] This section of the treatise has usually been misunderstood and mistranslated. Earlier in the treatise, under the rubric 'de notitia cantandi in quatuor voces', Salomonis explains the normal intervallic distribution of voice parts: that the first voice sings the plainsong, the voice above that, the second voice, sings a fifth above the bass, the next highest voice, the third, sings the octave above, and the fourth voice sings the twelfth. This explains the opening statement in the quoted excerpt concerning why the voices are not separated by identical intervals; Salomonis is pointing out that if they were, dissonant intervals would result. See Ernst T. Ferand, 'The Howling in Seconds of the Lombards', MQ 25 (1939), 313–24 at 315.

neumes' will become crucial to our understanding of medieval vocal sound. Arnulf agrees with the *Instituta* both in affirming that a good singing voice results from training both in vocal technique and theory, and in condemning those who sing without that training.

Anon., *Instituta*, 8. Let us abjure and forbid in our choirs voices like those of actors, or babbling, Alpine or highland, thundering or sibilant voices, neighing (as if the voice of a singing she-ass), lowing or bleating (like farm animals), effeminate voices, and every counterfeit, ostentation, and novelty of voices, since these practices smack more of vanity and folly than of religion. Such voices are not proper amongst spiritual men in the presence of God and his angels, in the holy land of the saints. Those who have such voices lack a natural manner, since they have not ever been trained in the skill of some musical instrument, and thus are incapable of having the flexibility of a voice required for neumes. Those people, therefore, although confused in their singing and in their morals, nevertheless, under pretext of religion, presume to be and appear as singers and rulers in choirs, although they know nothing, and wish to know nothing. For that reason they sometimes sow discord and destruction in choirs and they bring confusion on others, when they either speed up the chant with excessive frivolity, or else utter the sylla-bles with improper dignity (as one who drags a millstone up a mountain, yet at the top it always falls back down),[3] and therefore, chafing under any control, do not perceive the subtle sweetness of understanding, and seldom attain the delight of virtues; much less do they aspire to speculation on the divine mysteries, and to discovering the secrets of heaven. In any case, as far as the voices of such men are concerned, although they are not good, *Musica* knows how to put them to good use in opportune places; for they are igno-rant who hold such things in the treasury of their hearts.

Arnulf, 15:4. The first [category of musician] is that common among those who, being absolutely ignorant of the art of music, and lacking the supporting benefit of a natural [musical] disposition though not yet practised in plainchant, nevertheless through the rash venture of their silly presumptions strive to gnaw or rather gulp down musical consonances when precenting; while in the bark of their squabbling they bray louder than an ass. They blare like trumpets terrifyingly with brutish clangour; they disgorge a cacophonous expression; and by an organum that is in fact the opposite they commit barbarism in music against the rules. Blinded by the detestable false belief of their presumption they inwardly boast that they can disregard or take precedence over outstanding singers. They shamelessly present themselves among the rabble as if to correct or direct, so as to give the appearance of being trained musicians even though they do not even know enough about music to be led, and are always producing disso-nance with those who are concordant, and with their vicious solecisms defile whatever is correctly performed among the trained mass of musicians, so unbearable and harmful are they to singers.

One position that the five writers quoted above have in common is a dislike for ugly vocal sounds. Whether or not the French broke the notes in their throats, the Lombards actually 'howled', or the Alpine peasants had 'thunderous'

---

[3] This would seem to be an allusion to Sisyphus and his stone.

voices, we can see that the writers perceived these kinds of sounds as crude and unsuited to the needs of the music of the time. Although the quoted remarks cover a period of over 400 years, many of the basic concepts about singing appear to be the same. All five bemoan the poor vocal technique of those singers who do not have the ability to execute subtleties in the music, and in fact, they seem to have similar models for a good singing technique: clean articulation, flexibility of sound, expression, and a refined quality. This is closely related to the seventh-century values of Isidore of Seville, whose idea of the perfect voice was one that was loud, sweet, and clear:[4]

Isidore. The perfect voice, moreover, is loud, sweet, and clear; loud in order to reach on high; clear in order to fill the ears; and sweet in order to entice the souls of the listeners. If any voice should be at all deficient in any of these things, it is not perfect.

In addition, several of the writers were concerned with the correctness of the music that was sung, that the singers—especially the soloists and choir leaders, but also the members of the choir—should be well acquainted with the rules of mode and consonance. They seem to imply that the two traits, good singing practices and knowledge of the rules, are inseparable.[5] Arnulf makes the point that singers cannot attempt polyphony without a knowledge of the rules of plainchant; he and the *Instituta* author criticize those who are untrained and inept but who nevertheless offer themselves as leaders; the *Instituta* author describes problems caused by clerics who lead choirs without knowing the rules; and Elias labels as 'wolf howls' the sounds made by the singers in northern Italy whose singing practices stand alone outside of the modal practices common to laymen and clerics.[6]

Concern that singers should have knowledge of the rules of chant is a theme expressed frequently in the writings of the late Middle Ages, and is the basic premiss behind the inclusion of those rules in nearly every treatise of the period. By 'knowledge of the rules' is meant a thorough grounding in modal practices so that the correct notes, intervals, and formulas will be associated with each of the modes. This ability was absolutely essential in a tradition in which even the small amount of the chant that was written down did not notate accurate pitches. Both ignorance of the rules and differing opinions about their specific details created practical problems in performance, a subject addressed by Regino of Prüm in a

---

[4] Isidore's values were still current when translated and presented by Pietro Aaron as if they were his own observations on contemporary practice in Book 1, ch. 5 of his *Thoscanello* of 1523. See Bonnie J. Blackburn, 'A Lost Guide to Tinctoris's Teachings Recovered', *Early Music History*, 1 (1981), 29–16 at 64 n. 80.

[5] In addition to the theorists quoted here, comments can be found in many treatises concerning the difference between those musicians who know what they are doing and those who merely follow directions. For quotes and discussion see Müller-Heuser, *Vox Humana*, 32–44.

[6] For a discussion of this see Dyer, 'A Thirteenth-Century Choirmaster', 88–95.

treatise written for the church of Trier in the early tenth century. From Regino's statement we can see that because of a lack of agreement among the members of the choir as to the modes of the various psalms and antiphons, these items were often performed simultaneously in different modes, that is, with different arrangements of whole- and half-steps.[7] As will be seen in later chapters, knowledge of the modes was also necessary for a correct application of some of the ornaments.

Regino, 230. Since often in the church of your diocese the choir singing the psalms sang the melody with disorderly voices because of a discrepancy of the tone, and since I had often seen your worship unsettled on account of this, I seized an antiphonary and conscientiously read it through from beginning to end in order, and divided the antiphons that I found notated in it, according to what I think are their rightful tones.

There is also a recognition in both the treatise by Arnulf and the *Instituta* of the need for musical talent and aptitude, but that this must be accompanied by knowledge. These two theorists agree that leaders should be chosen only from those who possess both traits: knowledge and talent. This last sentiment is elaborated upon in a rather touching way by Arnulf in his description of the singers of his third category (15:41): those who have the knowledge but are unfortunately lacking in sufficient vocal talent to execute the music; these people have value as teachers!

Arnulf, 15:41. The third [category of musician] is visible in those who possess the glorious treasures of the art and discipline of music in the sacristies of their hearts, laudably acquired by virtue of study, who, although they suffer a defect in the instrument [i.e. the voice] so that they cannot properly perform what they know, nevertheless so compensate for their lack of natural ability by their knowledge of the art, that what they are unable themselves to perform harmoniously, they cause to be performed by their pupils, teaching those placed before them according to rule, by imparting musical riches and pearls to them, and by worthily unveiling the secrets of music to the worthy. For from the hearts of those men, speculative streams of musical instruction flow much more than from others; but yet by exercising themselves in that art they teach it in fact and deed; whence the ear and the eye of the wise man reveal the presence of the active musician worthy of praise, for the skill he possesses dispositionally he displays in active hearing and theorizing. Such men do not play tricks in musical matters, but profess real music, and however much the listeners dislike their singing, the eloquence they possess redeems this defect in that they expound the rules of the art through verbal instruction.

The *Instituta* goes further than the other treatises, however, in actually becoming involved with specific vocal qualities. While the pejorative remarks are quite colourful, unfortunately not all the words and phrases can be of assistance

---

[7] A statement that even master teachers did not agree on modes or melodies of the chant can be found in the 11th-c. *De musica* by Johannes Affligemensis, quoted here in Ch. 6, p. 114.

to a modern reader. Without too much difficulty we can probably arrive at the correct image of what is described as thundering, sibilant, babbling, bellowing, braying like an ass, or bleating like sheep, but some of the other images are far too subjective to be useful. The concepts of 'actors' voices', 'effeminate', 'ostentatious', and 'counterfeit' voices are all so general that to a present-day reader they could refer to many different sound qualities. The *Instituta* author's dislike of both 'ostentatious voices' and 'actors' voices', however, suggests that he might be referring not to a vocal sound but to the presence of too much drama in the singing voice. He also warns against interpretations that are either too frivolous or improperly serious, but there is no indication as to the amount of emotion that would be considered proper and not overly dramatic. From his remarks, however, we can see that expression of the text was clearly a part of good singing.

Advice similar to the above for the proper delivery of chant can be found in two other sources: the twelfth-century writings of St Bernard of Clairvaux, and the Canonical Rule of the Council of Basle from 1435 (110). Bernard makes a case for a dignified and controlled expression in music that supports the emotion as well as the sense of the text.[8] He, like John of Salisbury, Ailred of Rievaulx (below), and Elias (below, 17), is critical of performances that call attention to the singer at the expense of the text. The Canonical Rule concerns itself mostly with fairly elementary ideas for clear and reverent singing of the text (no talking or laughing), but the description of the attributes of a clear singing voice is quite helpful. Again we come across the admonition not to sing in the throat or to swallow the words, but also to open the mouth for proper enunciation.

Bernard. If there is to be singing, the melody should be grave and neither lascivious nor rustic. It should be sweet but not light; it should both enchant the ears and move the heart; it should lighten sad hearts and soften anger; and it should never obscure the sense of the words but enhance them. It is not a trifling loss of spiritual grace to be seduced by the levity of the song from the utility of the moral sense; and to pay more attention to the inflection of voices (or notes) than to the imparting of content.

Canonical Rule, 110. Whoever has elsewhere been beneficed or appointed to holy orders since they are obliged to perform the canonical hours, this holy synod warns them that if they wish their prayers to be acceptable to God, they must perform them neither in the throat nor between the teeth; nor by swallowing them down or hocketing the words; or by intermingling conversations or laughter; but both when alone and when joined by others, they must perform the daily and nightly offices respectfully and with distinct words. And let them not reduce devotion in that place.

John of Salisbury and Ailred of Rievaulx, both high-ranking English clerics in the twelfth century, write from a position that was common in religious orders

---

[8] The letter is in reference to an Office that he had composed for the Feast of St Victor, and he is referring to the music that should be set to it.

of the time, that it was improper to take pleasure in liturgical music, an opinion they copied from the writings of St Augustine.[9] For that reason both authors are extremely critical of any type of performance practice that would result in a sensual enjoyment of the music (a point made at the end of Bernard's statement quoted above). John condemns the extremes used by some singers who improvise preludes and postludes, as well as all types of ornamentation including counterpoint and polyphony, and Ailred adds to this the use of instruments—especially organs and bells—as well as specific expressive gestures employed by 'theatrical' singers. Many of these excesses are dismissed as 'feminine' and therefore 'lascivious' and unworthy of Divine service. Both point out (following Augustine's warning) that when music is performed in this manner the listener is likely to suspend all intellectual judgement and simply surrender to the charm of the music. In John's opinion, this type of performance replaces mental contemplation with sexual stimulation! Ailred condemns the excessive expression and ornamentation as the intrusion of the practices of the theatre into the church.

John of Salisbury. It also dishonours the very practice of religion that in the very sight of the Lord . . . with the lewdness of a lascivious voice and a kind of self-ostentation, with an effeminate style of diminutions, pauses of articulations, they attempt to effeminate the astonished little souls. Could you but hear the effete melodies of those singers who begin before the others, and of those who respond, of those who sing [first] and those who conclude, and those who sing in the middle, and those whose part is sung against their fellows's, you would believe it to be a chorus of Sirens, not a choir of men . . . Indeed such is their fluency in running up and down the scale, their subdivision or doubling of notes, their repetition of phrases and their combining of individual ones [phrases]—so that the high or even the highest notes are mixed with the low or lowest ones—that the ears of the singers are almost completely divested of their critical power, and the soul, which has yielded to the enjoyment of so much sweetness, is not capable of judging the merits of the things heard. Indeed, when such practices go too far, they can more easily occasion arousal in the loins than devotion in the mind.

Ailred, 97. Since we have decided to exclude evil persons from our discussion explicitly, let our discourse be concerned now with those men who clothe the business of pleasure under the pretence of religion; those who exploit in the interest of their vanity those things which the ancient fathers used to employ beneficially as types of the world to come. Now that types and symbols are not used, I ask from whence come so many organs, so many bells in church? For what purpose, I ask, is that terrible blowing of the bellows, expressing rather the crash of thunder than the expressive sweetness of the voice? Why that contraction and subdivision of the notes (lit. voice)? One voice joins in, another sings discant, another enters on a higher note, yet another divides and subdivides certain middle notes. Now the voice is reduced, then it is subdivided, at one time

[9] For additional discussion of this topic see William Dalglish, 'The Origin of the Hocket', *JAMS* 31 (1978), 3–20 at 7–12.

it is forced, at another it is enlarged into a more expansive sound. Sometimes, and this is shameful to say, the voice is distorted into horses neighing, sometimes manly strength is set aside and it is sharpened into the high pitches of the female voice; sometimes by a kind of artificial rolling the voice is twisted forwards and backwards. At times one might see a man gasping for breath with an open mouth as if suffocating, not singing, and ridiculously interrupting the song as if to threaten silence, and then imitating the agonies of the dying and the terror of those enduring eternal torment. Sometimes the entire body is agitated in actors' gestures: the lips twist, the eyes roll, the shoulders heave, and at every note the fingers are flexed to match. This laughable dissipation of the voice is called religion, and where these things are performed most frequently it is proclaimed that God is served with more honour. Meanwhile, the common people stand around trembling and terrified, and wonder at the noise of the bellows, the rattling of bells, the harmony of the pipes. But they also watch, not without derisive laughter, the lustful gesticulations of the singers, the harlot-like alternations and subdivisions of the voices, so that you would think they had assembled not at an oratory, but at a theatre, not for praying but for watching. And therefore should the sound be so restrained, so dignified, that it does not ravish the entire soul to delighting in itself, but leaves the greater part to understanding. As the most blessed Augustine said: 'The soul is moved to a disposition of piety when it hears divine song, but if the lust of hearing desires the sound of the song more than the sense of the words, it is condemned.' And, on another occasion: 'when the singing delights me more than the words, I confess that I have sinned punishably, and should prefer not to hear the singers. When therefore someone casts off that absurd and ruinous vanity and betakes himself to the ancient moderation of the Fathers: if honourable dignity arouses an unreasonable aversion in ears that prick with lust at the memory of theatrical trifles, as he thus contemptuously judges all their gravity as rustic backwardness, and to the style of singing taught by the Holy Spirit through those most holy fathers so to speak its instruments, namely Augustine, Ambrose, and especially Gregory, prefers Spanish ditties, as the saying goes, or the vainest trifles of I know not what pedants; if then this causes him torment, this grieves him, this makes him hasten back in breathless anguish to those things which he had vomited, then what, I ask, is the origin of this suffering: the yoke of charity, or the burden of worldly concupiscence?'

The statements associating the extremes of vocal expression and ornamentation with feminine manners are among the few to be found that ascribe particular practices (or more correctly, degrees of practice) to the different sexes. At first this may seem to be simply John's and Ailred's way of condemning a singing practice they find inappropriate, but the remarks are echoed by Arnulf of St-Ghislain, writing approximately two hundred and fifty years later (16:56). (This may be what was meant by the reference to 'effeminate voices and counterfeit, ostentation, and novelty of voice' in the *Instituta* excerpt, 8, above.) John, Ailred, and Arnulf consider this type of singing—extremely expressive, laden with ornamentation (and perhaps also singing in falsetto in the cases of John, Ailred, and the *Instituta*)—to be quite sensuous. The difference is that John and Ailred are attempting to provide guidelines for the singing of sacred music and therefore condemn the practice as unsuitable, whereas Arnulf is simply describing fine musicians.

Arnulf, 16:75. There is a second group among the fourth category, evidently of the favoured female sex, which is so much the more valuable the more it is rare; who in the epiglottis of the sweet-sounding throat divide tones with equipoise into semitones, and articulate semitones into indivisible microtones with an indescribable melody that you would think more angelic than human.

The *Statuta antiqua* of the Carthusian Order, compiled *c.*1250, are even clearer in pointing out that although various types of ornamentation are often performed, they are antithetical to the purpose of the monastic life. This position, similar to that put forward so vehemently by both John of Salisbury and Ailred of Rievaulx, associates ornamentation with delightful—and therefore undesirable—singing practices, at least undesirable in a sacred context. The *Statuta* advocate the avoidance of ornamentation in order to achieve the more proper monastic attitude of lamentation. From all three statements we receive the clear impression that the official position of the monastic orders was that singing should be as plain as possible. At the same time the fact that they feel the need to make such official statements suggests that ornaments must have been performed to some degree even though the practice was considered to be inappropriate. From this we can conclude also that expression of the text was a part of the approved practice as long as it was serious and controlled.

Statuta antiqua. Since it is the duty of a good monk to lament more than it is to sing, let us therefore use our voices to sing in such a way that delight in lamentation and not in singing shall be occasioned in our hearts, which . . . can be accomplished if those things which serve to delight in singing be removed, such as vocal diminutions [lit. breaking up of the voice], flowing over (*inundatio*), doubling the notes, and similar things, which belong more to curiosity than to simple chant.

Additional instructions on the proper expression and interpretation of sacred music, delivered in a tone not unlike that of John, Ailred, and the *Statua*, come from another of Elias Salomonis' passages (17). From the way in which Elias states his criticism of the laymen's practice of adopting for chant the performance customs of organum, it is possible to extract desirable principles for the interpretation of both organum and chant. To read his statements positively, the performance of organum is characterized by an uneven pace, anticipating the beat, accelerating and retarding within the phrase, and phrasing in small groups of notes as represented by the neumatic groupings. By contrast, chant is to be sung at a steady pace, avoiding any unevenness or variances such as those mentioned in reference to organum. Phrasing in chant is to be determined by factors other than the small grouping of notes within neumatic formations on the page. (Although Elias does not say so, the obvious guides would be those of text phrases and the melodic cadences.) This concern about the confusion of the two modes of performance practice is perhaps what is behind some of the criticisms quoted above from the *Instituta* (8). It is not that dramatic performance was excluded from sacred music, but that the more extreme or colourful expression was restricted to organum, whereas plainchant was to be more sedate.

Elias's final point brings up one aspect of performance that also bothered John and Ailred: that of the more flamboyant and less altruistic sacred music performers of the day who were interested in very showy performances. Elias also mentions the practice, apparently known to him in Rome in the late thirteenth century, of monetary gifts offered to lay church soloists.

Elias, 17. [Concerning the Laity.] What is more detestable, is that by scorning plainchant, which was truly ordained by the angels, the holy prophets, and by blessed Gregory, [the laity] at times adopt the practices of organum, which is itself based on the practice of plainchant.

And also, they scarcely deign at times to perform plainchant at its proper pace [lit. perform its feet] when they sing by anticipating, accelerating, retarding, and improperly phrasing [lit. joining] the notes—from which the effect of the science of organum is achieved, because they may happen to see the notes arranged in such a way on the page. But this [writing of notes] is done for the ornament and beauty of the notes on the page: for seeing, not for singing. Let them know this for certain, not inquiring whether the [practices] that they see are ours, rather than God's, or proper to the art of music (of which they are ignorant). But experimenting, they sing 'meow, meow' into the air, so that a stranger may turn up and listen; and what is even more damnable, they do this so that gifts may be brought forth more often, possibly to be diverted to unlawful uses and pocketed.

The largest set of straightforward instructions on ensemble singing and singers is found in the late thirteenth-century treatise of Jerome of Moravia (187:31—189:3); these touch on almost all the areas of singing seen above, while adding some new practical details. Jerome includes in his instructions some points that to the present-day reader would seem highly unnecessary, such as the statement about rehearsing in order to establish pitch, phrasing, and tempo (188:1), and the advice to follow a single director (188:5). At the same time he includes somewhat more sophisticated ideas, such as the direction to select and match the quality of the voices of the choir members (188:10), and to take care in selecting the pitch for a chant so as to avoid both the highest and lowest notes of the singers' ranges.[10] Most advanced of all is the final paragraph (189:3), in which he reminds singers that their voices will betray their true emotions, which is a plea for singers to become genuinely involved in the spirit of what they sing and to express it with sincerity.

---

[10] Actual directions in manuscripts of chant containing references to the spirit of the interpretation, the relative volume of the singers, and the improvisation of organum are discussed in Kurt von Fischer, 'Die Rolle der Mehrstimmigkeit am Dome von Siena zu Beginn des 13. Jahrhunderts',

In his discussion of the various types of incompatible vocal sounds (188:10), Jerome acknowledges the existence of three kinds of voices: chest, throat, and head. At first this might seem to be at odds with statements quoted earlier in which singers are admonished to project their voices from the front of the mouth and avoid swallowing the sounds in the throat. What he seems to be describing, however, is the three different vocal qualities: the bass voice that resounds in the chest; the falsetto voice in the head; and the mid-range male voice, which, for lack of any other word for placement, he terms as coming from the throat. These statements are made in the context of a discussion of matching voice qualities, and probably should not be read as indicating the method of voice production.

In paragraph 188:22 he advises the avoidance of extreme ranges so that the singers will not have to strain in order to sing pitches that are either at the top or bottom of their range. His stated concern here is that when a singer is at the extremes of the range the voice is strained and calls attention to itself, distracting the listener from the music and discomforting the singer—in Jerome's well-turned phrase, so that the 'song may not rule the voice, but the voice rule the song'.

Jerome, 187:31. Therefore, in order that ecclesiastical chant may be sung in such a correct and orderly manner simultaneously by two or more singers, five things are necessary:

188:1. First, that the song to be sung should be looked at with care beforehand at the same time and by all, and they should agree unanimously on the quality or quantity of harmonic time either according to the ancients or the moderns [i.e. agree on tempo, and note-values].

188:5. Second, as much as all may be equally good singers, nevertheless they must appoint one to be their precentor and director, to whom they must direct their attention most carefully, and only he shall determine how to perform the notes and rests; this indeed is most beautiful.

188:10. Third is that dissimilar voices ought not to be combined in such a way. This is because—to speak not by nature but by common image—certain voices are said to be chest voices, certain ones are throat voices, and certain are head voices. We say voices are chest voices when they produce notes from the chest, and those are of the throat that produce notes from the throat, and those are of the head that produce notes from the head. Chest voices are effective in low parts, throat voices are effective in high parts, and head voices are effective in the highest range. In general, coarse and low voices are chest voices, delicate and very high voices are head voices, and voices that are intermediate between these are throat voices. No voice, therefore, should be joined in song but a chest voice to a chest voice, a throat voice to a throat voice, and a head voice to a head voice.

Archiv für Musikwissenschaft, 18 (1961), 167–82; Agostino Ziino, 'Polifonia nella cattedrale di Lucca durante il XIII secolo', *Acta musicologica*, 47 (1975), 16–30; and id., 'Polifonia "arcaica" e "retrospettiva" in Italia centrale: nuove testimonianze', *Acta musicologica*, 50 (1978), 193–207.

188:22. But since every voice derives its energy from the chest, it is necessary fourthly that a song never be begun very high, especially by those possessing head voices, rather they should establish at least one note lower than the rest in their chest as a foundation for their voice; and not so low that they howl nor so high that they shout, but they should always begin moderately, that is 'sing'; that is so that the song may not rule the voice, but the voice rule the song; beautiful notes cannot be produced otherwise.

188:31. If anyone desires to know more fine notes he should take this for a rule: that he despise the song of no one, however uncultured, but he should be carefully attentive to the song of every man, because whereas the wheel of the mill sometimes renders a distinct screech without knowing what it does, it is impossible that a rational animal, desiring to direct all his actions towards a dutiful end, should not sometimes at least by chance or luck make a correct and beautiful sound. And whenever he should hear a note that pleases him, in order that he may possess the capacity of making it, he ought carefully to retain it.

189:3. The chief obstacle to making beautiful sounds is the sadness of the heart, because no sound has value, nor can it have value, if it does not proceed from the joy of the heart, because melancholics can have beautiful voices but they can not sing beautifully.

The above general instructions provide an overview of the desirable performance traits necessary for singing both monophony and polyphony in the Middle Ages. The concerns of the writers are for a bright and well-supported voice that is projected from the front of the mouth, one that has the agility to articulate gracefully and the technique to shade sounds and express the text. Expression should be adjusted to the text, occasion, and musical style, with the more showy and dramatic style reserved for organum and secular music (especially music of the theatre). To supplement that type of information, the following sections cover the more specific performance instructions for articulation, tempo, and expression.

ARTICULATION

The articulation of music is dealt with as early as Guido of Arezzo's *Micrologus* from the early eleventh century, where he associates ligatures with breathing places (162). His statement at first appears to be contradictory: he seems to say that one should breathe at neumes, and then he talks about connecting the 'sections'.[11] The seeming contradiction, however, is cleared up by the more detailed instructions from Jerome (183:21), who discusses the use of an articulated space between notes that are disjunct. Together, the two theorists are saying that non-ligated notes are to be clearly articulated by the use of a tiny silence, and that for purposes of articulation an entire ligature is to be treated the same

---

[11] For a somewhat different interpretation of Guido's remarks, see Nino Pirrotta, '*Musica de sono humano* and the Musical Poetics of Guido of Arezzo', in *Music and Culture in Italy from the Middle Ages to the Baroque* (Cambridge, Mass., 1984), 1–12 at 10–11.

as a single non-ligated note: the first note of a ligature is to be articulated but all succeeding notes within the ligature are to be joined together smoothly.

Guido, 162. Therefore, just as in metres there are letters and syllables, sections and feet and verses, so in music (*harmonia*) there are *phtongi*, that is, sounds, of which one, two, or three are fitted to syllables. Alone or doubled these [syllables] make a neume, that is, they constitute a section of a song; and one or more sections make a phrase (*distinctionem*), that is, a suitable place to breathe. Concerning which it should be noted that every section should be written and performed succinctly, and a [music] syllable even more so.

Jerome, 183:21. Second, that notes that are joined in notation shall be joined together in singing, but disjunct notes shall be separated. That separation is not a rest but a breath, and this is nothing other than the semblance of a pause or an entity the length of one *instantia*.

This same kind of information appears in the treatise of Johannes de Grocheio, in his discussion of measured music (176). The particular method Johannes is promoting in this section of the treatise is the notational practices of Franco of Cologne, and thus his major point is to advocate a mensural system. In his introduction to this section he tells us that problems arise when there is no text to guide the general rhythmic division of written notes, and that in those cases ligatures are used for assistance in recovering 'the composer's intention'. At first this would seem to refer to the identification of rhythmic modes by means of the ligated groupings, and no doubt that is one of Grocheio's meanings. But the statements by both Guido and Jerome quoted above indicate that there is much more to the use of ligatures, and a much wider meaning to Grocheio's words: the ligating of notes was also for the purpose of marking articulation and musical expression. Grocheio also points out that there are different versions of the same music, and that the variants are evident in the notation.

Johannes de Grocheio, 142:176 [in reference to measuring music]. Furthermore, since a song is sometimes without text and syllabic separation, in order that a sign might represent the thing signified, it was necessary to represent these things by ligating the notes.

142:179. They attributed meaning to those figures in various ways. Therefore, he who knows how to sing and perform a song according to one school of notation does not according to another. But the differences between them all will be obvious to anyone looking at the various strokes.

Guido also comments on the flow of the melodic line (174a), supporting the above implication that the performance of chant in the tenth and eleventh century was not in long smooth phrases. Stress was placed on many of the vowels, and as Guido says, the contrast between stressed and unstressed notes could be quite strong—so much so that a repeated note could seem to the listener to be either higher or lower simply because of the stress. Should there be any doubt about Guido's meaning here, the *Commentarius in Micrologum*

Guidonis Aretini, written a century later as an amplification of Guido's statements, confirms this interpretation (149:24).[12]

Guido, 174a. Likewise, we often place grave or acute accents above notes [with syllables]
because we often perform them with more or less stress, so much so that the repetition
of the same note often seems to be a raising or lowering [of the pitch].

Anon., *Commentarius*, 149:24. Whereof the book [i.e. *Micrologus*] goes on to say that
identical notes when repercussed appear at times higher, at other times lower, and calls
them 'changing tone' (*varium tenorem*) because of what it seems to be, when in truth it
is the same tone, since they remain on the same pitch.

From all the above statements we can conclude that all separate notes—
meaning both individual neumes and complete ligatures—were clearly articulated. The strength of the articulation followed the natural stress of the text, and
could be quite strongly differentiated. For untexted passages the presence of ligatures was also an indication of the desired articulation. In both texted and
untexted passages each ligature was to be clearly articulated at its beginning
while notes within the ligature were to be performed smoothly, that is, without
obvious separation. In texted music the amount of the articulation as well as the
other aspects of expression could be ascertained from the text.

An exception to the above-mentioned practice of articulation has to do with
the notes within ornamental organum passages. According to Franco of
Cologne, that type of passage was to be treated similarly to ligated notes whether
they were written as ligated or not (81:7). His description of ornamental 'flowers'
(*floratura*) in organum purum indicates that the entire passage was considered
to be a single melodic unit, unbroken by articulation once begun. (See a further
discussion of organum purum in Ch. 5.)

Franco 81:7. Likewise, it should be noted that in organum purum, when several notes
occur over a single note in the tenor, only the first should be articulated, and the remaining figures should be sung in the ornamental style (*in floratura*), as here: [See Ex. 2.1]

The conclusion is that medieval chant was clearly articulated, with individual
notes and the first notes of ligatures separated from one another by a tiny
silence. All notes within a ligature were unarticulated as were all notes within an
ornamental organum passage, and various syllables within a phrase were often
highly stressed. In Chapter 6 we shall see that some of this information can be
further refined.

TEMPO AND EXPRESSION

Some instructions for establishing tempo and pace in chant have been seen in
the section above on general singing instructions. What we can understand from

---

[12] Pirrotta, ibid. 10, interprets the passage as describing crescendo, diminuendo, rallentando,
and portamento.

Ex. 2.1. Franco's example of organum purum

those statements and those quoted below is that the general tempo of a chant was determined according to the solemnity of the service, the type of prayer, and the text. The writers are not in full agreement, however, on the amount of expression to be added to chant, nor on how much flexibility in tempo would be proper both for general artistic purposes and in order to mark off structural positions. In a statement quoted above, Elias criticizes singers for not performing chant at an even pace (17). He makes the same point with even more vehemence a little later in the same chapter (21, below), once again pointing to the difference in performance practices between chant and organum. His point in both cases would seem to be a protest against the adoption of the highly dramatic and uneven pacing that was suitable for organum, as opposed to the far more steady and subdued style in chant. In seeming contradiction, several theorists writing both before and after Elias make it clear that within a chant, cadences are to be heightened by the use of retard. Guido illustrates this with the colourful analogy of running horses, and even advocates the visual representation of tempo variation by spacing the notes closer together or farther apart on the page (175a).

Elias, 21. Mark well: we ought not place our scythe in another's harvest by adopting the style of organum and accelerating the notes; for whoever hastens each note, in destroying both, performs neither well. The infallible rule is that no plainchant in any of its parts allows a faster tempo than any other part, which is in accordance with its nature. That is why it is called 'plain chant', because it wishes to be sung in the plainest way possible.

Guido, 175a. Likewise, like a running horse, the notes should always approach the place of breathing at the end of the phrase more slowly, so that as if in grave manner they approach the resting place in a weary state. Notes crowded together or spaced out thinly as appropriate will often be capable of indicating this.

At first it may seem that Guido and Elias are giving contradictory advice, but a closer look reveals that they are probably referring to different things: Guido to the way in which phrase ends are given special treatment in an otherwise steady chant tempo, and Elias telling us not to employ a mid-phrase rubato, speed up or slow down entire phrases, or adopt any of the other devices that he believes are appropriate only in organum. Given the number of statements here and below that all cadences were treated with great attention—which included retardation—Elias's remarks should probably be taken as evidence that in Rome during the late thirteenth century the difference between a highly flexible organum tempo and a generally steady plainchant tempo was not always observed. The addition of slight retards at cadences as well as subtle expressive gestures that slightly delay or anticipate the general pace in plainchant would not be incompatible with this view. From other sources we know that in addition to retard, the sense of phrase ending in chant was further heightened by the addition of various kinds of 'reverberation' on the final and penultimate notes of phrases. The cadencing ornaments were known variously as tremula, morula, and procellaris, all of which are described in detail in Chapter 4.

Additional support for the use of expression within chant phrases can be found in the ninth-century letter from Notker, in which he explains the use of letters that accompany St Gall chant notation. As can be seen in the list below, the meaning of these symbols is far broader than simply an indication of direction or duration, as is usually thought.[13] While some marks could refer narrowly to pitch alone, for example 'a' or 'e' (higher, same pitch), a broader interpretation related to volume could be intended (louder, equal volume). Other marks clearly indicate expression: k = ringing sound; f = harsh; s = sibilant. Several of the St Gall manuscripts from before the twelfth century use these expressive letters rather liberally, as can be seen in Pl. I, which indicates that at least at St Gall, much attention was given to expression.

Notker. Notker sends greeting to brother Lantbert. At your request, I have taken pains to explain as well as I could what is signified by the single letters placed above the neumes (*cantilenae*).

'A' admonishes the singer that the note must be raised higher/louder (*altius*).

'B', according to the letters to which it is attached, signifies that the note rises or falls much further, or is held longer in a strident voice (*belgicat*).

'C' certifies that a note is performed quickly or rapidly.

'D' demonstrates that a note goes lower.

'E' elegantly explains that a note is sounded evenly/equally/at the same pitch.

'F' furiously demands that the note shall be begun with a harsh sound or the sound of gnashing teeth.

'G' genuinely grants that a note is to be gargled gradually in the throat.

'H' heralds that one aspirates on the note itself in the manner that one does when pronouncing this letter.

'I' indicates a lowering of the sound with the heaviness of the letter 'g'.

'K' for the Latins has no value, but among us Alemanni it replaces the Greek χ, signifying 'klenche', that is, a ringing sound.

'L' delights to lighten/raise the sound.

---

[13] For example, Willi Apel, *Gregorian Chant* (Bloomington, Ind., 1958), 117, classifies them as either 'melodic' or 'rhythmic'.

'M' mentions that the melody is moderated with supplication.

'N' signifies to take note of this.

'O' ordains that the mouth of the singer should resemble the letter itself.

'P' proclaims seizing or grasping the note.

'Q' Query: what is the signification of this letter for notes, when even in words it is written only in order that the following 'u' may lose strength?

'R' requires rectitude: the note must be shaven not to abolition but to a neat curl.

'S' shows that the note climbs upwards with a sibilant sound.

'T' testifies that the note must be lengthened or held.

'V' The value of this letter is that the force of the 'v' sound is diminished and is pronounced just as 'vau' in Greek or Hebrew.

'X' Although Latin words do not begin by X itself, nevertheless it expects that one should wait.

'Y' Among Latin speakers 'y' sings no hymn.

'Z' is purely Greek and by reason of this it is not at all necessary for the Romans. Nevertheless, it was taken over as aforesaid by the letter 'R', to inquire after other things, which is 'zitise' in one's own language.[14]

When two, three, or more letters are placed together, their significance will be understood easily from the above, especially from the instructions for the interpretation of the letter 'B'.

Some of these letters represent colourful sounds that are to be applied to the notes: f = the sound of gnashing teeth; g = gargled in the throat; h = aspirated sound; i = lowering the sound heavily; s = sibilant sound; v = the sound of the Greek or Hebrew 'vau'. As we shall see below, these types of sounds are an integral part of the singing style and were regularly employed in performance.

The use of these letters, however, was somewhat compromised by the fact that, contrary to what Notker's list might imply, there was no generally accepted key to their meaning. Johannes Affligemensis, writing approximately 200 years after Notker, pointed out the uncertainty (150). At the same time, his list of ambiguous meanings supports the point that in the eleventh century, notation included information about expression, even though the meanings were not universally agreed.

Johannes Affligemensis, 138. Some are accustomed to correct the uncertainty of neumes with certain letters, through which they seem not to inform the singer, but to hinder him twice as much with error. For though there is no certainty in the neumes, superscript letters do not present less uncertainty, especially since many words of various meanings begin with those letters, and so it is not known what they mean. If, however, some definite meaning should be assigned to the neumes, not all uncertainty would be thereby

---

[14] This alludes to the fact, known to the Romans, that intervocalic R in Latin had replaced an earlier Z sound. ζητησαι is Greek for to inquire. I am grateful to Leofranc Holford-Strevens for this clarification.

eliminated, since the singer still remains uncertain about the type of augmentation and diminution. For example, the letter 'c' is the beginning of various words, such as *cito* [quickly], *caute* [carefully], and *clamose* [noisily]; likewise 'l' begins *leva* [lighten], *leniter* [softly], *lascive* [playfully], *lugubriter* [mournfully]; and in the same way 's' in *sursum* [upwards], *suaviter* [pleasantly], *subito* [suddenly], *sustenta* [sustain], *similiter* [similarly], etc.

Information about tempo exists in a number of the sources. Jerome provides a view of performance tempos that are to change according to the solemnity of the day (this is also true in respect to the quantity of ornamentation) (187:20). The tempo is to be slower on Sundays and special feasts and faster on weekdays, a view supported in a more general statement in the Canonical Rule of 1435 (108).

Jerome, 187:20. Here we shall observe both the way of singing and the way of forming notes and rests in ecclesiastical song, to a greater or lesser degree according to the occasion. For if anyone indiscriminately employs either method itself, not determining the ferial days themselves or the weaknesses of the voices, he would be said not to use, but rather to abuse the said methods. Only on Sundays and special feasts are the ways described above to be carried out. On vigils the same method certainly ought to be followed with respect to the five special notes, but with the longas changed in value into semibreves, and semibreves into the shortest notes, and also with the tempus of the moderns changed to the tempus of the ancients [i.e. everything is sung much faster].

Canonical Rule, 108. The divine praises for the daily office are not to be sung quickly and hastily, but slowly and with a seemly pause especially in the middle of any verse of the psalms, while making a distinction between the solemn and the ferial offices.

Johannes de Grocheio addresses the subject of tempo in conjunction with expression. His descriptions include both sacred and secular musical forms, and he ascribes to many of the compositional types a tempo and emotional character, while at the same time relating the different compositional types to one another based on specific aspects of form, tempo, expression, or melodic characteristics. In order to describe the various aspects of sacred compositions he often uses secular forms as comparisons. His students obviously were more familiar with secular songs and dances, and thus when he wanted to contrast the devout and serious responsory and alleluia with the more spirited and joyful sequence, he chose for his comparisons the noble cantus coronatus and the two basic contrasting dance types: estampie and carol (276).[15]

Johannes de Grocheio, 164:276. These three chants, that is, the responsory, alleluia, and sequence, are sung immediately after the epistle and before the gospel, in mystery and

---

[15] On the dances and Grocheio's names for them, see Timothy J. McGee, 'Medieval Dances: Matching the Repertory with Grocheio's Descriptions', *Journal of Musicology*, 7 (1989), 498–517.

reverence of the Trinity. The responsory and alleluia are frequently sung in the manner of an estampie (*stantipes*) or cantus coronatus, in order that they may impose devotion and humility in the hearts of the listeners. The sequence is sung in the manner of a carol (*ductia*), in order that it may guide and gladden the listeners so that they can properly receive the words of the New Testament, for example the Holy Gospel, which are sung immediately afterwards.

Elsewhere in his treatise Grocheio describes the secular forms in a way that allows us to understand the elements they share with the sacred forms. His description of the vocal and instrumental estampie includes references to its complicated construction, which requires serious and spiritually uplifting concentration on the part of the performers (120, 141). The cantus coronatus is important for the quality of its text, which is serious, delightful, and noble in its aims. By contrast, the carol is a rapid dance with lively and morally positive movements (121, 140). Through the comparison, therefore, we can conclude that the responsory and alleluia were to be performed in a serious manner befitting a noble and complicated subject, whereas the sequence was lively and joyful.[16]

Johannes de Grocheio, 132:120. The song called estampie (*stantipes*) is that in which there is a diversity in the parts and in the refrain, in the rhyme of the words as in the melody . . . This song causes the souls of young men and women to concentrate because of its difficulty, and it also turns them away from perverse thoughts.

134:141. The estampie is also an untexted piece, having a difficult and carefully chosen set of concords, separated into versicles (*puncta*) . . . Because of its difficulty, the estampie causes the soul of the performer to pay close attention, and it also turns the soul of the listener and that of the wealthy from perverse thoughts.

130:112. A cantus coronatus is called by some a simple conductus (*conductus simplex*). . . . Cantus coronati are normally composed by kings and nobles and they are frequently sung in the presence of kings and princes of the earth, in order that their souls may be moved to be daring and resolute, magnanimous and liberal, characteristics that all make for good rule. This kind of song is made from delightful and lofty material, as, for instance, when it is about friendship and charity, and is made entirely of perfect longas.

132:121. The [vocal] carol (*ductia*) is a song that is light and rapid in its ascent and descent, and sung in a carol [i.e. round dance] by young men and women. This song indeed guides the hearts of young women and men and keeps them from vanity, and it is said to be effective against that passion which is called erotic love.

---

[16] Grocheio does not seem to be consistent with his references to the nature of the alleluia. Although he states in this passage that it is to 'impose devotion and humility', suggesting serious interpretation, elsewhere he describes it as a chant of joy (*cantus laetitiae*), which suggests a lighter performance.

134:140. A carol is also an untexted piece, measured with a regular beating of time . . . [the beats] measure the carol and the movement of the performer, and rouse the soul of man to move elegantly according to that art they call dance; and the regular beats measure the motion in carols and round dances.

The cantus coronatus, having a serious mood, a slow and stately pace, a noble and uplifting text, and an ornate melody is a useful comparison for several other sacred compositions as well. Grocheio mentions it to characterize the slow tempo and serious expression of the Kyrie and Gloria (270), the ornate melody of the hymn (241), and the manner of singing the offertory (280).[17]

Johannes de Grocheio, 162:270. The Gloria, however, is never found without the Kyrie eleison. These chants, moreover, are sung slowly and composed of perfect longs in the manner of a cantus coronatus, in order that the hearts of the listeners may be moved devoutly to praying and to listening devoutly to the prayer, which the priest, or the one appointed for this, says immediately.

156:241. A hymn is an embellished song that has many verses. By embellished I mean in the manner of a cantus coronatus, which has concords that are beautiful and elegantly arranged.

164:280. The offertory follows the Credo . . . It is sung in the manner of carol or cantus coronatus, so that the hearts of the faithful are awakened to devotion in sacrifice.

Grocheio obviously did not intend to be thoroughly consistent in his associations of various compositional types. His remarks were made in several different contexts within the treatise and therefore were intended to serve somewhat different purposes. He relates the compositional types to one another on the basis of one characteristic or another as a way of assisting his reader to understand specific aspects of various compositions, but without implying that all aspects of any two types would be the same.

One must keep in mind that Grocheio's treatise was on an introductory level, probably written for his students at the Sorbonne in Paris at the end of the thirteenth century.[18] Throughout the treatise he appears to be discussing music in terms that would have some recognition for his non-specialist students, and therefore the categories are undoubtedly simplified and unsophisticated. But even with that limitation it is possible to make use of his statements to gain an understanding of the relative tempos and affects that were to be applied in medieval sacred and secular compositions. In the absence of either more complete or higher-level statements for some of the compositions, the remarks

---

[17] As an example of the spirit used to sing the offertory, Grocheio cites the carol along with the cantus coronatus. Apparently, although the two forms are sung at different tempos, their rousing singing styles are similar.

[18] Ernst Rohloff, *Die Quellenhandschriften zum Musiktraktat des Johannes de Grocheio* (Leipzig, [1972]), 11. For a further discussion of this point see McGee, 'Medieval Dances', 516–17.

of Grocheio are a base from which one may begin to understand the medieval idea of the relationship between tempo, form, and affect. His statements are summarized in Table 2.1.

Guido of Arezzo advises singers to link the tone quality, volume, and speed of music to the subject matter of the text. He uses the word 'affect' (*effectus*), by which I believe he means tone colour, tempo, articulation, and expression:

Guido, 174b. Likewise, let the affect of the song express what is going on in the text, so that for sad things grave neumes are used, for serene ones they are delightful, and for auspicious texts exultant, and so forth.

The recommendations of Bonaventura da Brescia (42) and those of the anonymous author of the *Instituta Patrum de modo psallendi sive cantandi* (6)

TABLE 2.1. *Grocheio's comparative remarks on performance*

Type of composition	Emotion	Tempo and other remarks	Similar compositions	Basis of comparison
Responsory	devotion humility		estampie cantus coronatus	performance style
Alleluia	devotion humility joy		estampie cantus coronatus	performance style
Sequence	joyful gladden	solemn	carol	performance style
Hymn	to rouse the hearts of the faithful	embellished	cantus coronatus	construction
Kyrie	move hearts to devout prayer	slowly general praise	cantus coronatus cantilena	performance style form
Gloria	move hearts to devout prayer	special praise slowly	cantus coronatus	performance style
Credo			carol	construction
Offertory	devout giving		carol cantus coronatus conductus simplex	performance style form
Preface	devotion	solemn various solemnities	carol	form
Sanctus	fervent charity	ornate, slow		

TABLE 2.1 (*continued*)

Type of composition	Emotion	Tempo and other remarks	Similar compositions	Basis of comparison
Communion	contemplative		carol	form
Invitatory			conductus simplex	construction
hocket	mobility	pleases hot-tempered fast		
motet		learned not for vulgar		
round	vulgar	slow	cantus coronatus	tempo
cantus gestualis	heroic deeds martyrdom serious	for feasts		
cantus coronatus	daring resolute magnanimous liberal delightful lofty	embellished slowly excellence of text and melody	responsory alleluia Kyrie Gloria offertory conductus simplex hymn round	performance style identical construction tempo
estampie	concentration	complicated difficult	responsory alleluia	performance style
carol	rouse the soul	prevents love or Eros ornate elegant motion	sequence offertory Credo preface	performance style construction form

are to link expression to the solemnity of the occasion itself, although some of their reasons tend to be related more to practical than aesthetic considerations. Bonaventura's statements are intended for choir interpretation and indicate an awareness of an association between the affect of particular chant items and tempo. He claims that the practice he proposes is that advocated by Guido, although that has not been proved to be true.[19] The information, however, does come originally from the time of Guido: from the tenth-century *De musica* of Odo of Arezzo. Bonaventura has not taken his statement directly from Odo but

[19] Seay, in Bonaventura da Brescia, *Rules of Plain Music*, 39, states that the information is not in any of the surviving works by Guido.

TABLE 2.2. *Odo of Arezzo and Bonaventura da Brescia on the performance of chant*

Item	Affect	Reason
Nocturnal responsory	loud	arouse the sleepy
Antiphons	sweet and delicate	
Introits	public crier	rouse the people
Alleluias	delicate	
Tracts and graduals	moderate and pausing	
Offertories and communions	moderate	absolution

from the *Musices opusculum* of Nicolaus Burtius, published in 1487.[20] These suggestions are summarized in Table 2.2.[21]

Bonaventura, 42. On the method of singing according to Guido. Likewise note the manner of intoning in a choir, as Guido says in the third part of his *Musica*, that the responses of Nocturns should be intoned with a loud voice to arouse the sleepy; the antiphons intoned with a sweet and delicate voice; the introits intoned with the voice of a public crier to rouse the people to divine service; the alleluias should be intoned delicately; the tracts and graduals should proceed with a moderate and 'pausing' voice; offertories and communions should be sung as moderately as possible, and in this manner our consciences hear a true and heavenly idiom and the people of the world will be absolved.

The anonymous author of the *Instituta* deals only with the strength of the voice to be used, and makes a direct connection between the amount of enthusiasm to be expended and the amount of energy a singer needs to conserve for work. On special solemn occasions, those when everyone is excused from daily labours, the singers are fully rested and therefore can sing with a full voice; on Sundays and those feast-days when they must do some work they are to sing less vigorously; and on ordinary days when they will be working full-time, they should exert the least amount of effort:

Anon., *Instituta*, 6. Let us have three levels of melodies in respect to the three divisions of time. For example, at the time of principal feasts the melody ought to be sung with the whole heart and mouth, and with every affect of devotion. On Sundays, major feast-days,

---

[20] Nicolaus Burtius, *Florum libellus*, ed. Giuseppe Massera (Florence, 1975), 105–6; Odo (Oddo), *De musica*, in Gerbert, *Scriptores*, i. 276a. On the confusion of Odo of Cluny and Odo of Arezzo, see *New Gro ve*, xiii. 503–4. I am grateful to Bonnie J. Blackburn for calling these sources to my attention.

[21] I have not combined Odo's/Bonaventura's remarks with those of Grocheio (Table 2.1) because of the difference of location. The reader will see, however, that there would seem to be no contradiction in affect ascribed to the items that are in common: responsory, alleluia, and offertory.

and saints' days (on which days the lay people spend their time either partially or wholly in work), the melody should be sung in a more relaxed fashion. On weekdays, moreover, the psalmody of the night hours and the chants of the daily offices should be modified in performance, in order that everyone can chant the psalter with devotion, and sing attentively without a strained voice, and with affect but without defect.

Perhaps the most intriguing instructions concerning interpretation come from the *Summa musice*, which proposes a close association between the affect of a composition and the performer's hexachord selection, a concept that has serious implications for the application of *musica ficta* by adding a dimension to that subject that has not yet been explored by modern scholars. The writer proposes that 'light and joyful' compositions are to be sung in the soft hexachord, serious texts in the hard hexachord, and texts that are not at either extreme of emotion should receive a combination of the two hexachords:

Anon., *Summa musice*, 2055–65. If the theme of the text in the song is joyful, it is proper that the music be light and full of joy, as for instance a song concerning St Mary, St John the Baptist, the Epiphany, the Resurrection, and similar things. If however the text treats of some difficult matter in either its nature or appearance, then the music should be dignified and should mutate from soft 'b' to hard 'b' and the reverse . . . When the theme of the text is a mean between these two extremes, then the song should do so as well, something which fools believe to be without method.

TEMPO IN POLYPHONY

In the absence of statements to the contrary, we may conclude that the ideas expressed in regard to tempo and expression refer equally to monophony and polyphony. There are, however, two categories of polyphony for which special information is available: organum purum, for which a completely flexible tempo is advocated (see Elias, 17 and 21, above), and copula, which is singled out by Franco of Cologne (75) and Walter Odington (140) as having a tempo different from that ordinarily signified by the written neumes. The exceptional case of the copula supports the conclusion that otherwise monophony and polyphony were treated the same in terms of tempo.

By copula Franco and Walter are referring to passage of untexted polyphonic discant. A copula can be written with or without ligatures, but in either case it is to be performed faster than a texted passage in the same notation. Whereas Walter discusses the copula in binary ligatures as 'faster' than music written in rhythmic mode 2 (longas and breves), Franco speaks more specifically of this type being performed as if it were written in breves and semibreves, that is, nearly twice as fast. They state that a copula written in unligatured notation is performed faster than the written notation (Franco)—breves as in mode 5—but slower than the semibreves of mode 6 (Walter). In summary:

copula	*tempo*
binary ligatures	nearly twice written values
unligatured	faster than mode 5 breves but slower than mode 6 semibreves

Franco, 75. A copula is a rapid discant, coupled reciprocally. It can be either ligated or unligated. A ligated copula is one that begins with a simple longa and proceeds by binary ligatures with propriety and perfection similar to the second [rhythmic] mode. It is distinguished from the second mode in two ways, namely in its notation, and in its performance. In notation, because the second mode does not have a simple longa at the beginning, but the copula has, as can be seen here: [Ex. 2.2(*a*)]. If, however, a *divisio modi* is added between a first simple longa and a ligature, then it is not a copula, but is called the second mode, as here [Ex. 2.2(*b*)]. In performance, the copula is also distinguished from the second mode since the second mode is performed as a *recta brevis* and an imperfect longa, while the copula is performed rapidly all the way to the end as if it were semibreves and breves.

An unligated copula resembles the fifth mode, although it differs from the fifth mode in two ways: in its notation and in the manner of its performance. In the matter of notation it is distinguished from the fifth mode since the fifth mode, when without text, can be ligated in any manner, while the copula, which is never seen above a text, is never ligated, as is here evident: [Ex. 2.2(*c*)]. It is also distinguished from the fifth mode in performance, since the fifth mode is performed with *recte* breves, whereas the copula is more quickly sung (*copulatur*) [lit. connected] in performance.

Walter, 140. Another type [of part music] is that which moves by binary ligature like the second mode, but it is faster and has an unmeasured longa at the beginning, and it is called copula, taking its name from its meaning. A second kind of copula, which is written in separate notes, is slower than the sixth mode, and is named by what it is not, i.e. that its notes are not ligated.

Instructions for tempo in other kinds of polyphony are found a little later in Walter's treatise where he provides instructions for solo singers who are *improvising* their parts in polyphony. Once the singer of the top part has set the pitch by holding a first note—held without definite measure as in a copula—the others are to enter and then the ensemble is to proceed at a steady pace according to the normal way of measuring time. The differences between these instructions and those for singers of *written* polyphony would seem to be the need for the held first note in order to establish the pitch, and the change from polyphony to monophony for the final note.

Ex. 2.2. Franco's examples of the copula

Walter, 146. Let him who is to sing the higher part begin, and in such a way as to provide a copula, using that note which is held a long time. Let all the others follow him; let them sing clearly, moderately, and evenly, according to the proportionate measure of the *tempora*, softly, but listening, and let them drop out altogether after the penultimate note has been produced. There are other ornaments of psalm singing, however, that cannot be conveyed in words but only by means of a refined voice.

Walter's final sentence reminds us that the fine points of performance are not capable of being transmitted fully in writing, and that without actually hearing good performers, our understanding of medieval singing practices will be quite incomplete. At the same time, however, many of the values found in the passages quoted above are identical with those promulgated today. Singing with a clear voice, enunciating the text clearly, articulating cleanly, keeping a steady metre and rhythm, and expressing the text are values as easily understandable as they are unsurprising. Realizing that the musicians of the Middle Ages held to these kinds of basics provides the assurance that some of the performance values of today are applicable to the music of the Middle Ages. This is not to say, however, that the singing style in the Middle Ages was the same as that produced today by classically trained singers. Whereas many of the values are held in common between the modern and the medieval eras, their sound images are quite different from one another. As the next chapters will continue to make clear, the sounds, nuances, and techniques required by medieval music, as illustrated by the ornamental practices, are much closer to those found in the Middle East. The way in which similar values can be reconciled with separate techniques will be pursued in Chapter 6 once we have understood the demands on the medieval singing voice.

3

Written Ornaments

To complete our investigation of the medieval singing style and at the same time introduce the concept of ornamentation, we have the testimony of a set of 'ornamental' neumes and instructions on their performance. A study of these neumes and the special sounds that they require will bring the instructions of the previous chapter to the level of practical application. It will also assist us in comprehending the extent to which ornamentation was a part of basic musical practices of the late Middle Ages, and make clearer the fundamental concept of the vocal style as well as the specific techniques involved in singing medieval music.

The term 'ornamental' neume is used here in the modern sense, meaning something added to the musical phrase in order to grace it. As will become clear below, in medieval terms nothing about these neumes would have been considered ornamental in that sense: they were a normal part of the vocal style and were essential to the way in which a singer performed a musical phrase. The 'ornamental' neumes were not unusual additions to notes, but an integral part of the notational system;[1] the neumes that are termed 'ornamental' here were the only way to indicate a desired musical gesture. The kinds of sounds indicated by these neumes, therefore, were fundamental to the entire technique of medieval singing. In fact, it is most likely that what one might consider to be 'ornamental' about these neumes was the reason for the development of the early neume forms.[2]

In a discussion of neume shapes and their purposes, the author of the *Summa musice* (527–40) mentions clivis, plica, pes (podatus), pressus, and quilisma as requiring what we would think of as special vocal effects. He does not describe the neumes or the sounds as out of the ordinary, but merely includes the description as a part of the summing up of what he considers to be the shapes and their performance, and he implies that there is a direct relationship between the written shapes of the neumes and the sounds they represent. The neumes

---

[1] An observation made by David Hiley, *Western Plainchant: A Handbook* (Oxford, 1993), 361. See also Ferand, 'A History of Music', 465. Solange Corbin, 'Note sur l'ornementation dans le plain-chant grégorien', *International Musicological Society: Report of the Eighth Congress, New York 1961* (Kassel, 1961), i. 428–39 at 436–7, briefly discusses some of the same neumes.

[2] This topic is more fully investigated in McGee, ' "Ornamental" Neumes and Early Notation', *Performance Practice Review*, 9 (1996), 39–65.

discussed in the *Summa* are fewer than the number usually found in such lists, but it can be seen that the author believes that all other shapes, and therefore sounds, are formed from combinations of these. Although the *Summa* states (in the poem, 540–54) that the purpose of inventing the neumes was to 'record the various movements of the voice', the author is somewhat pessimistic about his reader's ability to gain much understanding without hearing them performed. This is partially true today, but by combining his descriptions with the statements found in several other sources, a fairly clear image of many of these sounds can be constructed.

Anon., *Summa musice*, 523–40. The punctus is formed in the manner of a point and sometimes it is attached to a virga, a plica, or a podatus; sometimes only to one and sometimes to many of the same kind, especially when the pitch descends. The virga is a simple (*simplex*) note, elongated like a staff. The clivis is named from [the Greek] 'cleo', that is, 'I turn back', and it is composed of a note and a half of a note, indicating that the sound must be bent. The plica is named from *plico*, 'I fold', and contains two notes, one higher and one lower. The podatus contains two notes, of which one is lower and the second is higher, ascending. The quilisma is called 'crooked' and it contains three or more small notes, sometimes ascending and again descending, or the reverse. The pressus is named from *premo*, 'I press'; the lesser contains two notes, the greater contains three, and it should always be performed evenly and quickly. A song, however, is not fully learnt through these signs, nor is anyone able to learn it better by using them, but it is necessary that it be heard from another person, and learnt by long practice. And that is why the usage of this singing is so called.[3]

lines 540–54 [a poem]. In former days singers were pleased with song, and it was their desire that their heirs might teach clever things. They therefore devised new figures to record the various movements of the voice. They called them 'notes' because from that [word] a certain type of music is named that is associated with the craft of singing. Their names are clives, plice, virga, quilismata, puncta and podati; the pressus should be united with them. The pes, growing with two small notes, desires to stretch upwards; the high one, liquifying (*liquescens*), abandons what it represents. The clivis wishes always to descend with two small notes, and the note at its end denotes an indistinct sound. It precedes a pause, or lingers in the mouth of one who is pausing as if it had the status of a complete note.

The neumes under discussion in this chapter are conventionally grouped under two headings: liquescent and repercussive.[4] Although these categories are not exact, they are a convenient way to initiate an investigation and so they will be used here. Some neumes actually belong to both categories, and we shall see that many more neumes than those discussed here could be considered to be

---

[3] According to Christopher Page, *The* Summa Music: *A Thirteenth-Century Manual for Singers* (Cambridge, 1991), 66 n. 59, the meaning of this last sentence is a 'reference to the derivation of the word *musica* from *muniens usu canentem* (strengthening the singer by practice)'.

[4] They appear as such in a number of studies, for example Apel, *Gregorian Chant*, 104–8.

'ornamental'. Table 3.1 provides a comparison of neume shapes in a number of traditions. The shapes used in the different traditions are recognizable as variants of a single idea in most areas, although there are some interesting idiosyncratic shapes that will be discussed later. In the following discussion my remarks

TABLE 3.1. *A comparison of neume types*

	St Gall	Aquitanian	English	Lorraine	Beneventan	square
virga	/	/	l	⸜	1	⌐
tractulus	–	–			⸍	▪
punctum	•	▪	•	⸍	•• ~	▪
clivis	∧∧∧	⌒⌐	ʃ ʃ	⸗	∧⌐	• ⌐
pes	∫∫∫	!	!⌡	⸝ ⸝	∫ ℐ	ℰ
plica	⸜∪ρ	⸜∪	⸜∪	⸜ ∪	⸍	η
quilisma	⍵	⸍⸜	⸟⸜	⸝⸜	⸝⍵	⅂
apostropha	⸝	▪	•	⸍	▪⸜	▪
bistropha	⸝⸝	••	••	⸍⸍	••⸜⸜	▪▪
tristropha	⸝⸝⸝	•••	•••	⸍⸍⸍	•••⸜⸜⸜	▪▪▪
oriscus	⸜⸝	⊬η	⊬	∞	⸍ η	↑
pressus	⸍⸍ ⸟⸜	⸍η	‖•	⸍∞ ⸍ℰ	⸝	⌐⌐
scandicus	⸜ ⸜	⸟⸜	!	⸝ ⸜	⸝⸜	⸞
salicus	⸜ℰ⸜	⸟⸜	⸝⸜	⸝⸜	⸝⸜	⸞
torculus	⸜⸜ρ	⸜ ⸝⸜	ʃ ʃ	∧⸜ρ	⸜η	⸜⸜
climacus	⸜• ρ	⸜⸝	ʃ•	⸗	⸟⸝	⌐⸝
porrectus	N	⸜	⸜	⸍⸜	℧	N

Table based on Corbin, 'Neumatic Notations', *New Grove*, xiii. 131

will usually be apropos of all or most neume traditions, but in order to retain some consistent reference, whenever there is a wide variation in shapes I shall be referring to those of the St Gall tradition unless otherwise stated.

LIQUESCENT NEUMES

'Liquescent' refers not to any specific neume but to an ornamental variant of many of the standard neumes.[5] Guido of Arezzo describes the liquescent sound as lacking precision in pitch (175b): made between two fixed notes, it seems not to stop as it travels from one note to the other. He further affirms that it does not have a full sound when he allows a 'full' note as a substitute. The first impression one would receive from the verbal description is that the liquescent sound is simply a glissando that takes the voice directly from one written pitch to the other. As we shall see below, this is true in some cases, but Guido gives an example of a more sophisticated ornament. The example provided with his statement involves the notes *g* and *f*, connected by a liquescent (Ex. 3.1). Instead of having the voice slide from *g* directly to *f*, however, the location of the liquescent 'dot' indicates that the voice is to slide from *g* to *d* before continuing its glissando to *f*. In other words, the placement of the liquescent dot indicates the tonal route that the voice is to follow. This is affirmed by several other manuscripts transmitting Guido's treatise in letter notation that specifically state *g d f*, etc.[6]

Guido, 175b. Notes, in fact, become liquescent in many places after the manner of letters, so that the passing from one note to another in a smooth manner (*limpide*) does not appear to have a stopping place. We put a dot like a blot beneath the liquescent note, in this way: (Ex. 3.1).

If you should wish to perform the note more fully, not making it a liquescent, no harm is done; in fact, it is often more pleasing. Indeed, you should do everything that we have said neither too seldom nor too constantly, but with good judgement.

Further details about the application of the liquescent sound are found in the *Metrologus*, a thirteenth-century amplification and elaboration of Guido's instructions (89). In the *Metrologus*, the sound of a liquescent is described as a compressed sound, and according to that author it can be applied only to

---

[5] For special studies of the liquescent neumes see Heinrich Freistedt, *Die liqueszierenden Noten des Gregorianischen Chorals* (Veröffentlichungen der Gregorianischen Akademie zu Freiburg, Heft 14; Freiburg, 1929); Johannes B. Göschl, *Semiologische Untersuchungen zum Phänomen der gregorianischen Liqueszenz: Der isolierte dreistufige Epiphonus praepunctis, ein Sonderproblem der Liqueszenzforschung*, 2 vols. (Forschungen zur älteren Musikgeschichte, 3; Vienna, 1980); and Haug, 'Zur Interpretation der Liqueszenzneumen'.

[6] There is some variation in notes given for this musical example. For a list see Guido of Arezzo, *Micrologus*, ed. Joseph Smits van Waesberghe (CSM 4; American Institute of Musicology, 1955), 176. The version given here is the one most often reproduced, and is taken from *LU* 318.

Ad te le - va - vi

Ex. 3.1. Guido's liquescent

specific consonants: reg, dig, leg, ag, vim, vem, tum, tem, and similar sounds. The treatise provides examples of the liquescent that expand on the single example in Guido. The first two examples for the syllables with consonants (Ex. 3.2(*a*) and (*b*)), demonstrate the liquescent motion that fills in an interval by ascending or descending from one written note directly to the next, rather than going beyond the next note and returning, as does Guido's example. In the next

Ex. 3.2. Examples of liquescents from *Metrologus*: (*a*) descending liquescents on syllables reg, dig, leg, ag, vim, vem, tum, tem, and similar consonants as well as for the diphthongs au, eu, luy, ley, and ey; (*b*) liquescents on ascending passages; (*c*) liquescents on descending scalar passages; (*d*) liquescents on vowels a, e, i, o, or u

sentence the author of the *Metrologus* explains the circumstances for the use of a liquescent in the model of Guido's example. He states that a liquescent is not performed directly between the notes of a descending diatonic interval (although this is possible for ascending passages; see Ex. 3.2(*b*), second liquescent). In order to liquesce in a descending scalar passage it is necessary to move beyond the next note for the liquescent and then return, as in Ex. 3.2(*c*). Although not described in the text, this example also shows that the same technique is employed in order to liquesce between notes on the same pitch; see Ex. 3.2(*c*), third pair, where the liquescent descends a second and returns to the same pitch for the first note of the next pair. The writer also states that other lower intervals can be used as the point of liquescence in these situations. This last point must include the interval of a fourth used in Guido's example as well as the seconds and thirds found in Ex. 3.2(*c*), but there is no information as to how much larger an interval a liquescent can encompass. It will be noticed that the syllables mentioned for liquescent treatment all end in 'g' or 'm', and thus involve a closure of either the throat or the lips. As we shall see below, the performance of a liquescent involves closing off or darkening of the sound, a technique that is directly related to the sound made when 'g', 'm', and other consonants are pronounced.

Vowels are treated differently. Specific syllables that make diphthongs—au, eu, luy, ley, and ey—can receive a 'liquescent' sound, performed in same manner as those for consonants, that is, the sound slides right up to and into the next note. But for the uninflected vowels *a*, *e*, *i*, *o*, and *u*, one may slide up to the next pitch as a 'liquescent', but once arriving at the pitch of the next written note, that tone is repeated, making a clearly articulated separation between the two neumes. (Ex. 3.2(*d*))

Anon., *Metrologus*, 89. [Guido's words are italicized] *Sounds become liquescent in many places after the manner of letters*: that is, syllables; *so that the beginning of one sound passes cleanly to another, nor does that first sound appear to be ended. Next,* for a descending liquescent sound, we place a punctus like a blot under the note for syllables such as reg, dig, leg, ag, vim, vem, tum, tem, and similar syllables that sound right up to the next note when that note is on the same pitch or the note above in this manner [Ex. 3.2(*a*)]. In ascent they are performed in this manner [Ex. 3.2(*b*)]. If the next note follows below [i.e. the half-step below], then it is not liquescent, but there are two notes following the liquescent [i.e. an interval of more than a half-step] in this manner [Ex. 3.2(*c*)]. Sometimes there is a different lower note following [i.e. larger intervals]; the same thing will happen after three notes.

On vowels one ought not to make a liquescent or a 'compression' except for au, eu, luy, ley, and ey. Above a, e, i, o or u, [the liquescent] is fashioned like this [Ex. 3.2(*d*)]. Then, the final [note] is considered as if two notes.

And if you wish to perform it (that is, a liquescent note) *more fully, not making it a liquescent, no harm is done; often, moreover, it is found more pleasing. All things that we have stated ought to be done neither too seldom nor unremittingly; rather they ought to be done with discretion.*

According to these instructions, the manner of performing the liquescent sound depends on the interval, the direction, and the syllable. Although all of them involve sliding the voice from one fixed pitch to another, certain sounds are to move directly to the next note, whereas others move indirectly, and some glide into the next sound while others stop to allow a separate articulation of the destination pitch. If the syllable ends with a sounding consonant (i.e. 'g', 'm', 'v', rather than one that causes a stop, for example 't'), or if it includes a diphthong, then the liquescent sound can move directly into the next note without an articulated stop. The change of sound quality from the closed sound of the liquescent to that of the full sound of the next note is considered to be sufficient articulation. If one adds a liquescent sound to one of the pure vowels (i.e. *a*, *e*, *i*, *o*, or *u*), however, there is not enough contrast since it is more difficult to make these sounds dark, and therefore the note following the liquescent must be articulated.

The singer is given some latitude in the matter of singing a liquescent. Guido tells us that one can convert a marked liquescent and sing it as a full note (i.e.

with a full and separately articulated sound). Further, the *Metrologus* implies that, given the proper syllable and interval, one can extemporize a liquescent between two written notes: a solid note can be converted to a liquescent sound, or an additional liquescent sound can be interpolated into the passage. Thus the singer has the option of converting notated liquescents to full sounds, and extemporizing liquescents where none is indicated, either in writing or as required by the syllable formation. The singer is admonished, however, to apply the ornament with taste and moderation.[7]

As an extension of the liquescent neume tradition, early notation in most traditions includes separate forms for liquescent and non-liquescent two- and three-note neumes.[8] Whereas the non-liquescent forms are made up of puncti, tractuli, and virgae, the liquescent shapes have curved or indefinite lines (see Table 3.1). In the liquescent forms the note represented by the curved mark is to be sung with an inflected tone and as a glissando, rather than sung with a stable full tone. Pl. I contains several examples of liquescent and non-liquescent neumes in an early manuscript. In line 1, for example, the lowest neume over the syllable exal*ta*vit is marked to have a liquescent sound as the first sound of a pes, whereas the last neume over the next syllable, 'it', is a pes without a liquescent.[9]

The manuscripts provide evidence that the use of the liquescent sound was not as restricted as the theoretical writings would have us believe. The liquescent neumes in Pl. I over the syllable Chris*tum* in the third line, and over angelo*rum* in the tenth, are placed exactly as described in the treatises: they are found over the liquescent syllables. On almost every line, however, liquescent neume shapes can be found as a part of extended melismas and not in conjunction with the consonant or vowel formations that are a part of the above descriptions. Since these examples are written by the same scribe who correctly assigned liquescent neume shapes to liquescent syllables, we can conclude that he intentionally chose those shapes in the melisma. The sliding liquescent sound, therefore, also could be used independent of any particular syllable formation. No early treatises describe an independent liquescent note formation (most likely because the term 'liquescent' referred to the sound of certain text syllables), but it is clear from the manuscripts that the liquescent sound had a prominent place in medieval vocal technique. In treatises from the thirteenth century forward a

---

[7] For variant examples from other MSS of the *Metrologus*, see Joseph Smits van Waesbergh (ed.), *Expositiones in Micrologum Guidonis Aretini* (Amsterdam, 1957), 89, 90. For more on liquescent notes see Dom Grégoire M. Suñol, OSB, *Introduction à la paléographie musicale grégorienne* (Tournai, 1935), 502–4.

[8] Haug, 'Zur Interpretation der Liqueszenzneumen', presents an interesting discussion of this point.

[9] The reader will note that in order to facilitate the liquescent sound on this word, the consonant 'v' must be included with the preceding syllable 'ta', rather than with the following 'it'. The reverse would be required if the decision were made to sing the marked liquescent as a full sound.

larger category of the liquescent sliding sound is covered by the word plica, and from those writings we can gain additional information about liquescent performance.

Plica

The word plica is often used in modern writings to describe the liquescent neume forms.[10] According to the late medieval theorists, however, the word actually had a broader application. Plica is always described as involving two sounds, but in some treatises it is considered to be the inflection, either ascending or descending, of a single note, whereas in others it described as a two-note neume.[11] All authors agree on what the neume is, but they differ in how they describe an ornamental sound that is added to a fixed pitch. In some of its aspects the sound description of the plica is identical with that of liquescent neumes, but whereas the liquescent neumes were thought of as connecting two fixed pitches and were linked to specific text syllables, the plica was a decorative ending to a fixed pitch and could be applied to any breve or longa, including those without text. The term plica, therefore, had a meaning that encompassed the earlier description of liquescent, but also included the same sound treatment applied without the syllable and interval constrictions. For that reason we should not be surprised that the shapes of the plica given in the treatises are nearly identical with the liquescent forms of the standard clivis and pes neumes. Especially in the St Gall tradition, the descending plica ' resembles the liquescent form of the clivis *ʔ*, while the ascending plica *ʸ* resembles the liquescent pes *ɪ*. The reader may find it convenient to think of the plica as a sliding and inflected sound that can be used in many situations, both in conjunction with other notes and by itself.

Information regarding performance of the plica is found in several treatises. The anonymous author of *Ars musicae mensurabilis secundum Franconem* (44) and Lambertus in his *Tractatus de musica* (273), both state that a plica must be formed in the back of the throat with the epiglottis. (This is probably what Guido is referring to (175b, above), when he differentiates between the sound of a liquescent and a 'full' sound.) Walter Odington also describes the plica as a half sound (129) by relating it to the semitonus and semivocalis in chant. This reinforces the idea that the sound of the plica is greatly reduced. He elaborates by saying that a plica is a 'bending of a sound by a sound', by which he also may be

---

[10] For a discussion of lack of consistency in the representation of the plica in theoretical writings see Mark Everist, *French 13th-Century Polyphony in the British Library* (London, 1988), 13–15. David Hiley discusses the relationship between the two neume shapes in 'The Plica and Liquescence', in *Gordon Athol Anderson: In Memoriam*, 2 vols. (Musicological Studies, 49; Henryville–Ottawa–Binningen, 1984), ii. 379–91.

[11] For example, it is described as an inflected one-note neume by Jerome (181:32–182:17), but as a two-note neume by the anonymous author of the *Summa music* (523–40).

referring to the use of a small inflection of pitch, for example, a quarter-tone.[12] The anonymous author of the *Breviarium regulare musicae* states that when added to a note, the plica receives exactly half the value of the written neume, that is, the fixed pitch and the plica inflection receive equal divisions of the time unit (26, 27). But Lambertus further refines that statement by pointing out that the value of the plica changes according to whether the note is perfect or imperfect. He agrees with the author of the *Breviarium* in the case of imperfect notes, where the plica shares the value equally with the written note, but if the note is perfect, the plica receives only one-third the value, not half. Lambertus also mentions the addition of a subtle vibrato in the performance of the plica.

Anon., *Ars musicae*, 44. Concerning plicas on simple figures. The plica is a mark of the division of the same sound into low and high, and must be formed in the throat with the epiglottis.

Walter, 129. The plica is the bending of a sound by a sound, written as a single neume. Only longas and breves are capable of receiving a plica. One type ascends, the other descends, which in plainchant are called semitonus and semivocalis.

Anon., *Breviarium*, 26. Secondly, we must speak of individual plicated notes. Wherefore it should be noted what a plica is, according to Master Franco, in the second chapter of his *Musica*: 'A plica is a note of the division of the same sound into low and high.' According to Walter of Odington, in book 6, chapter 2, 'a plica is the bending of a sound by a sound, written as a single neume'. From these definitions I offer a fourth conclusion. This Conclusion is that every note except a simple neume (*simplam*) [i.e. a semibreve] can be plicated.[13]

27. Therefore I set down these rules. The first rule is that the temporal value of any plicated note is neither increased nor diminished by the time [needed] for the plicated note. The second rule is that every plica is either ascending or descending; the ascending plica indicates that the sound is to be raised at the end, and the descending plica that it is to be lowered at the end.

Lambertus, 273. The first species of perfect plica when it descends is a certain figure with two stems in which the second is longer than the first, as this: ◗.

Ascending there is only one stem, as this: ◖. The perfect plica has the same property, value, and nature as the perfect longa, except that it contains two tempora in the body of the note, and one in the appendage [i.e. the plica]. The plica is produced in the voice by the closing of the epiglottis with a finely controlled and closed vibration of the throat.

The second species is the imperfect plica, which looks like the perfect plica, but has the same value and nature as the imperfect [longa] and contains one tempus in the body and the remainder in the appendage: ◗◖.

---

[12] Walter's exact meaning for 'bending' here is made even more difficult by another reference elsewhere in his treatise to a semivocal (94): 'A *semivocalis* transfers half its duration to another note, which is called a "semivocal" when descending, and a "semitone" when ascending.'

[13] By *simplam* I suspect the writer is referring to a semibreve, since all the other treatises discuss the plica in terms of plica longa and plica brevis.

As a result of all these descriptions it is possible for us to see the similarities and differences in the performance of liquescent/plica sounds according to whether they are accompanied by specific syllables or not. In all cases the sound is a diminished and sliding sound made in the epiglottis, and it can have a slight vibrato. When it is sung to accompany certain liquescent syllables it should slide smoothly to the next note, either joining with it or stopping for an articulation, depending on the syllables (vowels require an articulation, consonants and diphthongs do not). When sung without the prescribed liquescent syllables (either with other syllables or with none at all), the sound does not continue into the next pitch.

Gutturalis and Sinuosa

Walter Odington briefly describes two additional neumes whose notational representation and descriptions identify them as liquescents (94); see Ex. 3.3. Although the notation in the treatises resembles the plica neume, Walter treats them as separate. The sound of the gutturalis, he says, is made by a moving throat, by which I understand him to mean the gargling sound mentioned by Notker as signified by the letter 'g'. Alternatively, it could also mean a light vibrato similar to Lambertus' description of a plica. The sinuosa, which means 'winding', is described only as turning back in the fashion of a shepherd's staff, which at first would seem to be a reference to the physical shape of the neume itself, but it probably also refers to the sound: that it is to depart from the original pitch as do other plica-type sounds, and then turn back in the other direction. Because of the written description and the shapes of the neumes, I conclude that these are variations of the plica sound, meaning that for Walter, the plica is a semivocal sound that moves away from the written note in some fashion. Variations in its performance include the addition of a throat gargle or vibrato—gutturalis—and a return towards the written pitch—sinuosa. Lambertus (273, above) seems to think that all plicas are treated as gutturalis, but the other theorists quoted above are silent on the refinements. These differences are quite small and may be evidence of differing regional practices.

Walter, 94. A gutturalis is so called because it is formed in a moving throat.
    A sinuosa is so called because it bends back similar to a shepherd's staff.

Clivis and Pes

According to the *Summa musice*'s descriptions of the basic clivis and pes sounds, i.e. the non-liquescent forms, there is an aspect of the liquescent sound already

Ex. 3.3. Walter Odington's gutturalis and sinuosa

present in them (523–54, above). The *Summa* describes the clivis as having an indistinct sound on the second (lower) pitch, but at the same time warns that the inflected note is to be held full value and should not be cut short. The second note of the pes, too, is to receive an inflected sound. The *Summa* instructs the singer to sing the second pitch of the pes and then to make the voice move away from the true pitch, sliding lower with a liquescent sound. There are no additional performance directions, but the theorists seem to indicate that the articulation of the succeeding note depends on whether the change of sound on the ornament is sufficient to make it stand as a separate sound. Given the above descriptions, the difference between the liquescent and non-liquescent forms of clivis and pes would mostly be one of degree. The non-liquescent clivis includes an inflected second sound (although it does not slide), and the non-liquescent pes ends with a sliding liquescent sound. The inclusion of inflected and liquescent-like vocal nuances in what could be termed non-ornamental neumes strengthens the impression of the tonally flexible nature of the medieval vocal style, as described in Chapter 2, and the strong presence of indefinite and inflected sounds in all the music of the period.

Quilisma

The quilisma is a liquescent neume represented by a wavy or jagged line connecting two ascending (and occasionally descending) notes a third or fourth apart. Its interpretation has been the subject of several different theories, some based on suppositions drawn from its notational shape, and others from its resemblance to the *kylisma* in Byzantine chant.[14] The earliest known mention of quilisma is by the late ninth-century Aurelian of Réôme, who described it as being a 'tremulous and ascending note'. The *Summa musice* observes that the word quilisma means 'crooked', and that the neume contains three or more small notes (523–40, above), and Walter Odington likens it to moist earth; by which I infer that he is referring to the wavy marks left on the seashore at low tide.

Aurelian, 97:15. They sing a quilisma [lit.: a tremulous and ascending note] on the versus of these last parts.[15]

Walter, 95. Quilismas are so called by their resemblance, for *quilos* [i.e. moist] in Greek is 'soil' and *mus*, 'earth', as if the earth were moist from the reception of waters.[16]

---

[14] Many of the theories are summarized in Apel, *Gregorian Chant*, 113–15. See also Leo Treitler, 'Reading and Singing: On the Genesis of Occidental Music-Writing', *Early Music History*, 4 (1984), 135–208.

[15] See the explanation of Aurelian's statement with musical example in Treitler, 'The "Unwritten" and "Written Transmission" of Medieval Chant and the Start-up of Musical Notation', *Journal of Musicology*, 10 (1992), 131–91 at 191.

[16] The 'Greek' etymological origin of the word is pure fabrication on the part of the theorist. I am grateful to Leofranc Holford-Strevens for this information.

Additional information about the performance of a quilisma can be deduced from the simile drawn between the quilisma and the unwritten ornament called tremula by both Aribo (66:34) and the anonymous author of the *Commentarius in Micrologum* (153:59).[17] In context, the two writers were attempting to separate the tremula from a similar unwritten ornament called a morula.[18] They describe the tremula as 'greater and lesser pulses of the voice, as if trembling', whereas the morula consists of 'uniform pulses', that is, the alternation of sound and silence on the same pitch (perhaps something similar Giulio Caccini's trillo). In order to explain the difference between these two ornaments further, the tremula is likened to the quilisma.

Aribo, 66:34, and Anon., *Commentarius*, 153:59. The morula is twice as long or twice as short; [it is long] if the silence between two sounds is the double in relation to the silence between two [other] sounds. In the same manner the morula is twice as short if the silence between two sounds is single in relation to the silence between two [other] sounds [i.e. sounds and silences must be of equal length, either single length or double]. When Guido says 'or have tremula', I think it should be understood as follows: the tremula is the neume we call a stepped neume (*gradatam*)[19] or 'quilisma', which indicates length, of which he says 'twice as long', with an affixed virgula, without which it marks shortness, in his wording, 'twice as short'.

Anon., *Commentarius*, 149:22. The tremula is similar to a repercussed note, just as is a morula, but there is this difference, that in a morula the sounds are produced with uniform pulses of the voice, while in the tremula these same sounds are brought forth with now a greater, now a lesser impulse of the voice, as if trembling.

150:28. A repercussion is either a morula or a tremula, and that is what Guido means by 'that they have either a morula or a tremula, that is, a repeated tone', by means of a repeated impulse, but not changing pitch.

The graphic representation of the quilisma has always been interpreted as a representation of a waving pitch (see Table 3.1), but it has never been clear whether the waving line referred to pitch or intensity. By associating the tremula and quilisma, and from the specific statement by the anonymous writer that the tremula was a change in pulse but not pitch (*Commentarius*, 150:28, above), we can now be certain that in some performance traditions the quilisma was a volume pulsation without pitch change. This would mean that the *Summa* phrase 'ascending and then descending' refers to the shape of the mark rather than to the sound that is to be produced.[20] More information on the quilisma's

---

[17] The similarity of the two passages suggests that they have a common source.

[18] This subject is discussed at length in Ch. 4.

[19] The word *gradatam* is otherwise not known as technical musical term. Since it is used here as a synonym for quilisma, it perhaps refers to the shape of the neume as 'stepped', meaning varying sound levels.

[20] Page believes that the author has confused the quilisma with a porrectus. See *The* Summa Musice, 66 n. 58. For additional discussions of the quilisma see Walter Wiesli, *Das Quilisma im*

performance is provided by its consistent listing with liquescent neumes, meaning that there was an aspect of sliding and of reduced sound to its execution. In performance, therefore, a quilisma would signify a smooth motion between the two written pitches in which the voice pulses alternately strong and weak as it moves.[21] From this we can make a further distinction between the unwritten ornaments morula and tremula: the tremula belongs to the liquescent neumes because the pulses are connected, whereas the morula, which alternates sound and silence, is a repercussive neume.

Oriscus

The oriscus is often listed with the repercussive neumes. It has been considered by some scholars to be related to the stropha neumes (discussed below),[22] although only the simplest form of the oriscus resembles the apostropha (and the plica).[23] The other forms of the oriscus give visual evidence that it is probably one of the liquescent neumes. Whereas the strophas are composed of separated marks of a single gesture, all parts of the oriscus shape are joined as a single unit with a curved and indefinite ending similar to the liquescents. The connected curved shape of this neume suggests either the tremula-type ornament, in which the curves represent uninterrupted loud and soft pulses as in the quilisma, or possibly a change of pitch similar to a mordent; the oriscus shapes in the St Gall, Beneventan, and especially the Lorraine traditions bear a striking resemblance to the Baroque mordent symbol.

A recent comparative study by John Harutunian of the use of the oriscus in the introits of two Roman Graduals has resulted in the conclusion that it was

---

Codex 359 der Stiftsbibliothek St. Gallen, erhellt durch das Zeugnis der Codices Einsiedeln 121, Bamberg lit. 6, Laon 239 und Chartres 47: Eine paläographisch-semiologische Studie (Bethlehem Immensee, 1966), 100–1, 500–2; Eugène Cardine, *Gregorian Semiology* (Solesmes, 1982); Treitler, 'Reading and Singing'; and Göschl, *Semiologische Untersuchungen.*

[21] In support of this conclusion is a statement found in an 11th-c. gloss on the *Mythologiarum* of Fulgentius, found in the Vatican Library Reg. 1567: 'viva vox . . . potest enim et limmata subrigere et parallelos concordare et distonias mollire et ptongos iugare et ornare quilismata'. Quoted in Nancy C. Phillips, '*Musica* et *Scolica Enchiriadis*: The Literary, Theoretical, and Musical Sources' (Ph.D. diss., New York University, 1984), ii. 543. I am indebted to Paul Boncella for calling this to my attention.

[22] André Mocquereau, *Le Nombre musical grégorien*, 2 vols. (Rome and Tournai, 1908, 1927), ii. 163–5, classifies it as such. Apel, *Gregorian Chant*, 106–11, contends that it was at some point absorbed into the stropha forms, making the oriscus and apostropha identical, although he suggests that they may have been different sounds at an earlier stage. The information presented here suggests that for most regions this was probably not so.

[23] The most commonly found early shape of the oriscus resembles one of the contraction signs still in common use as the Spanish tilde. For a discussion of the shapes and various opinions on the origin and meaning of the word and the sign see Harutunian, 'A Comparison of the Oriscus', 1–21.

most likely of the mordent type.[24] Harutunian compared nearly 700 occurrences of the oriscus as it appears first in the diastematic notation of the eleventh-century Vatican MS 5319, and as 'translated' into heighted staff notation in the thirteenth-century Archivio di San Pietro, MS F.22.[25] He concluded that the symbol represented three notes: the pitch on which it was written, a note higher but possibly not as high as the next semitone, and a return to the original pitch.[26] Although we must be careful not to put too much weight on the evidence of later notational forms, in this case the graphic indication of the early neume shapes is in agreement with the later heighted translation.

Not all later notational traditions translate the oriscus into a mordent; in many it is a single neume with marks resembling ascending and descending plicas extending from it, or in other cases, simply a single neume. These conflicting translations of the oriscus, rather than being evidence of different traditions of singing this neume, more reasonably are the result the difficulty of representing in square notation the nuance of pitch inflection of less than a half-step.[27] From the information presented above as well as the evidence of the shape of the early neume itself, I would speculate that the performance of an oriscus probably involved a quick mordent-like sliding of the voice, possibly involving quarter-tone inflections of the written pitch. This kind of ornamental sound is compatible with what has emerged above as the vocal style of the period, and would fit in well with the kinds of ornaments described in this chapter and the next. The oriscus itself should be classified as a liquescent neume, but when it is added as a grace to the fixed pitch of a preceding neume, it would also be a repercussive neume since it would begin with an articulated repeat of the preceding neume.

[24] Harutunian, 'A Comparison of the Oriscus'. I am indebted to Thomas Connolly for drawing this study to my attention.

[25] For a detailed discussion of the relationship of the two manuscripts see Thomas H. Connolly, 'The *Graduale* of S. Cecilia in Trastevere and the Old Roman Tradition', *JAMS* 28 (1975), 413–58.

[26] Harutunian found that the three-note 'translation' occurred on the pitches A, B, A. He concludes that the reason for the three-note translation in the case of the oriscus in that position was the possibility of sounding both 'B' and 'Bb', whereas in all other cases the 'presence of a rigidly fixed whole or half step above made such a "translation" impossible . . . It would seem, then, that the oriscus, when used on other pitches, would have had the function of supplying that which was otherwise unavailable: a subtle upward inflection of an interval of less than a half tone'; 'A Comparison of the Oriscus', 62.

[27] Harutunian observed in reference to the two related manuscripts involved in his study, that in 53 per cent of the 686 cases the oriscus mark was translated as a single note. He concluded that this 'concurs with Dom Mocquereau's finding [*Le Nombre musical*] that the "tonal indecision inherent in the oriscus was often lost in the transcription" '; 'A Comparison of the Oriscus', 59. A similar discussion concerning the problem of translating indefinite pitches into specific pitch notation is found in Paul Anthony Luke Boncella, 'Toward a New Recension of the Frankish-Gregorian *Antiphonale Missarum*', in *Revista de musicología*, 16 (1993), 2229–45.

REPERCUSSIVE NEUMES

'Repercussive' refers to those neumes that consist of two or more marks on the same pitch. There are a number of these in early chant notation, some all on a single pitch, and others that involve the repetitive marks in conjunction with neumes on other pitches. They can be found in the manuscripts written as independent neumes of their own over a syllable of text, or joined to other neumes as composite forms. The distinctive graphic element of repercussive neumes is that the individual notes stand apart and unconnected, which distinguishes them from the liquescent neumes in which all the notes are joined together. In performance the notes of a repercussive neume are separately articulated, as is suggested by their graphic representation.

Stropha Neumes (Apostropha, Bistropha, Tristropha)

The apostropha, bistropha, and tristropha are variations of a single ornamental sound. Although they commonly appear in early chant manuscripts, especially in Graduals, very little is found in the treatises that describe or even mention them. The only theoretical statements about any of these ornaments appear to be that in the ninth-century treatise by Aurelian of Réôme, and a sentence with a written example in Walter Odington's treatise from *c*.1300. Aurelian's information is in reference to the 'Gloria Patri et Filio et Spiritui Sancto', in the third-mode verse of the introit. He relates the quick repercussions of the tristropha over the word 'Sancto' to the lashing of a hand.[28] Walter's statement makes it clear that the apostropha neume serves to aid in an elision of vowels; it is used when a word begins with the same vowel that ended the previous word, and thus the apostropha assists with the articulation (94). His graphic representations resemble plica and liquescent marks: apostropha *?*; bistropha *??*; tristropha *???*.

Aurelian, 122:45. O wise singer, note wisely, that when pure praise to the threefold name is sung in its entirety in two places, that is, on the sixteenth syllable, and afterwards on the fourteenth syllable, with a threefold note you may make a quick beat like a lashing hand.

Walter, 94. An apostropha is a type of accent that removes the last vowel of a word when the following word commences with a vowel.

Aurelian's choice of image, 'lashing hand', and even more the phrase 'quick beat' (*celerum ictum*), align the performance of these ornaments with the other

---

[28] Discussion of the stropha neume and Aurelian can be found in Treitler, 'Reading and Singing'.

written repercussive ornaments such as the unwritten morula and the pressus (discussed below). This conclusion is supported by Walter's statement and the written forms of the neumes themselves in as much as the marks in the stropha neumes are separated rather than joined together. (This is also the way they are written in later square notation.) The articulation of the stropha neumes, there-fore, is probably similar to that described for the morula: a quick alternation of sound and silence on the same pitch. In addition, the shapes of the separated marks of the stropha neumes are curved similar to a plica rather than to a punc-tum, which, together with Walter's statement that the stropha neumes are connected with a truncated vowel, suggests the performance practice described above associated with both the curved plica marks and the liquescent pes and clivis: a change of tone colour accompanied by a slide away from the pitch. From all this one can speculate that the performance practice indicated by apostropha, bistropha, and tristropha neumes is a rapid articulation in which the voice enters each new pulse on pitch and then slides flat with an inflected sound; they may be thought of as a series of quickly articulated plicas.

Pressus

Except for the instruction in the *Summa musice*, that the pressus should be sung 'evenly and quickly', the only hint we have as to what sounds this neume repre-sented is that when translated into square notation it is a repeated pitch followed by the lower auxiliary. In the manuscripts the pressus appears to act as a grace on the neume that precedes it. There is some diversity among the various scribal versions of this neume, but in most cases it has two distinct marks that are sepa-rated, which is probably a good indication that the pressus involves an articu-lated repercussion as part of its sound.[29] One of the two marks is a curved line, which in many of the traditions resembles the oriscus.[30] Based on both the visual representations and the *Summa* statement that the neume is executed 'evenly and quickly', it is possible to speculate that in all traditions the pressus involves both an articulated repercussion and a pitch inflection similar to that of the oriscus, ending one diatonic step lower than the original pitch. The notation traditions vary as to which of the sounds is separated and which is inflected, but both elements appear to be present in all of them. In that case the pressus could be classified as a member of both the repercussive and liquescent categories.

I have not found descriptions in the treatises for the performance of any other

---

[29] The *Summa* states that there are two forms—one with two marks and one with three. The reference is probably to pitches rather than to separate articulations, although a pressus with three separate marks is found in the English and Breton notations; see the chart by Hiley in 'Notation', *New Grove*, xiii.

[30] On the pressus in the context of a subdivision of the oriscus see Cardine, *Gregorian Semiology*. Also see the discussion in Harutunian, 'A Comparison of the Oriscus', 12–16.

neumes, but based on the obvious close relationship between the shapes of the ornamental neumes and the desired sound, I have speculated elsewhere that one of the principal purposes of the neume shapes was to represent performance nuances, both the kinds of sounds and the articulation.[31] Hucbald, writing at the end of the ninth century, suggests as much when he states that, although the neumes do not specify exact pitch as do a letter system he was advocating, they do assist the singer in determining vocal nuances and articulation:

Hucbald. In general, the usual notes are not at all considered unnecessary, for, inasmuch as they indicate the slowness of the melody and where the voice is to be tremulous, or in what manner the sounds themselves are grouped or separated, and also where the cadence occurs, lower or higher, according to the meaning of certain letters—all things which the artificial notes are not able to display—they are considered to be very beneficial.

Based on the preceding information, therefore, I would conclude that sound quality and pitch nuance are included in the notational signs: punctum, tractulus, and virga represent fixed pitch and full sound, whereas curved and indefinite marks represent unfixed and/or inflected sound. Further, since the purpose of the early notation forms was to represent the performance practices as graphically as possible, it would seem logical to conclude that the notation also provides articulation instructions: separated strokes mean separate articulation, whereas notes in ligature are not to be individually articulated. This last point is supported by Jerome, who directs the singer to join ligated notes and separate those not in ligature:

Jerome, 183:21. Second, that notes that are joined in notation shall be joined together in singing, but disjunct notes shall be separated. That separation is not a rest but a breath, and this is nothing other than the semblance of a pause or an entity the length of one *instantia*.

CONCLUSIONS

From these observations it is possible to speculate on a far broader use of the 'ornamental' sounds discussed above. Although treatises such as the *Summa musice* describe a relatively small number of neume forms and their performance practices, the early manuscripts from all traditions show a much larger variety of definite and indefinite symbols.[32] On close inspection one can see that many of the unmentioned forms are merely combinations of the basic shapes for which information is available. The oriscus, for example, when followed by a

---

[31] ' "Ornamental" Neumes and Early Notation'.

[32] A recent discussion of problems encountered in both interpreting some neume forms and in transcribing them into modern notation can be found in Theodore Karp, *The Polyphony of Saint Martial and Santiago de Compostela*, 2 vols. (Oxford, 1992), i, ch. 6, and ii, pp. viii–ix.

virga becomes a pes quassus: ⟋⟍ .[33] The scandicus ⸱⸱⟋ can be found written with several different marks in place of the second punctum: a plica connected with the final virga ⟋ (usually called a salicus), an independent descending plica ℈⟋, or with an oriscus ⟋ ⟋. Although no performance instructions have been found for these or many other composite early neume shapes, we do have information on the performance of all these components in other situations. It would seem to be a logical extension of the above information to assume that the various marks were intended to convey the same sounds regardless of their combination with other marks. In that case, we have sufficient information to be able to decipher nearly all the composite neumes.

Further, if the specific ornamental neume forms discussed above are considered to be merely categorical representatives or set combinations of basic shapes, it is possible to view the many different neume forms in the early manuscripts as records of an integrated vocal style that included a large number of sounds that are foreign to the later Western practice. If we observe the quantity of ornamental neume shapes in any one chant in the early manuscripts, the extent to which these 'ornamental' sounds were in use removes them from the category of 'ornamental'. In support of this view is the fact observed above that a part of the performance instructions for the non-liquescent clivis and pes included inflected and indefinite–i.e. 'ornamental'–sounds. We are left with an impression of a medieval vocal technique that had within its basic vocabulary such sounds as inflected tone, sliding and pulsing sounds, throat vibrato, and indefinite pitch as well as what we might think of as the more normal ingredients of full tone and stable pitch. Seen in this light, the improvised ornaments discussed in the next two chapters should fit smoothly into the overall picture of medieval vocal practices. The fact that neume shapes were closely connected with the desired performance practices also suggests that the differences in their forms from one region to another can assist us in identifying some elements of local performance styles, a subject that will be pursued in Chapter 6.

---

[33] The word *quassa* is found in the St Emmeram treatise (102), in conjunction with a 'shaking' sound that could be used as a morula. See the discussion of morula below in Ch. 4.

4

Graces

THE ornaments described in this chapter under the general heading of 'graces' are those to be added directly to a particular note, as differentiated from those added between notes, which are discussed in the next chapter. All ornaments discussed here were to be improvised, both their content and placement: there are no marks or signs in the music for their addition. Information about the nature of the ornaments, the technique of performance, and their placement is found only in theoretical writings. Much of what is discussed here is an extension or variation of the kinds of vocal techniques and nuances that were a part of the execution of the written ornaments discussed in Chapter 3.

Whenever possible I have grouped and labelled the ornaments according to their modern classifications. This has been done for purposes of organization and in order to assist the modern reader to understand the various ornaments. When there is a specific medieval name for an ornament it is given as well, although the writers of the late Middle Ages often grouped under a single name or concept several ornaments that we would consider today to be separate items. In reading the descriptions of ornamental practices in this chapter and the next the reader will receive the best mental impression if the vocal techniques and sounds discussed in Chapters 2 and 3 are kept in mind.

TRILL/VIBRATO

The grace most often discussed in the treatises is the ornament that oscillates from one pitch to another: the decoration we would call 'trill' when it involves the interval of a half-step or wider, or 'vibrato' if it occupies an interval smaller than the half-step. Although the word 'trill' is not used by the medieval writers, the words *vibro* and *tremolo* are often found in conjunction with the description of how this ornament is executed.[1] Whereas in present-day vocal training the

---

[1] The issue is further complicated by Giulio Caccini's use of the word 'trillo' in his *Le Nuove Musiche* of 1602 to describe an ornament that is depicted in notation as an accelerating repetition of a single pitch with a clear articulation. Although a discussion of Caccini's ornaments is beyond the scope of the present study, the use of the word 'trillo' to describe a pulsation of the same pitch, and our later use of the same word to indicate change of pitch, suggests that at some point the word must have had a broader meaning: it described an ornament that involved multiple repetition of a

two ornaments—trill and vibrato—are considered to be separate techniques, the early treatises discuss fluctuation of pitch as a single thing, no matter what the distance of the interval involved.

The clearest statement about the placement and execution of a trill is that by Jerome of Moravia when he describes, in unusually unambiguous terms (for this subject), how to execute a trill on an organ and how that differs from the same ornament executed by the voice (184:14). He directs the performer to hold down the organ key of the written pitch and then repeatedly to strike the key above it:

Jerome, 184:14. The quality and diversity of these flowers is shown on an organ in this way. When we play a song on an organ, if we want to embellish any note, for example a G in the bass, then we leave that note unchanged and strike not the note immediately below it, F, but the note above it, namely a. Then, we trill [vibrate] vigorously and a most beautiful harmony arises that we call harmonic flower (*flos harmonicus*).

What will result from Jerome's instructions, of course, is an intermittent dissonant clash: one organ pipe keeps sounding while the note above it is rapidly opened and shut, illustrated in Ex. 4.1(*a*).[2] Jerome goes on to describe three different types of trill ornaments for the organ (184:22): the 'open' trill, which is performed at medium speed and involves a whole-step above the written pitch, illustrated as Ex. 4.1(*a*); the 'long' trill, which is slow and involves a half-step above the written pitch, as in Ex. 4.1(*b*); and the 'quick' ornament,[3] which is a half-step trill that begins slowly and accelerates, as in Ex. 4.1(*c*):

Jerome, 184:22. When the immobile key and that to be vibrated constitute a semitone and the vibration is slow, it is the flower called 'long'. But when they are a tone apart and the vibration is neither slow nor quick but halfway between, this is an 'open' flower. And when the interval is a semitone and the vibration is slow in the beginning and is extremely fast as it progresses and as it ends, the flower is called 'quick'.

Earlier in the treatise Jerome had introduced the concept of 'harmonic flower' as an ornament of the voice (184:4). (His instructions in this chapter are mostly for the voice; the passage about organ trills quoted above is one of the few statements about instruments in this chapter of the treatise.) In his elaboration of

pitch, whether alternating with another pitch or simply pulsating without change of pitch (as, for example, the *quilisma*; see Ch. 3). As the discussion of *morula* later in this chapter will show, according to several medieval treatises all kinds of trills as well as pulsations and vibrato (in modern terms), were considered to have been generically related. It is not difficult to imagine that during the time of Caccini and later many or most aspects of that same general category still existed.

[2] These 'trill' examples all begin on the upper auxiliary. Although Jerome does not mention this technique in the passage quoted here, he states in another passage (185:4) that all trills begin this way. See the discussion of 'reverberation' below.

[3] There does not seem to be an entirely satisfactory English equivalent for Jerome's word *subito*. The word can also be translated 'unexpected', or 'immediate'. A more correct term would be 'accelerating', but I have chosen to use 'quick' because Jerome frequently uses that word to distinguish aspects of other ornaments.

Ex. 4.1. Jerome's organ trills: (*a*)'open'; (*b*) 'long'; (*c*) 'quick'

this concept for the voice he separates the 'trill' ornament into four different types—one more than for the organ—('long', 'open', 'quick', and *procellaris*), and it becomes clear here that he includes within the category of 'flower' the oscillation of any interval from one smaller than a half-step up to at least a step, thus encompassing in modern terms both trill and vibrato:

Jerome, 184:4. By 'harmonic flower' (*flos harmonicus*) is meant an ornamental and extremely fast and wave-like (*procellaris*) vibration of the voice or the sound [of an instrument]. Some of the flowers are 'long', some 'open', and others are 'quick'.

Similar to his description of the types of organ trills, Jerome presents the three basic types of vocal 'harmonic flowers': 'long', 'open', and 'quick' (Jerome 184:7, 9, 11), but with some differences between vocal and instrumental execution

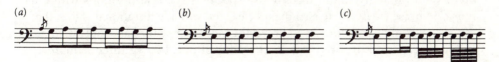

Ex. 4.2. Jerome's vocal trills: (*a*) 'open'; (*b*) 'long'; (*c*) 'quick'

(see Ex. 4.2). He points to the differences by prefacing the remarks about organ flowers with a notice that the 'quality' of the flowers is different on the organ (184:14 above). One difference is obvious—vocal trills involve alternate rather than simultaneous sounding of the written note and its auxiliary. Also, in vocal performance both the 'open' and 'long' trills are described as slow (184:7, 9), whereas for instruments the 'open' trill was of medium speed. Jerome emphasizes that for an organ the embellishment always is the note above the written pitch and not below it, and we shall see that vocal trills sometimes involve a lower pitch. But even more interesting is that when describing the intervals of the vocal trills he uses the phrase '*does not exceed* the limits of a semitone', and '*does not exceed* the limits of a tone', rather than stating simply the pitch of half- or whole-step as he did when describing the instrumental version. This suggests that vocal trills can include intervals different from our standard division of the half- and whole-step:

Jerome, 184:7. Those flowers are 'long' whose vibration is slow and does not exceed the limits of a semitone.

184:9. There are 'open' [flowers] whose vibration is slow and does not exceed the limits of a tone.

184:11. There are 'quick' [flowers] whose vibration is slow in the beginning, and is extremely fast in the middle and at the end, and does not exceed the limits of a semitone.

Jerome's 'quick' vocal trill can be understood in modern terms both as a vibrato and an accelerating narrow trill, both of which in singing could encompass an interval smaller than a half-step. We would call the 'long' and 'open' ornaments 'trills', but Jerome uses the same word, *vibratio*, to describe the sound of all these ornaments. The difference between the two varieties of 'long' and 'open' ornaments in singing, since they are both performed slowly, seems to be only the width of the interval.

Three of Jerome's four trill ornaments begin slowly; the 'long' and 'open' trills remain slow throughout their length, whereas the so-called 'quick' trill begins slowly and then accelerates. Only the *procellaris*, discussed below, moves rapidly throughout its length.

In addition to the clear descriptions of the different types of trill ornaments, Jerome also gives some information about their application.[4] The different kinds of trills serve different purposes and are associated only with notes of longa and breve values that are found in only five specific structural positions within a musical phrase (184:30). He also makes clear the variable durational values that can be assigned to both longa and breve: the longa can be the value of two, three, or four breves, and the breve can be the value of one, two, or three semibreves (*instantia*) (181:8, 13):

Jerome, 184:30. Fifth, therefore it ought to be noted that the above-mentioned flowers must not be performed on notes other than the five separately measured notes, and that they are performed in different ways. . . .

181:8. The longa note, when it is used in ecclesiastical chant, has and ought to consist of two modern tempora, equal to six tempora of the ancients. The longer form has three modern tempora the equal of nine ancient tempora. In its longest form it has four modern tempora, equal to twelve of the ancients.

---

[4] A similar description of these passages can be found in John Caldwell, 'Plainsong and Polyphony, 1250–1550', in Thomas Forrest Kelly (ed.), *Plainsong in the Age of Polyphony* (Cambridge Studies in Performance Practice, 2; Cambridge, 1992), 6–31 at 10.

181:13. Likewise, the breve note, when used in ecclesiastical chant, has and must consist of one modern tempus, which is the equal of three tempora of the ancients. The shorter form has two *instantiae* of the moderns, equal to two tempora of the ancients. The shortest form has only one *instantia* of the moderns, equal to one tempus of the ancients. This [value], according to both the moderns and ancients, is indivisible.

Jerome states that all the notes in chant have the value of a perfect breve with five exceptions, all of which are longas: (1) the initial note of the phrase; (2) the second note of a syllable having more than one note; (3) a plicated note; (4) the penultimate note of a phrase; and (5) the last note of a phrase (181:19–182:26). But to receive the longa value rather than that of a breve, the notes in cases 1, 2, and 3 are subject to specific conditions:

To be a longa the first note of the phrase (case 1) must be the pitch of the modal final. The second note of a multi-note syllable (case 2) is only a longa if it is not preceded or followed by another one of the five exceptions. A single plicated note (case 3) is a longa when the note plicated is itself written as a longa. If it is separately written it has the value of an imperfect longa, but if it is ligated it could be a perfect longa or even a four-unit longa. (The actual value would depend on neume shape and notational context.) Also, a pair of plicated, ligated notes with the written value of two breves could have the value of breve–longa if they are followed or preceded by a longa. (This last part is essentially the same rule as in case 2 above, but includes the possibility of a plicated version.) The fifth position—last note of a phrase—will be a longa of two to four units of time (breves) depending on the grammatical disposition of its text. If the text is merely pausing as at a comma, the note will be an imperfect longa; if the pause is more substantial, it is a perfect longa; and if it is the end of a thought, the pause is of four units.

Jerome, 181:19. Concerning all these things such rules are given:

All plainchant and ecclesiastical chants have first and foremost equal notes, namely of one tempus of the moderns but three tempora of the ancients, that is breves, except for five [notes].

181:24. First is the note by which each cantus begins, which is called the principal note, and which is always a longa provided it is the final of the chant, otherwise it is a breve like the others.

181:27. The second exception is that which is called the second note of the syllable when any syllable has more than one note. For then the second note, following the first, is a longa, provided it is not preceded or followed immediately by a note from the aforesaid excepted five notes; otherwise it is a breve like the others.

181:32. The third is the square note tailed from both sides, which is of two [kinds]. When the right tail is longer than the left, ascending or descending, it is called the plica longa, as it is here: ♩ ♩ . This [note] has two forms, namely simple and ligated. The simple form has already been shown. The ligated notes have longer tails, either ascending or descending, [and can encompass the interval of] up to a third in three [pitches], or less, or even more, and they are called long and ligated plicas, like this: ⚹ ⚹ .

182:8. When, on the other hand, the left tail is longer than the right, it is called the plica brevis, either ascending or descending, like this: ⚹ . Accordingly it is a breve like the other [notes]. Similarly, this [neume also can be] of two [types], namely simple, as has already been shown, and ligated when there are two notes descending; when ligated they cannot [encompass] more than a tone or semitone in ecclesiastical chant, as here: ⚹ ⚹ .

182:15 The first note is a breve like the others and the second is a longa, provided it has one of these five positions; otherwise it [the second note] is a breve like the others.

182:18. The fourth of the five notes is the penultimate note.

182:19. The fifth is the last [note] before each and every pause, which is not always a longa. Only in a short pause of an incomplete phrase is the last note a longa of two tempora. But in a pause of a complete phrase, which is the length of two tempora, [the last note] is longer, namely of three tempora. In the pause of a perfect phrase, which is longer, that is of three tempora, the [longa] is the longest, namely [of] four [tempora].

Referring to longas in these five positions, Jerome assigns the 'long' trill orna-ment for use only on the first note of the phrase and to the interval between the penultimate and final note of a phrase when that interval is an ascending half-step (184:30, continued below). The slowly oscillating half-step 'long' trill, there-fore, is used to frame a phrase. When sung on the initial note it will gently open the phrase. When sung at the end of a phrase, since it encompasses the half-step interval that separates the two last notes, its performance will result in a smooth glide from the penultimate to the final, where, as we shall see below, an addi-tional ornament is placed.

Jerome, 184:30, continued. For 'long' flowers must be employed on the first, the penulti-mate, and the last notes when there is an ascending half-step.

By contrast, the trill of a larger interval, the whole-step 'open' ornament, is applied in the case of a descending interval (184:30, continued below). This would include a longa in any descending situation, but Jerome makes a point of also including the special situation (181:27, above), where a syllable is shared by two or more notes and the second note is a longa. The element that makes the 'second note' situation different is that in the other placements the 'open' trill would be performed on a note that receives a syllable, whereas the second note has none. This would divert the emphasis of ornamentation to the second pitch, causing the first note—the note with the syllable—to act as an accented appog-giatura to the second. The application of a trill on a descending interval also permits the selection of a note below in place of the note above for the trilling interval; this would be useful mostly in situations where the following note is no farther than a step below the trilled note.

Jerome, 184:30, continued. But if it should be one of other melodic shapes [i.e. other than an ascending half-step] used in descending form, then the 'open' flower is applied, which is also the flower used for the second note of a syllable.

Jerome explains both the nature and the placement of the 'quick' trill by describing its use with a plica longa (184:30, continued below). This is a reference to his earlier description of one of the special longa placements that is in conjunction with a plicated neume (181:32–182:7, above). The presence of a plicated longa, therefore, would itself be the indication for the possible placement of a 'quick' ornament, although nothing in the statement would suggest that application of that trill is limited only to longas marked to be plicated. The 'quick' ornament would seem to have had a much wider possibility of placement. Further, since plicas are both ascending and descending, the 'quick' trill could involve either the note higher or lower than the basic pitch.

Jerome, 184:30, continued. 'Quick' flowers are used only on plicae longae between which and the note immediately following the shortest notes are placed to ornament the harmony.

Use of the plica longa as a way of discussing the execution of this ornament provides a fairly clear idea of the desired sound. As discussed in the previous chapter, a plica is a neume with two sounds, and its execution includes the use of the epiglottis in the performance of the second note. The 'quick' ornament, therefore, begins with a full sound on the written pitch, moves quickly to the plicated note above or below with an inflected sound, and then gradually accelerates (see Ex. 4.3). Since the trill itself starts with a darkened sound, a gradual change to full tone would probably accompany the acceleration.

Ex. 4.3. 'Quick' vocal trill on ascending half-step with (*a*) reverberation; (*b*) full tone; and (*c*) darkened tone

REVERBERATION/APPOGGIATURA

In order to begin all the trill ornaments, Jerome tells us that one first precedes the written note with a 'reverberation' (185:4). Earlier in his treatise he introduces the idea of 'reverberation' while discussing the interval of a unison, which he describes as the repetition of a pitch (59:3). In the previous chapter we have seen that the term 'reverberation' is used in conjunction with several different ornaments, all of which involved pulsations of a single pitch, including tremula and morula, which is probably what Jerome is referring to in conjunction with his description of the performance of a unison. In the context of an ornament that preceeds the trill ornaments, however, it would seem likely that instead of referring to a pulsing of the written pitch, Jerome's meaning for 'reverberation' in this context would be an appoggiatura, since he says (in 185:4) that the interval of reverberation is to be the same (tone, semitone, or other interval) as the following trill.

Jerome, 185:4. Sixth, reverberation must precede the flowers themselves, at [the interval of] a tone or semitone or any other melodic interval, on all the five [special] notes, except on the last [note of the phrase], which receives a reverberation of a semitone . . .

59:3. Unison is the doubling of many notes in a space or on a line at the same pitch. It is called unison, as it were, 'one sound', because, according to John [Affligemensis], 'although it is one voice, it reverberates without cease'.

This instruction would mean that one begins all ornamented trills on the upper or lower auxiliary, depending on the direction of the trill, before proceeding to the note. From Jerome's wording—that the reverberation 'precedes' the ornament (*praecedere*), rather than 'begins' it—it is possible to infer that after singing the reverberation there is a hesitation on the written note before proceeding to the trill. (This inference is reinforced by his statement about the exception to the rule in conjunction with the procellaris, below.) On the other hand, it would also be possible to interpret 'precedes' as referring to metric position, meaning that the ornament is sounded just prior to the correct metrical placement of the written note, as in the examples above. But his description of the reverberation in respect to the final note of the phrase (185:4, below) makes it clear that in all positions except for final, the reverberation is not simply the first note in a smooth running trill/vibrato beginning on the upper auxiliary. The reverberation is sounded quickly, the principal note is sustained, and then the trill—whatever its type—begins its motion.

A preceding reverberation is to be applied to all 'long', 'open', and 'quick' trills, with the only exception having to do with a trill on the last note of a phrase. Jerome points out that on the final note of a phrase the reverberation can only be a small interval, and that once it is begun in this manner, the final note proceeds without hesitation with a light, slow vibrato that he calls the procellaris. Jerome's description of the procellaris is both clear and colourful, associating the unintrusive sound of this vibrato with the gentle rippling effect of a breeze on water. Since all other trill/vibrato ornaments have been described in terms of the trilled interval, the description here that the procellaris does not interrupt the sound must refer to a very tiny pitch variation.

Jerome, 185:4, continued. It [i.e. the last note], however, is to end with a procellaris, which is no more than the slow vibration of a voice or [an instrumental] sound in the form of a semitone. Thus it belongs to the class of long flowers. The procellaris is so called because, just like a turbulence on the river when air is set in motion by a slight moving breeze without breaking the water, so the sound of the procellaris must be performed in song, with the appearance of movement but without the interruption of the [instrumental] sound or the voice.

Jerome states that the final note 'receives' (*assumit*) the reverberation and continues on to the end with the vibrato. I interpret this to mean that there is no hesitation or pause in the flow of the final note of the phrase. This might be more simply described as singing the last note with a vibrato starting on the upper auxiliary. This would support my interpretation of the contrasting instructions regarding the execution of a reverberation preceding all other trills ('open', 'long', or 'quick'): that instead of proceeding immediately into the trill, there is a hesitation on the written pitch after sounding the reverberation, and that for these trills (but not for a vibrato on the final note) the reverberation begins before the 'beat'.

Jerome's mention of the procellaris is interesting not only for the clarity of the description, but also for his statement about its placement: the light vibrato is to be used as a way of gently finishing a phrase. He does not advocate its use as an ornament elsewhere in a phrase, perhaps because, as he describes it, the procellaris would tend to bring the phrase to an end rather than to propel it forward. Later in the treatise, while discussing other vocal practices of a certain group of French singers, Jerome gives yet another reason for restricting the use of the procellaris (187:15): if it is used constantly, he says, the voice sounds as if it is trembling, although he admits that it is employed in this way by singers from other locations.[5]

Jerome, 187:15. They generally reject the use of the vibrato (*procellares*), claiming that all peoples using it have trembling voices.

If one envisions, therefore, a typical phrase ending with the interval of an ascending half-step, the sequence would be one of a long trill with reverberation on the penultimate note, followed by a procellaris on the final note, as in Ex. 4.4.

Reverberation can also be applied to longas, breves, and semibreves without necessarily proceeding to a trill, and Jerome presents rules for those applications, noting that reverberation is only applied to those breves (and semibreves) that

Ex. 4.4. Half-step cadence with (*a*) reverberation; (*b*) 'long' trill, and (*c*) procellaris

___

[5] By ascribing this view to 'some singers', Jerome may be referring to a smaller group than in his earlier reference to 'the French'.

Ex. 4.5. Reverberation without trill applied to ligated breve–long: (*a*) full tone; (*b*) half tone; (*c*) quarter tone; (*d*) quarter-tone reverberation applied to unligated breve and semibreve

are not ligated (183:26). The reason for avoiding reverberation on ligated notes has to do with the practice of articulation: each separate neume is articulated with a tiny silence, and a ligature is treated as a single neume (183:21). To sound a reverberation at the beginning of a note within a ligature, therefore, would cause a separate articulation on a note that is not to be separated. The interval used in the reverberation can be quite small—from less than a semitone up to a tone. He also alludes to other intervals ('all other types'), but his reference is not clear and he may be including here a pulsation on the same pitch. In modern terms the application of reverberation without trill would be similar to an appoggiatura (see Ex. 4.5).

Jerome, 183:26. Third, that no breve ought to be begun with reverberation except those in the above-mentioned five exceptions, which are measured individually. This is done in different ways, for some of them are begun with a reverberation of a semitone, others [with a reverberation] of a tone, but others with a reverberation of all other types [of intervals].

183:21. Second, notes that are joined in notation shall be joined together in singing, but disjunct notes shall be separated. That separation is not a rest but a breath, and this is nothing other than the semblance of a pause or an entity the length of one *instantia*.

In the case of the smallest ornamented note (a semibreve of the shortest value), Jerome tells us that the reverberation is done very quickly (183:32). The reason for this different treatment of the semibreve is probably the practical matter of the speed and function of the semibreve. The particular choice of words used here to describe when the ornament is sung, 'anticipation' (*anticipatio*), and 'before' (*ante*) the note, rather than at its beginning, reinforces my impression that a reverberation is always sung in anticipation of the metrical position of the written pitch:

Jerome, 183:32. Reverberation of the shortest note before the note to be sung, however, is the quickest anticipation by means of which the following [written] note is begun.

ACCENTED APPOGGIATURA

Another of the 'graces' described in the treatises is similar to an accented appoggiatura (i.e. an ornament beginning on the beat of the written note). Johannes de Garlandia mentions it in the context of two different ways in which one may

Ex. 4.6. Johannes de Garlandia's appoggiaturas: (*a*) from a single note; (*b*) variable intervals

embellish each note of a scalar descent (95:10). One way is to precede each note of the descending passage with a grace from the first note of the phrase, which will result in a series of appoggiaturas enlarging from the first interval of a second (step or half-step depending on the scalar intervals), to a third, fourth, and fifth; he limits this ornament to intervals no larger than that of a fifth (Ex. 4.6(*a*)). He also demonstrates a variation on this same scalar descent, in which each note of the passage is preceded by an appoggiatura of a step, half-step, or third. His example demonstrates the use of both the upper auxiliary and the upper third on each step of the passage (Ex. 4.6(*b*)). He recommends the use of this ornament for enhancing the melodic attraction of tripla and quadrupla in polyphony:

Johannes de Garlandia, 95:10. In well-ordered sound, colour is created in a twofold fashion: either by means of a single note within the range of a fifth, as here: [example]; or by means of various notes, strictly within the range of an octave, as shown in the example, and by extension as far as the twelfth. We employ such decorations in composing (*instrumentis*) the triplum and the quadruplum [literally, in threefold and fourfold instruments].[6]

---

[6] Another translation of this last phrase could be 'We employ such decorations on instruments capable of the third or fourth octave', if one were to translate the word 'instrumentis' as 'instruments', which is the way it is usually translated. I have chosen to translate it as 'composing' because there is no other evidence in this section of his treatise that Garlandia is considering instrumental music. The recent publications of Christopher Page and others concerning the completely vocal nature of polyphony would seem to support this conclusion.

Ex. 4.7. Triplum from *Partus fuit virginalis/Beata viscera*: (*a*) as written; (*b*) and (*c*) with Johannes de Garlandia's appoggiaturas

Garlandia's statement about employing these ornaments 'in composing' tripla and quadrupla may mean that some of them are improvised in those voices in addition to similar appoggiaturas already written in by the composer. It is not clear exactly to whom Garlandia is addressing his treatise. The title of the treatise itself, *De mensurabili musica*, and the extent to which he goes into notational details indicate that he is directing his remarks to serious students of music, but he seems to discuss written and unwritten practices intermixed throughout this section of the treatise.[7] As noted in Chapter 1, Erich Reimer doubts that these chapters (14–16) are by Garlandia, which would explain their lack of conformity with the remainder of the treatise.[8] Ex. 4.7 demonstrates the application of Garlandia's appoggiaturas to a phrase of a triplum.

REPEATED PITCH: COMMINUTIO, TREMULA, MORULA

Another type of 'grace' described by Garlandia as a colour in his section on ornamentation of the triplum is a called *comminutio* (fragmenting, or subdividing), a repercussive ornament related to trill and vibrato that he illustrates as a rapid subdivision of a note. The information about rhythmic subdivision is clear because of his musical example (see Ex. 4.8), but there is uncertainty about its execution because the text does not state whether there is a break in the sound or simply unbroken pulsations, as in the tremula and quilisma.[9] Apparently the comminutio can be applied to several adjacent notes in a phrase, but only in passages where the notes are conjunct and each one at least the value of a breve.

[7] For example, immediately following the paragraph quoted here Garlandia presents his idea of the *commixtio*, which is undoubtedly an improvised practice.

[8] Reimer, *Johannes de Garlandia*, ii. 39–42.

[9] The notation is of no help in this case, since in square notation there was no way to indicate a difference between loud–soft pulsations and separately articulated notes, as there was in earlier notation. On this subject see McGee, 'Ornamental Neumes and Early Notation'.

Ex. 4.8. Johannes de Garlandia's comminutio

Garlandia does not make any statement concerning the restriction of this ornament to any particular point of a phrase, and so we can probably conclude that the comminutio ornament was simply one method of ornamenting adjacent notes within a phrase.[10]

Johannes de Garlandia, 95:14. Colour occurs in the embellishment of the sound, as a comminutio [lit. fragmentation, i.e. subdivision] of notes in a simple conductus. That comminutio always occurs in conjunct sounds, not disjunct, as here: [Ex. 4.8].

Pulsing subdivision of a single pitch is described in earlier treatises as two different ornaments: morula and tremula. One of the earliest mentions is by Guido of Arezzo, who in his *Micrologus* calls for both morula and tremula as performance practices related to phrase ends in a monophonic line (163):

Guido, 163. A hold (*tenor*)—that is, a delay (*mora*) on the last note—which however small it is for a syllable, is larger for a section, and longest for a phrase—is a sign of division in these. And so it is necessary that a song should be clapped as if with metrical feet, and that some phrases should have a morula twice as long or twice as short compared with others, or a tremula, that is, a hold of variable length, which sometimes is shown to be long by a simple horizontal dash added to a letter.

Although Guido does not describe either morula or tremula in clear detail, his equation of tremula with 'hold' suggests some type of ornament, and the sentence following implies that he is discussing the subdivision of a written note. Fortunately for our understanding, two other writers, Aribo and the anonymous author of the *Commentarius in Micrologum*, elaborate on Guido's passage in a manner that explains how one executes these two different subdivisions. The anonymous writer makes it clear that both morula and tremula consist of a repetition of a pitch, but whereas the morula consists of all equal sounds, the tremula is performed by alternating loud and soft pulses (*Commentarius*, 149:21).[11]

Anon., *Commentarius*, 149:21. Not only ought one morula be compared with another, but also with a tremula and related notes, and the converse, according to the way they are arranged in the chant. The tremula is similar to a repercussed note, just as is a morula, but there is this difference, that in a morula the sounds are produced with

---

[10] Reimer, *Johannes de Garlandia*, ii. 41, associates this ornament with the tremula described by Jerome. Edward Roesner, 'The Performance of Parisian Organum', *Early Music*, 7 (1979), 174–89 at 176–8, identifies some compositions from W1 as possibly including composed examples of the comminutio. The word found in the single manuscript source is *commixtio*, but both context and the musical example indicate that this is a scribal error.

[11] The word *mora* means 'pause, or delay', and is usually translated as such in modern editions of treatises. It apparent from the discussion below, however, that when this type of retarding was employed it was coupled with a pulsating ornament.

uniform pulses of the voice, while in the tremula these same sounds are brought forth with now a greater, now a lesser impulse of the voice, as if trembling.

Aribo's commentary does not include the passage quoted above, but he and the anonymous writer transmit nearly identical passages in which they clarify both techniques by describing the morula as having a silence between the tones, and the tremula as being related to the performance of the quilisma (Aribo, 66:34, *Commentarius*, 153:59; also quoted and discussed in Ch. 3 in a different context).[12] The morula is described by both commentators in the process of elaborating on Guido's statement that they could be 'twice as long or twice as short'. Through a combination of the statements we may conclude that the morula is a repetition of the same pitch with the sounds clearly detached from one another but all performed at the same volume, whereas the tremula is sung by alternating loud and soft without a break, in the same way one performs the pulses in a quilisma (see Ch. 3, p. 54). According to the anonymous writer, tremula and morula (and therefore quilisma) do not change pitch when being pulsed (150:28, also quoted in Ch. 3).

Aribo, 66:34 and Anon., *Commentarius*, 153:59. The morula is twice as long or twice as short; [it is long] if the silence between two sounds is double in relation to the silence between two [other] sounds. In the same manner the morula is twice as short if the silence between two sounds is single in relation to the silence between two [other] sounds [i.e. sounds and silences must be of equal length, either single length or double]. When Guido says 'or have tremula', I think it should be understood as follows: the tremula is the neume we call a stepped neume (*gradatam*)[13] or quilisma, which indicates length, of which he says 'twice as long' with an affixed virgula, without which it marks shortness, as is shown in his wording, 'twice as short'.

Anon., *Commentarius*, 150:28. A repercussion is either a morula or a tremula, and that is what Guido means by 'that they have either a morula or a tremula, that is, a repeated tone', by means of a repeated impulse, but not changing pitch.

At this point we might return to the relationship between the tremula and quilisma. Since both Aribo and the anonymous author of the *Commentarius* equate the two, a question arises as to why Guido would not have stated simply that at the ends of phrases a quilisma should be performed. It is not that the quilisma was unknown in Guido's time (the eleventh century); it is mentioned in the ninth century by Aurelian of Réôme, and appears as a written sign in some of the earliest-known notated chant books. In his description of the tremula, of course, Guido seems to be discussing an improvised practice, rather than one that is marked in the notation, and that may be the distinction.[14] To his

---

[12] Joseph Smits van Waesberghe, who edited both treatises, believes that Aribo and the anonymous author of the *Commentarius* do not agree on their definition of morula and tremula. See Aribo, *De musica*, ed. Waesberghe, p. xxiii.　　　　　　　　　　　　　　[13] See Ch. 3 n. 19.

[14] For comparison, see Guido's remarks on the liquescent (Ch. 3, p. 46), where he speaks of how it is indicated in writing.

commentators later in the century, it was clear that the written quilisma and the improvised tremula were very similar ornaments. From this it would be possible to conclude that as late as the eleventh century the two ornaments were still somewhat different from one another—perhaps two different kinds of pulsation—but that by the late eleventh century they had melded into a single practice. It is more probable, however, that at all times the only differences were whether or not the ornament was notated, and whether it remained on a single pitch or moved between two pitches. When this pulsing ornament was to be used to join two pitches a third apart, it was written as a quilisma. At the same time, however, the singer was to insert the identical pulsing sound of a tremula (without changing pitch) at phrase ends as a matter of custom without relying on a written mark.

The word morula had other meanings than a pulsing motion interpolated at the end of a phrase. Another function, as implied by Guido (163, above) and the two commentators (Aribo and *Commentarius*, above), has to do with the lengthening or shortening of phrases. Since Guido makes it clear that morula and tremula ornaments are applied at the ends of phrases, it is significant that shortly afterwards he states that phrase ends are to be slowed (Guido 175a, below). At the same time he warns that the singer must take care when retarding certain phrases not to make such a difference in phrase lengths that equal-length phrases would become unbalanced in length (Guido, 165, below). One meaning of these statements seems to be that corresponding phrases should be retarded to a similar degree in order to keep the balance, but it could also include the idea of matching the quantities of ornamental passages interpolated at the phrase ends.

Guido, 175a. Likewise, like a running horse, the notes should always approach the place of breathing at the end of the phrase more slowly, so that as if in grave manner they approach the resting place in a weary state.

Guido, 165. Special care should be taken in the assignment of neumes, that, since neumes are produced either by the repetition [lit. repercussion] of the same sound, or by the linking of two or more [sounds], they should nevertheless always be related either in the number of notes or in the proportions of the holds (*tenorum*), and correspond equal to equal or double or triple to simple, or else three to two or four to three.

The writer of the *Commentarius in Micrologum*, in his amplification and qualification of the *Micrologus*, adds to our understanding of the way in which the morula and tremula ornaments were intended to function. The anonymous writer seems to be pointing out that normal articulation involves a slight lengthening. He observes that this happens at the end of all separately written neumes, and that the amount of the lengthening and the presence or absence of ornamentation depends on the function of the neume in its phrase: those neumes at the ends of phrases are ornamented with a morula or tremula.

Anon., *Commentarius*, 150:27. A held note is sometimes repercussed and sometimes it is not, and it is through this that we distinguish syllables and neumes when we linger for some time at the end of some notes.

Rudolf of St Trond supplies the missing details with regard to the purpose of the above discussions: the writers were all referring to metrical chant—rhymed texts that were to be sung in such a way that the phrases were matched metrically. To take up the slack caused by a missing syllable or to allow for subdivided syllables and those set to melismas, the performer was to lengthen or shorten particular notes of the matching phrases. The word 'morula' did not refer to a particular pitch or neume, but to any note that corresponded to a long syllable. As Rudolf states (and the other writers imply), singers could alter these morula points by shortening or lengthening them as long as they compensated at another morula in order to make the phrases match. It would seem, therefore, that when a note was held long at one of these points, it would also be pulsed; morula referred to both the function of a note within a metrical phrase and to its performance practice. To complicate the issue from our point of view, the performer could chose to execute the morula note as a tremula.

Rudolf. To sing metrically is so that it may be observed where he ought to use the longer and shorter morulas. Since it can be observed which syllables are short and which long, similarly one should note which sounds should be lengthened and shortened so that the long run together properly with the short and that the song (*cantilena*) can be beaten in metric feet. Therefore let us sing by practising this exercise. I shall beat time, you will follow and imitate me. Only the final longa receives the value of three breves [example missing].[15]

In order to sing metrically, set morulas should be measured in long and short notes and the sound should not be shortened or lengthened in places more than is proper, but we should keep the notes within the law of scansion so that the melody may end on the same mora as it began [i.e. balance the length of the phrases by adjusting the morulas]. Or if you wish to change the mora at any time, that is to make the beginning and ending of a phrase either shorter or more elongated, you may do this in two ways, that is you may change the lengthened morula to be twice as short, or the shortened morula to be twice as long. Let us undertake to sing a melody first shortened and then lengthened, so that first the long morulas are shortened, then correspondingly we should lengthen those which are short. Let us now sing: [text examples].

First let there be a short mora, a long one added, then a short again. This measuring of rhythm is the greatest distinction of learned song, whether it is sung by one or by many, either drawn out or more quickly. And it happens as well when someone sings

---

[15] The manuscripts do not include an example at this point. This section of Rudolf's treatise is copied from the *Musica enchiriadis* (written *c*.900 and often attributed to Hucbald), in which an example is written in Daseian notation. See Rudolf Steglich, *Die Quaestiones in Musica: Ein Choraltraktat des zentralen Mittelalters und ihr mutmasslicher Verfasser Rudolf von St. Trond (1070–1138)* (Leipzig, 1911; repr. 1970), 60 n. 2.

metrically along with someone else who lengthens and contracts neither more nor less, as if from one mouth the voice of the multitude is heard. Likewise, in alternating, that is leading and responding, it is as important to preserve the morula as to preserve the harmony of sounds [i.e. when performing metrically in *alternatim*, the observation of correct phrase lengths—by correctly employing morulas—is as important as keeping the correct mode and pitch].

There is an agreement of phrase length [lit. a harmony of morulas], if that which must be added corresponds either in equal morulas or for good cause—morulas twice as long or twice as short.

In the latter half of the thirteenth century the Parisian theorist known to us as the Anonymous of St Emmeram used the word morula in a way that tends to enlarge its possible performance practices (102). He too uses morula rather broadly as a way to describe a longer note-value (*recta brevis*). According to the St Emmeram author, the vibrating or shaking note (*quassa*) is only one way of performing a long note; it could also be sung full value by the voice, performed with an instrument that somehow does not sound the note fully,[16] or omitted. The description of *vox quassa* here is so unclear that in addition to the articulated repetition of a single pitch, the description could also be construed to encompass trill, vibrato, or even a small 'passaggio'. On the other hand, knowing the descriptions of the morula quoted earlier, the reference to the *vox quassa* as a half-complete note that is subdivided may be an attempt to describe the alternation of sound and articulated silence.[17] Walter Odington describes the *pes quassus* as a turbulent note performed with a trembling and shaking voice (95), which would fit with all the above descriptions of its performance.

Anon. of St Emmeram, 102. A unit of time (tempus), therefore, as it is used here, is a morula wherever a *recta brevis* can be made. The *recta brevis* is that which contains only one unit of time, and that is indivisible according to that which has been said before, that is, with respect to the *recta brevis*. Note that the tempus can be correctly performed in three ways, and that by proportion, that is either by use of a full sound (*vox recta*) or a shaking sound (*cassa*, lit. empty) or one that is omitted (*omissa*). A *vox recta* is produced by natural instruments [i.e. the voice]. The *vox cassa* is the same as a sound—not a voice [i.e not a natural vocal sound]—artificially produced as on musical instruments in which the sound is heard and perceived proportionally [i.e. the sound is intermittent]; or it is a shaking sound, so named from 'quassa'—agitated—which is the same as an imperfect or a half-complete sound, subdivided by means of different sounds. The *vox omissa* is made for the restoration of the spirits [i.e. to catch a breath], and it is produced by [making] a pause equal to the duration of the previously mentioned note, for the unit of

---

[16] The author does not describe this, but it might refer to the observation that a sound from a plucked string will diminish in volume even though assigned the correct length of time.

[17] The phrase 'subdivided by means of different sounds' could also be taken to refer to the use of a passaggio of notes of varying pitches rather than just to the repetition of the same pitch. If this is what is intended by the phrase, the St Emmeram writer has assimilated into the idea of morula the short passaggio executed at various places as described in Ch. 5, p. 103.

time is subdivided by a *vox quassa*, as has been said, and imperfected as to semibreves, which are named after the word s*emus, sema, semum* [= adj. 'deficient'], that is, *imperfectus, imperfecta, imperfectum*, as if imperfect breves.

Walter Odington, 95. The *pes quassus* is so called because it is formed by a trembling and shaking voice.

It is clear from these statements that there were two accepted methods of ornamenting a single note without changing its pitch: repetition with clear detachment between sounds, and pulsations where the voice alternates between strong and weak but does not break the flow of sound. Since Garlandia's term comminutio is different from both words used in the earlier treatises, and since comminutio—fragmenting, or subdividing—could be translated as either the articulated or pulsated version, it is not possible to ascertain which of the two ornaments he was describing, and in fact, he could have been describing both. And although Guido, Aribo, and the author of the *Commentarius* describe morula and tremula only in conjunction with cadencing, Garlandia, Rudolf, and the St Emmeram writer do not. It would seem, therefore, that articulated repetition (morula) and pulsating repetition (tremula) were ornaments to be used both in the midst of phrases and at cadences. The difference in execution in the two placements would have to do with the retard that should be introduced at phrase ends but not elsewhere.

A more artistic description of the practice of inserting pauses—moras—in musical performances is given in the mid-fifteenth-century treatise by Giorgio Anselmi, where he likens it to a rhetorical gesture: as an interpretative device to be employed effectively by trained singers (Giorgio III:229). He describes the mora only as a pause, however—one of the possibilities allowed by the St Emmeram author—but does not mention the placement of a vocal ornament as a substitute.

Giorgio, III:229. For just as the orator often soothes the weary listener with some joke and makes him well disposed, so the trained singer mixes some delays (*moras*) with the melody and makes the listener more eager and attentive to the rest of the phrases of the song. These morulas, or rests, are called pauses in a song.

The information quoted so far concerning repetition of a single pitch has applied to monophonic chant and the highest part in organa tripla, but there is also information about the use of the tremula in the tenor voice of organum. A statement by Walter Odington indicates that a tremulo pulsation was regularly added to enhance the sustained notes of the tenor even when a dissonance was involved:

Walter, 141. Organum purum is composed in this way. One phrase, or two or three, is selected from some plainchant and the tenor arranged in a certain way, and the superius moves with it in any number of consonances and concordant dissonances. The superius begins at the octave, fifth, or fourth above the tenor and ends at the octave, fifth, or

Ex. 4.9. Walter Odington's organum purum example

unison. It should be sung gently and precisely, the descent should be quick and even, and the tenor should be held tremulo even when it participates in a dissonance [Ex. 4.9].

Walter's reference to the tenor still sounding through a dissonance is at odds with the instructions of Franco of Cologne, who states that in times of dissonance the tenor is either to 'feign concord' (which probably means to alter the tenor note to a pitch that is concordant with the superius), or to be silent (80:1). Since there is evidence that Walter was a follower of Franco, there can be little question that the two instructions are contradictory and probably demonstrate the differing regional practices between France and England at the end of the thirteenth century in regard to how a sustained dissonance in organum is to be treated. With reference to vocal practices for the tenor of organum, we can be sure that the English sang the part with a tremulo, but little can be assumed from Franco's silence on that matter. On the other hand, the statement by Jerome quoted above (187:15), that the 'some singers' (presumably some of those in Paris) did not sing with a constant vibrato and that they claimed that those who did had 'trembling voices', may have been a reference to the English.[18]

Franco, 80:1. The longas and breves of organum are understood through three rules. The first is: whatever is notated in the shape of a longa simplex is long, and whatever is notated in the shape of a brevis is short, and whatever is notated in the shape of a semibrevis is half-short. The second rule is: whatever is long [in the upper voice] must be concordant with respect to the tenor; but if it occurs as a discord, the tenor should be silent or feign concord.

INTERVAL AND PITCH VARIATION

An important element of medieval singing practice involves freedom with pitch—both the substitution of one interval for another and the selection of pitches other than the standard whole- and half-steps. The use of variable pitches as a part of medieval vocal technique was mentioned in Chapters 2 and 3.

---

[18] For a discussion of these passages and another interpretation of what may be intended see Roesner, 'The Performance of Parisian Organum', 176, 183.

Several of the statements about singing technique imply that a minute variance of pitch is one of the desirable subtleties of vocal technique, and the performance of many of the written ornamental neumes includes the use of quarter-tones along with sound inflection.[19] Jerome of Moravia mentions pitch variation more extensively than does any other theorist. He calls for trill intervals that do not exceed a tone or a semitone (see Jerome 184:7, 9, 11 above, p. 64), and he includes the filling in of a half-step interval as one of a set of 'passaggi type' ornaments (see Ch. 5, p. 91). When describing the ornamentation practices of certain Parisian singers and how they differ from those of others, he addresses the subject of pitch variation directly and explicitly states that in addition to rearranging the tones and semitones of a chant, thereby altering its mode or introducing non-modal intervals, these singers also employ the chromatic and enharmonic intervals (187:8).

Jerome, 187:8. They [certain singers] take pleasure in adding organum (*modum organicum*) to ecclesiastical song [i.e. plainchant], which the first mode [i.e. the diatonic genus] does not reject, and also in introducing the two remaining genera, for they unite enharmonic quarter-tones (*diesis*) and chromatic trihemitones (*trihemitonium*)[20] with the diatonic genus. They exchange the semitone for a tone and the reverse, in which they are in discord with all nations.

The identification of the three genera—diatonic, enharmonic, and chromatic—is an echo of Greek theory from a much earlier period, but it is clear that Jerome is referring to contemporary practices. A number of other theorists also make reference to the three genera or to subdivisions of the whole tone, and although not all of them are describing melodic coloration in the same way as Jerome, some do present evidence that indicates a similar use of variable pitch.

The author of the *Duo semisphaeria quas magadas vocant*, Anonymous I (G), writing in the twelfth century (but possibly as early as the tenth), refers to the three genera in a manner that would suggest he is discussing practical, rather than theoretical, matters. He expresses a preference for the employment of the diatonic genus in ecclesiastical chant because of its character, which he describes as 'vigorous' and 'hard', which prevents a weakening of the souls from the excessive sweetness that results from use of the chromatic genus. He excludes the

---

[19] Related to this topic is the use of chromatic tones that are not a part of the regular modal scales. John Snyder presents evidence for the presence of many chromatic changes in orally transmitted chants that were later regularized when written down; see 'Non-diatonic Tones in Plainsong: Theinred of Dover versus Guido d'Arezzo', in Marc Honegger et Paul Prevost (eds.), *La Musique et le rite sacre et profane* (Actes du XIIIᵉ Congrès de la Société Internationale de Musicologie, Strasbourg, 29 août–3 septembre 1982; Strasbourg, 1986), ii. 49–67. Perhaps this is part of what Regino of Prüm intends when he advocates the removal of non-modal variants from the chant in order to make it conform to theory. This is discussed in Calvin M. Bower, 'Natural and Artificial Music: The Origins and Development of an Aesthetic Concept', *MD* 25 (1971), 17–33.

[20] The trihemitone is a minor third that is available in the diatonic genus. What Jerome seems to be saying, however, is that these singers employ it where it is foreign to the diatonic genus.

chromatic genus completely from ecclesiastical use because it is effeminate, but he seems to support the occasional use of the enharmonic genus, which combines the vigorous and sweet qualities of the other two genera. The chromatic genus is not excluded from all music, however, only from ecclesiastical, and although it is his opinion that the diatonic genus has the most suitable character for ecclesiastical music, he does leave the door open for the occasional use of the enharmonic genus in that repertory.

Anonymous I (G) 331. This genus is called diatonic according to the range and arrangement of tones, an arrangement that the other genera do not have, since one [i.e. chromatic] is produced through semitones, while the other [i.e. enharmonic] is produced through *dieses* [quarter-tones], which will be explained in what follows. The diatonic genus is acknowledged to be rather vigorous and hard. This genus is chosen for ecclesiastical use lest the souls of the hearers or the singers be softened by the sweetness of the chant. That music is capable of wholly altering souls by its sweetness and capriciousness anyone can learn through personal experience, and we know that the writings of wise men attest it. The chromatic genus is called, as it were, coloured. This is because it is the first departure from the diatonic and is as if it were of a different colour; indeed, the Greek word *croma* means 'colour'. This genus is acknowledged to be most soft [i.e. effeminate], for which reason it is not put to ecclesiastical use. The enharmonic genus, however, because it is composed and blended with moderation from both the other genera, receives its name from 'harmony', which is the harmonious accord of different things. This genus occupies the place of the mean, as it were, because it is neither hard nor delicate, but it is sweet since it is composed from both.

The most highly developed theoretical writing that includes elements of both the non-standard pitches and the chromaticism of the enharmonic and chromatic genera can be found in the writings of the early fourteenth-century Italian theorist Marchettus of Padua, who goes to some length in his *Lucidarium* to describe the division of the whole tone into five parts, including enharmonic, diatonic, and chromatic semitones. Each of the fifth subdivisions he called a 'diesis', which he explains as the smallest division of the whole tone that can be sung. Two of the dieses can be joined to make up an 'enharmonic' semitone, which would be the interval between A and B♭, or B♮ and C; three make up a 'diatonic' semitone, the interval between B♭ and B♮; and four, the 'chromatic' semitone, is four-fifths of a tone, a very wide semitone.[21] Jan Herlinger presents a convincing argument that Marchettus was not simply theorizing, but discussing practical performance.[22]

---

[21] See Jan Herlinger, 'Marchetto's Division of the Whole Tone', *JAMS* 24 (1981), 193–216 at 203–5.
[22] 'Once dismissed by scholars as out of touch with the musical reality of the time, Marchetto's examples are now known to reflect Italian practice at the dawn of the Trecento' (ibid. 193). This is similar to the earlier conclusion in Marie Louise Martinez-Göllner, 'Marchettus of Padua and Chromaticism', in *L'Ars nova italiana del Trecento*, 3 (1969), 187–202 at 189.

Of importance to the present discussion is not only the existence of the differ-ent sizes of semitones, but the use of these chromatic alterations within a melodic phrase. Although chromatically altered pitch was well accepted in particular situations, Marchettus' chromatic progression is unusual in that it was not restricted to use as a leading-tone, but was used within the body of a phrase. Further, although the theory of the time allowed for the replacement of, for example, B♭ with B♮ (or the reverse), it did not allow the use of both pitches in succession except in rare circumstances (Marchettus calls this 'permutation').[23] Marchettus, however, presents melodic sequences such as the descending chro-matic progression D, C♯, C♮, a sequence that calls for the interval of one diesis followed by another of four. And whereas the use of C♯ would normally be acceptable as a leading-note to D, here both forms of C are used melodically in a descent from D to C. (Marchettus describes this type of motion as 'feigned colour' (2.8.9–10), which brings yet another dimension to the use of 'colour'.)

Marchettus, 2.8.9–10. This division of the tone into two should be made with feigned colour, so that whoever uses it feigns it in the first descending interval (which is a *dyesis*) as if he wished to return upwards after this descent, and then descend a chromatic semi-tone. Thus a consonance follows, though less naturally and less properly.

Marchettus' treatise was widely disseminated, especially in Italy, and some of the chromaticism it describes can be found in Italian music of the fourteenth century.[24] Because the symbols used in the written music for chromaticism were limited to sharp and flat, however, it is not possible for us to know if performers during that time would have employed Marchettus' pitch variants as Herlinger suggests, that is, whether in performance any given half-step or chromatic alter-ation would have been subject to the several possible pitches discussed by Marchettus.

The subject of chromatic alteration continued to appear regularly in the music treatises of the late Middle Ages and the centuries to follow, but the discussions were usually in the context of describing the application of *musica ficta* in polyphonic music where the chromaticism was confined to leading-note use. Still, the inclusion of the 'enharmonic' genus in some of these discussions—especially when the writer is familiar with Marchettus' subdivisions—brings with it the possibility that non-standard pitches could have been a part of the performance practice.

[23] See Herlinger, 'Marchetto's Division', 196–7.

[24] See the list of copies of Marchettus' treatises in Jan Herlinger, 'Marchetto's Influence: The Manuscript Evidence', in André Barbera (ed.), *Music Theory and its Sources: Antiquity and the Middle Ages* (Notre Dame, 1990), 235–58 at 256–8. Chromatic musical examples in Herlinger, 'Marchetto's Division', 194–6. The theorist Prosdocimo de' Beldomandi, in his *Tractatus musice speculative* of 1425, condemns Marchettus' subdivisions as erroneous. See D. Raffaello Baralli and Luigi Torri, 'Il *Trattato* di Prosdocimo de' Beldomandi contra il *Lucidario* di Marchetto da Padova per la prima volta trascritto e illustrato', *Rivista musicale italiana*, 20 (1913), 731–62 at 731.

(a)   (b)   (c)

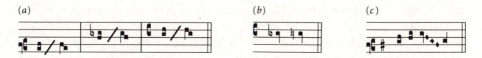

Ex. 4.10. Bonaventura da Brescia's semitones: (*a*) 'enharmonic' (minor); (*b*) 'diatonic' (major); (*c*) 'chromatic' or 'excellent'

Bonaventura da Brescia was well acquainted with the treatise of Marchettus, and in his *Regula musice plane* of 1497 he describes the three different sizes of semitones: enharmonic for those that occur normally in the scale, diatonic for major semitones such as between B♭ and B♮, and chromatic for those that are altered through *musica ficta* to make a leading-note (Ex. 4.10). But in his description and use of the chromatic semitone he differs from Marchettus: whereas Marchettus' chromatic semitone was composed of four dieses—an extra-large melodic semitone—Bonaventura approaches the chromatic change only from above as a leading-note, and assigns it one diesis. Bonaventura, therefore, is not describing Marchettus' type of chromatic melody, but the usual method of altering a cadencing interval, though his use of the terms and the variable divisions of the semitone do give evidence of the continuing use of different sizes of half-steps, that is, variable intervals.

Bonaventura, Ch. 12. Likewise note that there are three types of semitone, that is to say, the enharmonic semitone, the diatonic semitone, and the chromatic semitone, or in other words, the minor semitone, the major semitone, and the 'excellent' semitone, etc. The enharmonic semitone, that is to say, the minor semitone, happens everywhere one finds 'mi fa' in ascent and 'fa mi' in descent, as is seen in the figure above: [Ex. 4.10(*a*)]. Likewise, the diatonic or major semitone happens everywhere one finds 'fa mi' in ascent and 'mi fa' in descent, and the two of these are found in the [Guidonian] hand according to the natural order, that is, where there are 'b fa♮ mi'; and this semitone is found from the first 'b' to the second as here: [Ex. 4.10(*b*)]. Likewise, the chromatic or excellent semitone is made through *musica ficta*, that is, when we make a semitone by means of *musica ficta* in place of a tone in ordinary music. And such chromatic or coloured semitones are made in descent, that is, when of 'fa' or 'ut' of the natural hexachord we make an accidental 'mi', as is evident here: [Ex. 4.10(*c*)].[25]

Along with those theorists who describe variable pitch positively in terms of actual practice (Anonymous I (G), Jerome, Marchettus, and Bonaventura), there are those who make it clear that it was not in use. In a somewhat ambiguous passage the author of the twelfth-century *Summa musice* seems to be rejecting

[25] Other treatises containing similar statements are: Berkeley Treatise (1375); *Sciendum quod antiquitus*, which appears in three 15th-c. manuscripts; and Ciconia's *Nova musica*. These and other sources are cited and discussed in Herlinger, 'Marchetto's Influence'. I am grateful to Prof. Herlinger for advice on this subject.

all but the diatonic intervals. He uses the terms 'diatonic', 'enharmonic', and 'organicum' to discuss what he introduces as the property of tones (*proprietas tonorum*), but which seems to be a discussion of vocal ranges. He calls the lowest range 'organicum' rather than 'chromatic', as one would expect in this context, but in his description of 'organicum' he uses the same term employed by Anonymous I (G) for rejecting the 'chromatic' genera from ecclesiastical use: *mollicies* = softness, or effeminacy. The exact meaning of the passage is not clear, but it is obvious that this writer associates the word 'enharmonic' and anything other than diatonic as unacceptable (478–88):

Anon., *Summa musice*, 478–88. Such a threefold song the discoverers and first scholars of music called 'diatonic', as it were, after the property of tones. A song that is lower than the lowest range of the gamut they disregarded on account of its softness, having little or no value. They called this *organicus*, because the instrument of the human voice is deficient in it. Similarly, they did not bother about music that is beyond the highest range of the gamut on account of the insupportable labour [required to produce it]; besides, no pleasure is to be found in it. They called such music enharmonic, because it is placed outside the harmony of diatonic music, and it wearies and annoys the singer and the listener, giving no pleasure of delight.[26]

There is no ambiguity in the 1323 statement of Johannes de Muris (262), who refers to the chromatic and enharmonic genera as 'contrary to the natural inclination of the human voice', although he concedes that they could be used with some difficulty by instruments. According to de Muris, only the diatonic genus was used for ecclesiastical chant or any other sacred or secular music, including music for instruments.

Johannes de Muris, 262. In these regions where the catholic religion of the faithful flourishes just as anywhere in all lands, it astonishes me and I do not understand why those two types of melodies, chromatic and enharmonic, have never come into use: rather, all ecclesiastical chant that the holy fathers, venerated doctors, and men of good memory and most mild and worthy mind used—and all chant measured by specific time-value as in conductus, notas, organum, and the remaining types of song—and all secular chant sung by men or women, young or old—and all music for instruments—[all these] are understood to fall into the diatonic genus.

I do not know by what spirit (except divine), by what pleasure and spontaneous will it [music] falls naturally into and is realized into sounds through the diatonic genus. I do not know in which part of the world, in which corners of any region, and under which part of the heavens or by what method they hide the other two genera.

I can think only that they were devised for singing so to speak against the natural inclination of human voices. [But] I know that scarcely or never would the human voice conform well with these two genera, and certainly not by itself, although on instruments

---

[26] This excerpt is somewhat confusing and suggests that the theorist may have confused the harmonic genera with range. In any case it is clear that he does not know of the chromatic and enharmonic versions as being in practice.

a great deal is possible. Nor do I doubt that the music of these two genera was harsh and uneven and joyless to [all] those imbued with the third genus, the diatonic, as we are. Moreover, I am well aware that a fourth (*diatesseron*) can also be divided into five semitones and into greater or lesser commas, but this would exceed the tetrachord; for an example of the aforesaid see the figure.[27]

Thirty-two years after de Muris's treatise, the Dutch theorist Johannes Boen discusses the variable subdivisions of the tone as an unrealized theoretical possibility, something that could result from the development of new instruments and vocal skills (45)—a more positive attitude than that of de Muris:

Johannes Boen, 45. According to the diversity of time and place, many new and unheard-of things will arise, as for example the performance of the comma and the three minor semitones, and of many similar things which, although they have not been heard thus far, perhaps in the course of time will be heard through the use of new instruments and vocal skills: just as there was not as much subtlety in music before Pythagoras as there is now, nor do we use such subdivisions of melody (*fracturam in cantu*) as do the English, the French, and the Lombards.

At the same time, Boen did acknowledge the use of notes that were outside the normal hexachords, referring to the addition of sharp and flat signs and their use on notes that were not part of the traditional scale system (63). He associates these chromatic changes with 'lascivious' songs, a statement that is reminiscent of Anonymous I (G)'s reason for dismissing the chromatic genus from ecclesiastical music.

Johannes Boen 63. Lest the foregoing conclusion lie undiscussed, it should be said with more exactness that in modern use the aforesaid notes that exist outside the natural monochord are allowed in the scale only according to the suitability or the lasciviousness of the particular song; for at present men are more involved than in the past in the practical extension of any song because they are drawn to lascivious things. And so that this wanton new delight outside the structure of the monochord may be designated in writing, it is represented just as it is produced in sound; and in order that the sign may correspond to the thing signified, those letters and their performance are reasonably allowed in the various clef locations (*clavibus*).

What, then can we conclude about the use of non-diatonic tones in medieval music since there seems to be contradictory evidence? There is no doubt that Jerome and Marchettus discuss chromaticism and variable subdivisions of the tone as part of the melodic coloration practice of the time, and Anonymous I (G) seems to allow enharmonic intervals in some chant, and both enharmonic and chromatic intervals in other (unspecified) repertory. At the same time, de Muris rejects any possibility of the presence of any but the diatonic genus in either the sacred or secular repertory, and the *Summa* seems to agree with this.

---

[27] This refers to a diagram of note ratios within the tetrachord.

Bonaventura discusses the use of chromatic change, but much of his discussion is directed towards describing a leading-note function rather than the selection of chromaticism or variable-pitch half-steps for the purpose of melodic colour, and Boen's discussion could also be seen as referring that same use.

One possible solution to the contradictory statements could be that the non-diatonic notes were part of the performance practices only in certain regions. Perhaps this is what the author of the *Summa* is telling us when, during his discussion of the six syllables of the hexachord, he states that it is his under-standing that Italians did not use the same note names as many of the other Europeans (573–81).

Anon., *Summa*, 573–81. These names of the notes [i.e. ut, re, mi, fa, sol, la] are used by the French, English, Germans, Hungarians, Slavs, and Danes, and other people on this side of the Alps; the Italians, however, are reported to use other notes and names, and whoever wishes to know should inquire from them.

It is possible, of course, that his meaning is just that the Italians used syllables other than ut, re, mi, etc., but that would seem odd, given the fact that the assign-ment of these syllables originated in Italy. The possibility exists, therefore, that he is telling us something about an Italian preference for notes not encompassed by the usual syllables. The excerpt from Marchettus of Padua lends some support to that interpretation of the *Summa* distinction.

At the same time, there is reason to doubt that the practice of chromatic change and variable pitch could be so easily separated according to geography. Whereas the negative statements in the treatises of Boen (from the Netherlands), and the *Summa* (from Wurzburg), and the limited use described by Anonymous I (G) (possibly from Austria) could suggest a more conservative practice north of the Alps, we are left with opposite sides of the issue taken by Johannes de Muris and Jerome of Moravia, both of whom were from Paris at approximately the same time (*c*.1300). Also confusing the issue is the existence in the manu-scripts from nearly all geographical areas of the many ornamental neumes that require non-diatonic tones.

The problem of the conflicting views on the practical use of non-diatonic tones will have to remain without a complete resolution for the present. There is little difficulty in accepting that the practice existed in Italy as late as the four-teenth century and perhaps later, but the extent to which it was used in other areas is not clear. Jerome says that the use of these sounds by a certain group of singers in Paris sets them apart from 'all other people', and Garlandia, also from Paris, advocates colouring the sound, although he did not specifically mention the chromatic and enharmonic genera. In this light the only way I can reconcile the absolute rejection of the use of the enharmonic and chromatic genera by de Muris is to suggest that he may have been referring to their complete adoption for melodic composition, rather than the occasional use of their intervallic properties for the coloration of melodies that are basically in the diatonic genus. As we have seen in the previous chapters, non-diatonic sounds were a part of medieval singing style, but it is not clear whether all regions went to the same extent in the adoption of chromatic and enharmonic intervals into their performances as Jerome claims was done by some Parisians.

5

Passaggi

THE ornaments referred to here as passaggi are those that were used to connect written notes, or in some cases to replace what was written. The number of notes in a passaggio can vary from one to dozens, and there are statements in theoretical treatises that describe where and how they should be added. Petrus dictus Palma ociosa defines them very clearly when he speaks of them as flowers, and states that they consist of many sounds performed in the place of one. Arnulf of St-Ghislain mentions the addition of diminutions in a number of different contexts. In his description of musicians of the second class, for example, he notes that clerics add virtuoso passages to instrumental compositions (15:32):

Petrus. That which they call flowers (*flores*) of mensural music occurs when many sounds, or small notes (which is the same thing), variously ornamented according to the quality of each mode, are placed in one voice against a single sound or a simple note of the same duration [in another voice].

Arnulf, 15:32. We see among them some clerics who, on the instruments known as organs, perform the most difficult musical compositions, such as the human voice would scarcely undertake. They compose and perform them through a certain wonderful prodigy of inventive music innate in them. There are others who, only a little less laudably, remember those things which were then composed and performed and sometimes the graceful labour of him who remembers matches the merit of the composer.

Arnulf's statement is made in the midst of a description of musicians without formal training who imitate the performances of more learned musicians (Arnulf, 15:24). The beginning of the passage is revealing for its expressed values, including those towards the use of improvisation. For Arnulf the most praiseworthy musicians are those who have both talent and knowledge; these are the people who can create in an artistic manner. On the other hand, he acknowledges the contribution of those who have musical talent without knowledge. They learn by imitating, and if they work hard enough at it they too can perform musically. Arnulf includes in his discussion of the things this class of musician imitates 'collecting whatever bundles of the harvest of musical flowers . . . they can' (*florum musicalium*), a phrase frequently found in the treatises referring to the addition of ornaments (see Ch. 1, p. 10),

Arnulf, 15:24. The second category [of musician] is evident in those laymen who, although they are devoid of all musical art, nevertheless, guided by the zeal for sweetness, give their fastidious ears to anything musical. These laymen more intently and deeply love musicians and follow them, and just as all animals follow the sweet-smelling panther, and the bee buzzes on account of the sweetness of the honey, those laymen in their enthusiasm more eagerly follow those who have been put forward for their study as musicians, collecting whatever bundles of the harvest of musical flowers and corn-ears they can, so that in babbling about most matters they are in agreement with the more talented singers, and thus they are in a way qualified and appear to be experienced, because whatever of the art of music is lacking in them they supply through practice and natural industriousness.

In context, therefore, in mentioning the addition of ornamentation, Arnulf would seem to be describing the approved mode of performance practice, even though the singers in the second category are merely imitating what they hear from the schooled musicians rather than understanding what they are doing. In his fourth category, trained and intelligent musicians with good voices, he once again brings up the subject of ornamentation, this time as praise for women who employ rapid diminutions (Arnulf, 16:56). These women subdivide 'tones into semitones' and 'semitones into indivisible microtones', by which Arnulf must be referring to the replacement of written notes with rapid passaggi and probably also to the use of non-diatonic pitches.[1]

Arnulf, 16:75. There is a second group among the fourth category, evidently of the favoured female sex, which is so much the more valuable the more it is rare; who in the epiglottis of the sweet-sounding throat divide tones with equipoise into semitones, and articulate semitones into indivisible microtones with an indescribable melody that you would think more angelic than human.

The Dutch theorist Johannes Boen tells us that not everyone ornamented to the same degree. As a way of pointing out differences in regional practices, he mentions that the people of his area—the Low Countries—do not subdivide to the extent done by the English, French, and Italians (Boen, 45).

Johannes Boen, 45. According to the diversity of time and place, many new and unheard-of things will arise . . . nor do we use such subdivisions of melody (*fracturam in cantu*) as do the English, the French, and the Lombards.

The statements quoted above attest to the use of ornamental passages, but their references are all quite general and do not tell us what music is to receive this type of elaboration nor exactly where it would be placed. Some of that more

---

[1] Christopher Page, 'A Treatise on Musicians from ?c.1400: The *Tractatulus de differentiis et gradibus cantorum* by Arnulf de St-Ghislain', *Journal of the Royal Musical Association*, 117 (1992), 1–21, is not sure how one may interpret this reference to women. From other references in the treatise it appears that Arnulf is somewhat antifeminist, and in that case Page finds it difficult to know how much of this reference is intended to be sarcastic. Their inclusion in Arnulf's highest category of musician would seem to verify the participation of highly skilled female singers in musical performances of the day, and as has been seen in Ch. 2, a particular type of dramatic performance practice is attributed to women by several other theorists.

specific information is available from other theorists. Both Anonymous IV (87:10) and Franco of Cologne (81:7) discuss the elaboration of certain positions of a section of organum purum. In that type of passage, if one encounters two or more notes in succession on the same pitch in the upper part, after the first note is sung a florid ornament is to be substituted for the remainder. One of the conventions in performing organum purum, therefore, is that the repetition of a pitch is to be considered a signal for the invention of a passaggio. In this context the theorists are describing only organum purum, but we shall see below that the same principle of ornamentation is also to be followed in plainchant.

Anon. IV, 87:10. Likewise, two notes on the same pitch, whether consonant [with the tenor] or not, are rendered as an ornamented *longa*.

Franco, 81:7. Likewise, it should be noted that in organum purum, when several notes occur over a single note in the tenor, only the first should be articulated, and the remaining figures should be sung in the ornamental style (*in floratura*).

Although a number of theorists provide some information about performing various types of passaggi in plainchant, it is Jerome who gives the most detailed instructions. Following his detailed discussion of the use of trills and reverberation (see Ch. 4), he states that not all song should be performed with these ornaments (185:15) (in a later passage he says that ornaments should be used 'only on Sundays and special feasts' (187:20); see discussion in Ch. 2), and then he proceeds to discuss the ornamentation of intervals up to that of a fifth. He begins with a 'unison', a term he has earlier described (59:3) as two or more notes on the same pitch, which are to be performed with continuous reverberation— probably referring to the tremula or morula (see Ch. 4). As in the statements above, a unison can be replaced by an ornamental passage, and Jerome's instructions concern the rhythmic subdivision of the written values. The performer is to sing all the notes quickly (semibreve = the smallest written note), changing to a continuous trill/vibrato for the last two notes of the series, which, he seems to imply, are given more time (185:23):

Jerome, 185:15. Certain of the French follow this manner of singing, indeed not in all songs, but in some, for since many nations are charmed because this manner of singing is luxuriant [lit. substantial], it is likewise not displeasing to say more substantial things about it. But I do not think it would be otherwise well or adequately described unless the melodic intervals (*modis*) from which every song is constructed were separately and particularly described. Therefore, one must first speak of the unison.

185:23. If a unison should have more than two notes, all are semibreves with the exception of the penultimate and the last, which alone is performed by them with reverberation. This is true even when the two [written] notes are of the same value, on one or more syllables, or one or more words.

Jerome does not actually state whether the added semibreves are to be all on the same pitch, similar to the morula and tremula described in Chapter 4, or a more florid passage, but in the light of the description by Anonymous IV and Franco of Cologne of the ornamentation of unison passages in organum purum, a florid passage is probably what was intended here. Jerome also says that the last two notes of the passage are to be performed with reverberation. Although the word 'reverberation' has been used in various contexts meaning both a repeated note on the same pitch and a vibrato/trill, in the light of his ensuing discussion of other intervals, he is probably referring here to a vibrato/trill. These last two notes of the passage are not to be sung as semibreves, although he does not say how much value they are to be given. (Undoubtedly, their value is determined by the value of the written unison, minus however much time is devoted to the embellishment.) The function of the trill on the last two longer notes would be to add a feeling of cadence to the ornamental passage.[2] Ex. 5.1 is my conjecture of how one might ornament such an interval.

The remainder of the statements in this section of Jerome's treatise refer to the filling in of intervals from a second to a fifth using a combination of pitches and vocal inflections. The intervals may be filled either by definite pitches or inflected sounds, including the plica. The duration that is devoted to the ornamental fill-in is to be subtracted from the value of the first written note, and part of the description of the ornamental addition is devoted to the durational possibilities as well as those of pitch and inflection. The statements concerning the treatment of some of the ornamental additions as plicas, therefore, has implications for both sound quality and duration. As described by Lambertus, and discussed in Chapters 3 and 4, the plica is an imprecise pitch, sung in the throat with a darkened sound and vibrato. Its value is one-half of an imperfect note (breve or longa), or one-third of a perfect note.

Jerome informs us that the interval of a second, either a whole or half step, is to be filled by a pitch that he calls a *mediata* (185:28). If the written interval is a whole tone then the mediata would obviously be the half-step between (or an inflected pitch near there), and in the case of a written half-step it would necessarily be the quarter-tone. Jerome provides several suggestions for executing the filling-in, depending upon the direction of the notes and their values. When the written value of the first note is an imperfect breve, the duration is to be shared equally between the written pitch and the mediata, but when it is a perfect breve

Ex. 5.1. Possible ornamentation of a written unison

---

[2] The instruction here to apply reverberation to the last notes of a unison is similar to that given just before for the application of the same ornament to the final note of a phrase (185:4; see Ch. 4).

Ex. 5.2. Examples of a filled second: (*a*) imperfect breve with mediata 1:1; (*b*) perfect breve with mediata 2:1; (*c*) ascending perfect breve with mediata 2:1 and reverberation

the mediata can receive two-thirds of the value (Ex. 5.2(*a*) and (*b*)). In a descending interval where the first written note is a longa, it and the mediata are performed as a plica longa, meaning that the plica receives half the value if the longa is imperfect, or one-third if it is perfect. And from what follows in Jerome's instructions for all other intervals, I infer that a reverberation is also performed between the mediata and the final note of the interval. That is, the mediata forms the upper note of a trill (or mordent) on its descent to the final note. At no point does Jerome specify the value of the final note for these filled intervals, but from the discussion it would seem that they must be no shorter than a breve.

If the interval is an ascending second, in addition to singing a mediata between the two written pitches, a reverberation is made on the last note, and as per earlier instructions, the reverberation must come from above (185:28). In this last case, therefore, first a mediata is sung between the two ascending written pitches, and then the last note is preceded by a mordent or trill that begins on the note above it, as in Ex. 5.2(*c*). No additional information is given concerning the durational values in ascending intervals and so we may assume that they are the same as those given for descending intervals. Jerome makes a point of stating that the interval of a second, as well as those of the third, fourth, and fifth described below, are filled in the described manner whether they are written as separate notes or ligated, but he seems to imply that the interval he is describing for ornamental treatment must be set apart as a unit with no more than a single syllable. Because of the nature of the ornamental sounds, this kind of filling-in probably would not apply if there were a change of syllable on the second written note.

Jerome, 185:28. Also, when two notes, either ligated or separate, are the distance of a semitone or tone apart, they are joined by a third note in the middle, called a mediata, which is attached to the second note. It is usually a semibreve equal in value [lit. in unison] to the first note, but sometimes is a breve the value of three semibreves (*tres instantias*), so that a descent is more rapidly perceived between the two [written] notes.

Sometimes, when the notes are unligated yet descending, an ascending plica longa is placed with mediatae interposed as before. In ascending intervals a reverberation is made on the second [written] note.

The intervals of a third, fourth, and fifth are similarly filled by the addition of notes between the written pitches. For the interval of a minor or major third, the interpolated middle note can have a value of half, two-thirds, or one-third the value of the written first note, depending on its value (186:4). When the written value is an imperfect breve the mediata takes half of the value, but when the written value is a perfect breve there is a choice of either a 2:1 or 1:2 distribution of the three semibreve units (Ex. 5.3(*a*)). If it is a longa then a plica longa may be performed (Ex. 5.3(*b*)).

Although Jerome does not elaborate on other possible durational choices for the interval of a third when the value is a longa, his statement that 'sometimes . . . one moves . . . as a plica', suggests that any number of other subdivisions of the value are also possible. For descending intervals of a fourth and fifth the only durational possibility mentioned is that of a plica longa, which means that these intervals can only be filled in when the first written value is a longa. For all intervals, descending and ascending, when the value of the written note is a longa and the singer chooses to sing the mediata as a plica, the value of the longa is shared according to the rule stated above concerning plicated imperfect and perfect longas.

When filling an interval of a descending third with a plica longa, a reverberation is sung beginning on the median note and leading into the final note (Ex.

Ex. 5.3. Examples of a filled third: (*a*) descending breves, perfect and imperfect; (*b*) descending longa with plica; (*c*) ascending longa with plica; (*d*) ascending longa with plica and reverberation. * = plica with inflected sound, not necessarily an exact pitch; any other diatonic or non-diatonic pitch between these two notes could be selected

5.3(*b*)). The ascending third can also be performed in this way with the mediata interpolated as a plica longa (Ex. 5.3(*c*)) but in this case the reverberation leading into the final note cannot begin on the plica since it must come from above (Ex. 5.3(*d*)).

Jerome, 186:4. Likewise when two notes are separated by either a major or minor third, either ligated or separate, the second note is joined on for singing by means of a semibreve, or even a breve when the equivalent of three semibreves. Sometimes in descent one moves from the first note that is a plica longa descending as far as the middle note, from which a reverberation is performed leading to the third [note], as above, and the converse in the ascent, or as is more common, [in ascent] a reverberation is performed on the third [note].

To fill in the intervals of a fourth and a fifth much the same process is followed, although in these cases only a written longa may be ornamented and more than one median note is used. For the descending fourth this requires filling the interval with two additional notes (186:11). The first interpolated sound will be a plica on the note a second below, followed by a third sound which is reverberated down to the other written note (Ex. 5.4(*a*)). In ascending fourths the same procedure is followed except that the third note is not reverberated: the reverberation is performed from above the final note (Ex. 5.4(*b*)):

Jerome, 186:11. Likewise when the two notes are separated by a descending fourth, one moves to the second [note] with a plica longa and [performs] a reverberation on the third [note] [leading] into the fourth. But in ascent, the reverberation is made on the fourth note.

For the interval of a fifth I infer that three notes are filled in, since Jerome states that it is treated similarly to that of the fourth, including the difference in placement of the reverberation between ascending and descending intervals (186:15). As with the other ornamented intervals, in descent the reverberation is placed on the penultimate note, but in contrast to all other filled-in intervals, there is no reverberation applied to the final note of this ascending interval (Ex. 5.5(*a* and *b*)).

Ex. 5.4. Examples of a filled fourth: (*a*) descending; (*b*) ascending. * = plica with inflected sound, not necessarily an exact pitch; any other diatonic or non-diatonic pitch between these two notes could be selected

Ex. 5.5. Examples of a filled fifth: (*a*) descending; (*b*) ascending. * = plica with inflected sound, not necessarily an exact pitch; any other diatonic or non-diatonic pitch between these two notes could be selected

Jerome, 186:15. Among certain singers the same is done for the interval of a fifth as for the fourth, both ascending and descending, although in descent a reverberation is more commonly performed on the fifth note. No reverberation is made on the ascent, and the same applies to all the subsequent intervals.

In summary, for two-note intervals Jerome presents formulae for filling in the interval of up to a fifth. The durational value of the first note is to be shared with one or more interpolated median notes that fill the space between the written pitches, although the added notes need not be full sounds nor standard diatonic pitches. The descending and ascending intervals are treated similarly except for the execution of the reverberation: for descending intervals the reverberation comes from the last of the interpolated notes; in ascending, the reverberation is from a new note—that above the second written pitch (with the single exception that no reverberation is performed on the ascending fifth).

EXTENDED PASSAGGI, INTRODUCTIONS, CADENZAS, *CAUDAE*: ADDITIONS IN POLYPHONY

Related to 'passaggi' are the more extended embellishment sections to be added by the performer at fermatas, phrase beginnings and ends, or as preludes and postludes to compositions. John of Salisbury refers to them in an unkind light as inappropriate for the Divine Service because they distract the listener from the proper sober attitude. But in making his criticism, he thereby establishes that such things were done. His remarks lack the type of detail that would be helpful for our purposes, but in the light of the excerpts from Anonymous IV that follow, he seems to be referring to preludes ('singers who begin before the others'), postludes ('those who conclude'), diminutions ('subdivisions or doubling of small notes'), and improvised counterpoint ('sung against their fellows').

John of Salisbury. Could you but hear the effete melodies of those singers who begin before the others, and of those who respond, of those who sing [first] and those who conclude, and those who sing in the middle, and those whose part is sung against their fellows', you would believe it to be a chorus of sirens, not a choir of men . . . Indeed such is their fluency in running up and down the scale, their subdivision or doubling of small notes, their repetition of phrases and their combining of individual ones [phrases]—so that the high or even the highest notes are mixed with the low or lowest ones—that the ears of the singers are almost completely divested of their critical power, and the soul, which has yielded to the enjoyment of so much sweetness, is not capable of judging the merits of the things heard.

Anonymous IV discusses these types of additions more clearly and in a more positive tone at several points in his treatise. We have already seen his instructions, along with those of Franco of Cologne, for the insertion of an ornamental passage when there are two notes of the same pitch in organum purum (see above, p. 90). He augments that statement by pointing out that within any melodic line there are numerous longas that should be ornamented, and that not all of them are on perfect consonances (88:30). These dissonant ornamental notes must be internal, because he goes on at some length in describing how one begins a polyphonic composition by ornamenting the first note of the upper part (88:6). This last statement seems to address four different points about the method of beginning a two-voice composition: (1) that the upper voice is to begin with the tenor when concordant and before the tenor if discordant; (2) that the ornament can be in the form of one or more notes; (3) that the tenor should enter only when the upper part is concordant; and (4) that the total duration given over to this passage is the value of a duplex longa. Each of these points requires elaboration.

Anon. IV, 88:3. Likewise, sometimes there are many longas [intended] for the purpose of embellishment (*coloris*) or the beauty of the melody, irrespective of whether they are concordant or not, which is indeed self-evident in the way they function.

88:6. Likewise, there is an embellished double-length longa (*duplex longa florata*). This [note] is placed at the beginning, in the name of the most holy *alpha*, and it is called 'the beginning before the beginning'; and it will always be concordant. Likewise there are some who put two or three notes in place of one. In that case, the first note may be either concordant or discordant, and it always begins shortly before the tenor, and the tenor begins with the second note if it is concordant, or with the third. The third note is lengthened and embellished (*florificandam*), as we said above. Some people are able to place three or four ligated notes before the beginning of the tenor. If the last of those notes should be concordant, the tenor will begin with it; if it is discordant, the tenor will begin with the first concordant note following.

The opening phrase of the second excerpt at first seems to be discussing a note-value in the superius voice that is written—a duplex longa. But in the light of the information that follows, it would seem also that this value is interpolated when not present. Further, there is some leeway for performers to choose whether the superius will begin with the tenor or slightly before it. If one or more of the initial notes are discordant, they are to be performed prior to the entry of the tenor, but it would seem that the performer may also choose to perform a concordant note prior to the entry of the tenor.

The interpolated passage, if it is a single note, must always be concordant with the tenor. But it is also possible to substitute two, three, or four notes prior to the entry of the tenor, and these can be either concordant or discordant; the only restriction is that the tenor cannot enter until the upper voice has reached a concordant pitch. These points all seem to be quite clear.

The most problematic aspect is reconciliation of the phrases concerning the number of notes preceding the tenor with the concept of *duplex longa florata*. Certainly an addition of from one to four notes could be considered to be an embellishment—instructions quoted earlier relate to ornaments of as little as a single note. But when associated with the rather large time-value allotted to this embellishment (and in the light of the same theorist's statements about organum purum passages, 84:4, below), it is probable that the author had something far more extensive in mind. If the reference to single notes is read instead as 'basic pitches', from which quick-moving flourishes depart and return, the passage would have a somewhat different meaning. Read in that way the instructions would mean that the singer of the upper voice-part has the freedom to add a highly ornamental passage either simultaneously with or prior to the entry of the tenor, and that the passage could include from one to four 'basic pitches'. If the elaboration revolves around only a single 'basic pitch', that pitch must be concordant. But the singer also has the option of choosing a more elaborate introductory passage, using up to four basic pitches, which also would allow some of these basic pitches to be discordant. This kind of treatment can be found in the composed repertory. In Ex. 5.6 the passage of organum is based on three notes, *d*, *a*, and *e* (only the *e* is discordant). Since the beginning note is concordant, the two voices could enter simultaneously.[3]

Ex. 5.6. Organum passage with three basic notes, from the Las Huelgas Ms. Transcription from G. A. Anderson, *The Las Huelgas Manuscript*, CMM 97, p. 69. By permission of Hänssler-Verlag.

---

[3] Roesner, 'The Performance', 180, demonstrates some possible examples of dissonant beginnings in which the tenor entry probably would have been delayed until a consonance.

At the end of the same paragraph, Anon. IV makes a point of instructing singers to apply the same type of ornamentation at other appropriate places within the composition when the opportunity arises (88:6, below). Although he does not say exactly where these places are, it would seem logical to conclude that he is referring to any place where the top voice sings before the tenor enters—at the beginning of a new phrase following a rest in the tenor part, for example, and in those places where the tenor sounds a long note. In the last case the 'basic notes' used for the interpolated embellishment must all be concordant with the tenor.

Anon. IV, 88:6 concluded. This same procedure is followed should there be a change (*modulatio*) of the melody on account of some beautiful or appropriate ornaments (*coloris*) or something similar to that which pertains to 'the beginning before the beginning'.

For several of the theorists the addition of this type of ornamental flourish in polyphony is discussed in terms of the creation of organum purum passages, as in the statement by Anon. IV, where their addition is advocated as a method of ornamenting beginnings and endings of compositions and phrases (84:4). The preludes, postludes, and embellished phrase endings he describes are to be added as organum purum interpolations to other types of polyphonic compositions. To this writer, the addition of a postlude will provide a 'more noble ending' to a composition.

Anon. IV, 84:4. Certain people add a section of organum purum after the previously mentioned points in order to create a more noble ending, and in a similar manner, at the beginning they add (through the method of making organum) two or three notes that are appropriately concordant and are in conformity with a more noble beginning. They do this by making an embellishment before a long rest, just as is the custom in organum purum and in such genres, etc.

The style in which these additions are to be constructed is made clear by the reference to organum purum, which is the practice in polyphonic music of sustaining a single note in the tenor while a treble passage is sung against it, as Franco of Cologne clearly states in the following passage (80:1; partially quoted in Ch. 4). Franco contrasts organum purum and discant, depending upon whether the tenor sustains or moves. There also must have been some disagreement at the time as to whether the florid passages in organum purum were to be sung rhythmically or not, because Franco feels the need to state that within organum the relative values of the notes remain similar to those described earlier in his treatise. Anon. II also emphasizes that the ornamental aspect of organum is rhythmic as well as melodic and harmonic (307).

Franco, 80:1. Organum, strictly speaking, is a song that is not measured in all its parts. It ought to be known that organum purum can be made only above a tenor where a single

Ex. 5.7. Franco's organum examples. From *Ars cantus mensurabilis*, ed. Reaney and Giles, 80–1

note is in unison [i.e. sustained], for when the tenor has several notes at once there is automatically discant, as here: [Ex. 5.7(*a*)]

The longas and breves of organum are understood through three rules. The first is: whatever is notated in the shape of a longa simplex is long, and whatever is notated in the shape of a brevis is short, and whatever is notated in the shape of a semibrevis is half-short. The second rule is: whatever is long [in the upper voice] must be concordant with respect to the tenor; but if it occurs as a discord, the tenor should be silent or feign concord, as is evident here: [Ex. 5.7(*b*)]

The third rule is: whatever note occurs immediately before the rest that we call *finis punctorum* is a longa, because every penultimate note is long.

Anon. II, 307. What is organum? Organum is a musical chant produced from various consonances of tropes with a sweet concord, decorated with harmonies and various ornaments (*coloribus*) of rhythm.[4]

The attribute that sets organum purum apart from other types of compositional formats is the sustained tenor that allows the singer of the upper part the freedom to improvise without the confinement of strictly measured note durations—in the words of Anon. II, 'harmonies and ornaments of rhythm'. The upper voice in these sections is composed of notes in irregular rhythmic patterns of longs and shorts that need to be concordant with the sustained tenor note only at the beginning of its phrase, the end, or at any internal pause ('longas' in Franco's terms). Jacobus of Liège (7) affirms Franco's statement that in a section of organum purum the upper part has long and short durational values as indicated by their shapes, although he makes it clear that these durations are not exactly measured. Neither the individual durational values of the long and short notes nor the total amount of time allowed for any single passage is confined by exact measure.[5] At the same time, the author of the *Quatuor principalia*, while

---

[4] Numerous descriptions of organum similar to these exist in the treatises, as for example in the Vatican organum treatise; see Irving Godt and Benito Rivera, 'The Vatican Organum Treatise—A Colour Reproduction, Transcription, and Translation', in *Gordon Athol Anderson: In Memoriam*, 2 vols. (Musicological Studies, 49; Henryville–Ottawa–Binningen, 1984), ii. 264–345, esp. 293.

[5] On this topic see a summary of opinions in Jeremy Yudkin, 'The Rhythm of Organum Purum', *Journal of Musicology*, 2 (1983), 355–76; and Edward Roesner, 'The Emergence of Musica Mensurabilis', in Eugene K. Wolf and Edward H. Roesner (eds.), *Studies in Musical Sources and Style: Essays in Honor of Jan LaRue* (Madison, Wis., 1990), 42–74 at 69.

supporting the idea of the temporal freedom within a passage of organum purum, seems to contradict the other theorists on the subject of durational values when he refers to the upper voice singing 'without measure' (297).

Jacobus, 7. [On polyphony] The mensural art requires these and many other things, just as is touched on above in the first book, chapter 16. This type of song is termed measurable because separate voices are performed at the same time within some span (*morula*) of exact or inexact time. I say 'inexact' because organum duplum is not always measured with an exact measure of time, as for example during flourishes (*floraturis*) on penultimates, where many notes may sound in the discant above the single penultimate note of the tenor. This type of song [i.e. organum duplum] is considered to be measured music because discant occurs and requires separate notes to be performed simultaneously, which would not be performed by one and the same singer simultaneously.

Anon., *Quatuor principalia*, 297. It ought to be noted, moreover, that organum purum cannot be made unless it is above a single tenor without measure, in this way: the one singing the tenor ought to fashion himself artfully in certain places, namely when he perceives through a consonance that some perfect concordance is imminent, and particularly on the penultimate, where he must sign himself for concordance. The one singing the organum above the tenor must regulate the time in such a manner that, for as long as the organum purum lasts, it is proper to run hither and thither through notes without measure, up to the concordance. When the organal voice reaches a perfect concordance, at that very moment he will draw out a delay (*moram*), and particularly on the penultimate, as here: [Ex. 5.8]

It is not reasonable that theorists would differ so radically on such an issue, and in fact in the passage immediately following that quoted above, the *Quatuor principalia* repeats Franco's statement almost word for word (Franco, 80:1, above), that in organum the values of long and short are to be observed. The correct interpretation of the statement that the superius is to be 'without measure', therefore, is that it is a reference to 'exact measure', meaning that the notes of the upper part need not be sung in exact metric ratio to one another, nor should they be an exact subdivision of the durational value of the note(s) in the tenor. This impression of the freedom of tempo in organal passages receives further support from Elias Salomonis in his affirmation of steady tempo for plainchant, where he contrasts proper plainchant tempo with that performed

Ex. 5.8. *Quatuor principalia* example of organum purum. From Warren, 'Punctus organi', 180

during organum passages, which he states were 'accelerated', i.e. subject to irregular pacing:

Elias, 21. Mark well: we ought not place our scythe in another's harvest by adopting the style of organum and accelerating the notes; for whoever hastens each note, in destroying both, performs neither well.

Franco and Jacobus both point out that once the tenor begins to have more than one note—i.e. once the tenor has exact temporal measure—the composition loses this aspect of temporal freedom, and becomes another type of composition: discant, a format in which all parts proceed according to a strictly measured rhythm, and thus the amount and type of improvisation and ornamentation is restricted by the regular measure.

The technique being described in the above excerpts for the invention of an upper part in the style of organum purum is to be applied at specific places, such as beginnings and ends of phrases. At those points the tenor note is sustained while the singer of the upper part improvises a melodic-rhythmic passage. The improvised passage must begin on a consonance and end on a consonance, and the singer of the organal part is responsible for correct harmonies in these places. There are no harmonic constraints on the upper line other than when it changes notes simultaneously with the tenor voice. Since responsibility for establishing consonances within the phrase is delegated to the singer of the tenor, the organal singer is free to concentrate on making the improvised passage melodically and rhythmically interesting. If the tenor part is to change notes in mid-phrase it is the responsibility of the singer of that part to make these changes on consonances. According to the author of the *Quatuor principalia* (297, above), the singer of the tenor does this by 'perceiving that a concordance is imminent', but it is also clear that the singer of the upper part must signal these occasions through the use of particular consonances (or particular kinds of consonances), and especially by retarding. When the tenor wishes to draw the passage to a close he signals for the penultimate note, and the organal singer makes a final retard, holding the penultimate note (*mora*)—which in Ex. 5.8 above is at the interval of a major seventh. The words *mora* and *morula* are correctly translated above as 'drawn out' or 'lengthening', but from the instructions in Aribo and the Anonymous *Commentarius in Micrologum*, we know that the words also referred to the performance of a pulsation or repetition of the pitch while drawing it out (see the discussions in Ch. 2, p. 29, and Ch. 4, p. 73), a meaning it may well have in both the *Quatuor principalia* and in the quoted passage from Jacobus.

The instructions above for sustaining one part while another is free to proceed without the necessity of accurate measure are quite similar both for short applications of the technique (Jacobus), and for protracted sections of improvised organum (*Quatuor principalia*). In the case of extended sections

Ex. 5.9. Opening organal section from Paris, BNF, Ms f. fr. 1139, fo. 44ᵛ. Transcription from T. Karp, *The polyphony of Saint Martial and Santiago de Compostela*, 1992, Vol. 2, p. 184. By permission of Oxford University Press.

with several note changes in the tenor, the actual execution is somewhat complicated and would take some rehearsing to learn. But for a short passage inserted on the penultimate note of a phrase as described by Jacobus, the tenor would simply treat his penultimate note as if it were marked to hold indefinitely (modern fermata practice), and await the signal from the organal singer (possibly a sustained and pulsated dissonance—a morula) to proceed to the final. Ex. 5.9 is an opening organal section that would require this type of coordination between the two singers. If this were an improvised passage the singer of the upper part would retard his last four-note embellishment and sing a morula on the penultimate note, c', as a way of signalling the tenor to move to the cadential note.

One can understand this practice of melodic interpolation, in which the singer strays from the concord for the purpose of melodic ornament and then returns to the proper consonant intervals, as a basic concept in conjunction with the theory of monophonic chant composition. While describing the similarities between kinds of musical phrases in monophonic chant and grammatical punctuation, Jerome states that passaggi—'flourishes' in his words—are used as a way of punctuating chant phrases (153:34). In context he is describing how a composer creates melody within the rules of mode, but at the same time he presents us with a clear concept of how a melodic flourish (*ornatum*) is employed and understood. He singles out and describes two analogous musical ornamental situations: *diastema*, a pause within a compound phrase in which a flourish of a few notes departs from and then returns to the modal pattern; and *systema*, a much smaller flourish that is used to connect sub-phrases, presumably done in the same manner. Jerome does not describe a musical equivalent for the third grammatical simile, *teleusis*, the pause at the end of a completed section, but it is clear from the rest of his discussion that the melodic flourish connected with this gesture would be similar to that for the other two except that it would be longer than the *diastema*. The simile drawn between these ornamental passages and grammatical punctuation indicates their functions: all are pauses of different degrees. The *diastema* and *teleusis*, respectively colons and periods, are minor and major points of cadence. The *systema*, a comma, is only a minor pause within a thought. Ornamental flourishes at these three different points, therefore, cause an interruption of the melodic flow corresponding to that of their grammatical counterparts.[6]

Jerome, 153:34. That, moreover, which the grammarians call the colon, comma, and period, in song some call *diastema*, *systema*, and *teleusis*. By a *diastema* is signified a distinct flourish (*distinctum ornatum*) of the song, which occurs when the song pauses in a seemly fashion not on the final but in another place; *systema* indicates a connecting flourish (*conjunctum ornatum*); a seemly pause on the final at the end of a song is called *teleusis*.

Diastema is properly vocal space or an interval [of time] shared by two or three or more sounds of a definite range of delivery. *Systemata*, however, are properly the principal parts of music. To arrest movement (*sistere*) means occasionally to stop or to be prevented; that is, it permits one thing to stand in place of another, 'to assist', 'to be present in the middle', 'to consist', 'to dwell', 'to remain'.

As can be seen in this excerpt, the principles of ornamentation, flourish, and departure from the set rules and patterns were basic to how one composed and considered melody. From this point of view, for the performer to interpolate short ornamental flourishes at the end of the parts of a compound phrase and on penultimate and final notes would be the extemporized version of the composed *diastema* and *teleusis*, and those that link one sub-phrase to another would be similar to the *systema*. In musical terms the difference between the *diastema* and *teleusis* would be the absence or presence of a rest at a point of cadence.

This simile is also useful in clarifying where and to what extent a medieval performer would probably place the more elaborate embellishments in a texted phrase: corresponding to the grammatical structure of the text itself. In many cases, of course, the composer has already elaborated the melody at exactly these points—as indicated by the statement in Jerome—but this would not necessarily inhibit the addition of extemporaneous ornamentation as well.

---

[6] In the first paragraph Jerome paraphrases Johannes Affligemensis, pp. 79–80. In the second he explains his terms, but instead of explaining *teleusis*, explains *celeuma*. I am indebted to Bonnie J. Blackburn for this observation.

(a)

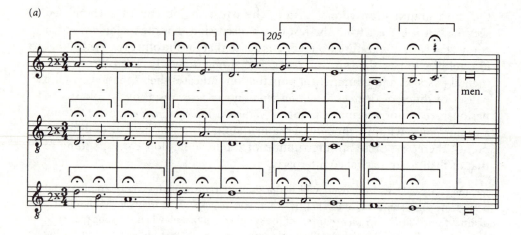

(b)

Ex. 5.10. Fermatas in Dufay's works: (*a*) *Missa Sancti Jacobi*; (*b*) *Resvellies vous*, from *Opera omnia*, CMM 1, Vols. 2 and 6. By permission of Hänssler-Verlag.

FERMATA AND SIGNUM CONGRUENTIAE

Another location for a free-flowing ornamental passage, both in monophony and polyphony, is any note marked with a fermata or a similar symbol, as Charles Warren has demonstrated.[7] These locations are sometimes found at section ends and final cadences, including 'Amen' passages in various sacred works (see Ex. 5.10(*a*)), but they also include marked notes within particular phrases where special attention to the text is desired. In this same category one could also include a secular polyphonic example, Dufay's ballade *Resvellies vous*

[7] Warren, 'Punctus Organi'.

et faites chiere lye, written for Carlo Malatesta, in which the four mid-phrase notes over the text 'Charle gentil', are written with fermatas (Ex. 5.10(*b*)).

Ex. 5.10(*a*) is an interesting case, since in the unique manuscript source (Bologna, Civico Museo Bibliografico Musicale, MS Q 15) this section is marked 'chorus'. One can hardly imagine a group of singers improvising flourishes together, and so if the symbol does indicate a flourish, it must have been executed by only one of the singers. There is no problem in the case of Ex. 5.10(*b*), since there is little suspicion that in the fifteenth century secular polyphonic music was sung by more than one person per part.

It is Warren's conclusion that the shape of the fermata mark is an indication of the performance practice: a note (the centre dot), surrounded by other notes (or a note adorned by a flourish of notes of unspecified pitch—written as a curved line).[8] In a polyphonic setting this would mean that where such a mark is placed, the superius soloist sings a florid embellishment around the written pitch while all other singers hold the written notes. If this interpretation of the meaning of fermatas is correct, then the passages so marked within numerous thirteenth-, fourteenth-, and fifteenth-century compositions are all to be executed with improvised ornamental passages similar to those described in the instructions above for the creation of passages of organum purum. It is not difficult to speculate that this same practice also might have been carried out in other such locations within a composition—those without fermata marks but having long, sustained chordal passages with significant text, as for example in the Gloria (and Credo) of the Machaut mass (Ex. 5.11). This would be in accordance with the idea expressed by Jerome (153:34, above) concerning the relationship between ornamental passages and grammatical position.

We have already encountered several theoretical statements concerning the prolongation and embellishment of final notes of phrases and compositions in monophony. There is evidence that this tradition was carried on in polyphony, at least at the final cadences (see the statements above concerning the insertion of organum purum passages at various points within a phrase). Ex. 5.12 is the 'Amen' for a Gloria by Estienne Grossin from Trent, Museo Provinciale d'Arte, MS 87, in which two versions of the final cadence have been supplied for the superius: one with fermatas over the penultimate and antepenultimate notes,

---

[8] Warren's conclusion is supported by the relationship between other early notation marks and their intended sounds that I have pointed out in 'Ornamental Neumes and Early Notation'. The meaning of the fermata symbol through the centuries is in need of further study; although the mark has been used as the indication for cadenza up to the present time, in 1540 Sebald Heyden described it only as indicating a general pause in all voices: 'Hemiciclus cum punctulo inserto, instar Iridis, Notulae imminens superne, communem omnibus vocibus cessationem indicit, ita [fermata mark]': *De arte canendi* (Nuremberg, 1540; facs. edn. New York, 1969), 54. Translation and transcription in Clement A. Miller, *De Arte Canendi* (American Institute of Musicology, 1972), 64.

Ex. 5.11. 'Jesu Christe' from Machaut's mass. From Guillaume de Machaut, *Messe de Nostre Dame*, ed. Leech-Wilkinson, Oxford University Press, 1990. Reproduced by permission.

matching the same markings in the other two voices; and a written-out embellishment for the same location of the type that would ordinarily have been improvised at the sign of the fermatas. The embellishment is exactly according to the instructions seen above for the extemporaneous invention of a passage of organum purum at final cadences. The signal that the soloist has reached the end of the florid section undoubtedly would have been the inclusion of a morula or tremula with retard on the final embellishing note, thus notifying the other singers to move to the next consonance or section. From the information gathered above one may speculate that this practice of interpolating passaggi also could have been extended, at the will of the performers, to endings not marked with fermatas.

Ex. 5.12. 'Amen' from Estienne Grossin's Gloria, from Warren, 'Punctus organi', 181

Observation of the fermata as an embellished hold would apply in all cases where the mark is written over a single breve or longa, or a series of longas. But when the mark is placed over notes of different values, as in Ex. 5.10(*a*), it is Warren's conclusion that the embellishments are to be performed, not as an indefinite held note, but within the time of the written metrical values. Again this would be in accordance with instructions for the retention of relative durational values in a passage of organum purum, as discussed above in conjunction with the statements by Franco of Cologne (80:1) and Anonymous II (307). (The exception would be when the note is the penultimate, as in Ex. 5.12.)[9]

The signum congruentiae, according to Warren, represents a variation of this same idea: instead of marking the place of departure, this symbol marks the point of arrival. Whereas under the fermata mark the embellishment begins after the written pitch is sung, the note written under the signum congruentiae is to be the final note in an improvised passage. In a polyphonic setting this would suggest that the lower voices must remain silent during the embellishment, joining the superius only when the written pitch is reached (probably indicated by some signal similar to that specified in the *Quatuor principalia*, 297, above, for the singing of organum purum).

ADDITIONS TO MONOPHONIC MUSIC

The most elaborate of the ornamented compositions uncovered in Warren's investigation of the performance practice associated with fermatas is the cantus coronatus, which, according to Johannes de Grocheio's statement (112; partially quoted in Ch. 2), is a song 'crowned around the sounds' (*circa sonos coronatur*), which Warren interprets as meaning that the notes are treated as if they had fermatas—that is, sung with flowing ornamentation.[10]

Johannes de Grocheio, 130:112. A cantus coronatus is called by some a simple conductus (*conductus simplex*). This [song], because of its excellence in text and melody, is crowned around the sounds by masters and students, just as the French *Ausi com l'unicorne*, or *Quant li roussignol*.[11] Cantus coronati are normally composed by kings and nobles and they are frequently sung in the presence of kings and princes of the earth, in order that their souls may be moved to be daring and resolute, magnanimous and liberal, characteristics that all make for good rule. This kind of song is made from delightful and lofty

[9] In these cases the composer probably wished to make the written values visually correct in terms of subdivisions of perfections. The placement of a fermata over a shorter note, however, would have indicated that it was to be extended as an elaborate ornament regardless of its indicated durational value.

[10] Warren, 'Punctus Organi', 134–5. The cantus coronatus is also known as the 'grand chanson courtois'; see Christopher Page, *Voices and Instruments of the Middle Ages: Instrumental Practice and Songs in France 1100–1300* (London, 1987), 67.

[11] Hans G. Spanke, *Raynauds Bibliographie des altfranzösischen Liedes, neu bearbeitet und ergänzt, erster Teil* (Leiden, 1955), nos. 2075, 1559.

material, as, for instance, when it is about friendship and charity, and is made entirely of perfect longs.

The last phrase of Grocheio's statement, that a cantus coronatus is made of all perfect longs, is at first rather confusing since the surviving versions of the two composed examples cited by him have a variety of rhythmic values (see Pll. II and III).[12]

The solution to the apparent contradiction between the theoretical statement and the extant music may be assisted by a similarly puzzling statement in a later paragraph in the same treatise (270; also quoted in Ch. 2), where Grocheio discusses the Kyrie and Gloria:[13]

Johannes de Grocheio, 162:270. The Gloria, however, is never found without the Kyrie eleison. These chants, moreover, are sung slowly and composed of perfect longs in the manner of a cantus coronatus, in order that the hearts of the listeners may be moved devoutly to praying and to listening devoutly to the prayer, which the priest, or the one appointed for this, says immediately.

To my knowledge there are no surviving Kyries and Glorias in manuscripts of French provenance that are composed only of perfect longas, and therefore both here and in his description of the cantus coronatus Grocheio must have intended something else. It is possible that he was referring not to the actual notes of the music itself, but to the tempo of the composition in reference to the mensural values in the musical forms under discussion. In another place Grocheio refers to pacing some chants more quickly than others on certain occasions (see Ch. 2). In the excerpt above (270), therefore, he may simply be referring to the pacing of the tempo for Kyrie and Gloria, which is to be slow, similar to the cantus coronatus (which he also describes as a solemn piece). And in describing the pace of the cantus coronatus as sung with 'perfect longas' he could be referring to the fact that perfect longas are sung more slowly than imperfect longas, again a reference to the dignity of the piece. The Kyrie and Gloria, therefore, similar to a cantus coronatus, are composed (or performed) in 'perfect mensuration' in contrast to 'imperfect'. Presumably this attribute is another symbol of the dignity of these pieces.

I propose that this is all that is being said here, although it does have some performance implications for the cantus coronatus. Given the fact that the pacing unit of the music of that time was the breve, when the longa (and its equivalents) are perfect, the composition moves 50 per cent slower on the level

---

[12] For a comparative study of eight manuscript transmissions of the first three lines of *Ausi com l'unicorne* see Jean Baptiste Beck, *Die Melodien der Troubadours* (Strasburg, 1908); and Hendrik Van der Werf (ed.), *Trouvères-Melodien* II (Monumenta monodica medii aevi, 12; Kassel, 1979), 290.

[13] For another view of Grocheio's meaning see Van der Werf, *The Chansons of the Troubadours and Trouvères* (Utrecht, 1972), 153–5.

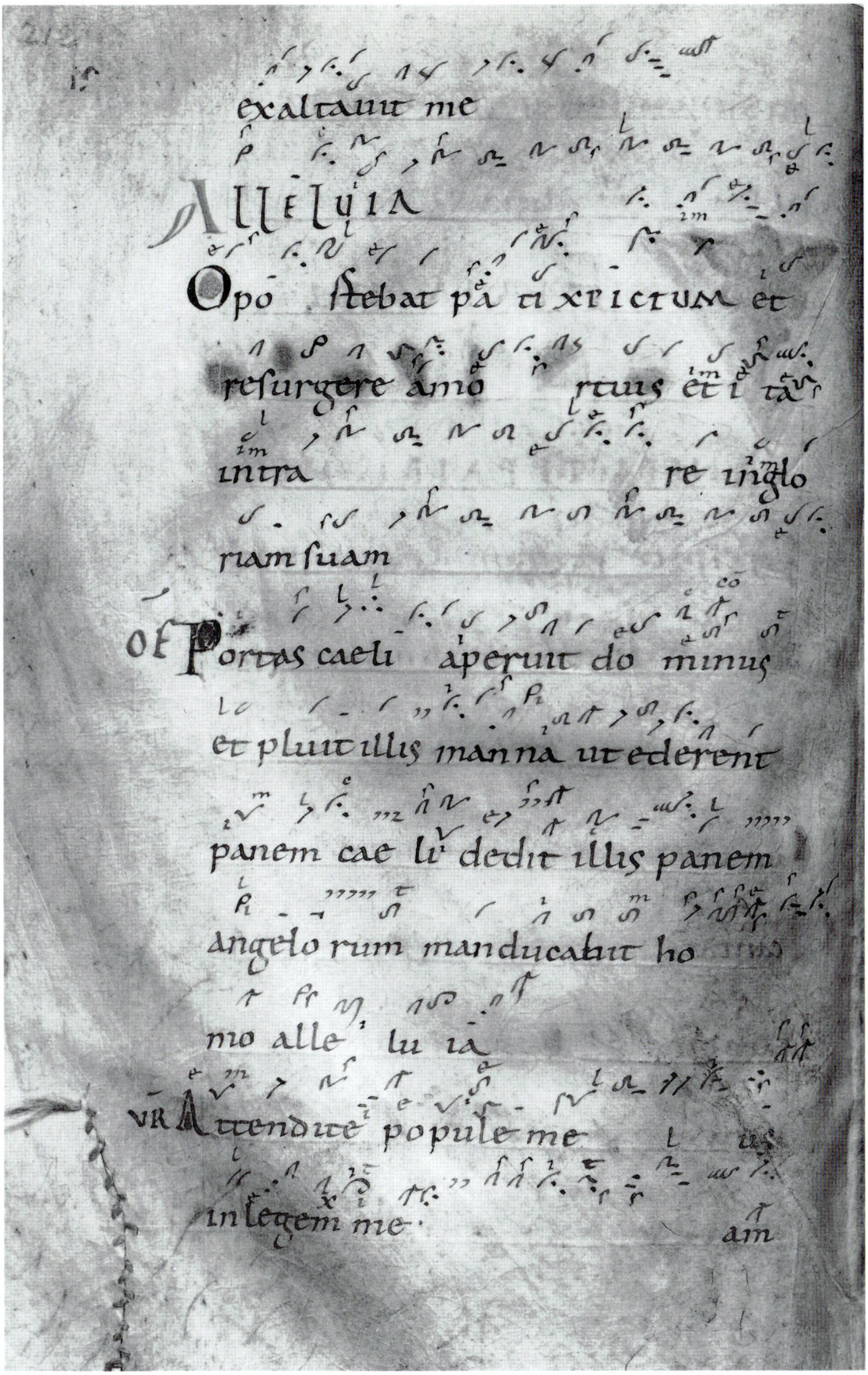

Pl. I. St Gall and German notation. Einsiedeln, Benediktinerkloster, MS 121, p. 216

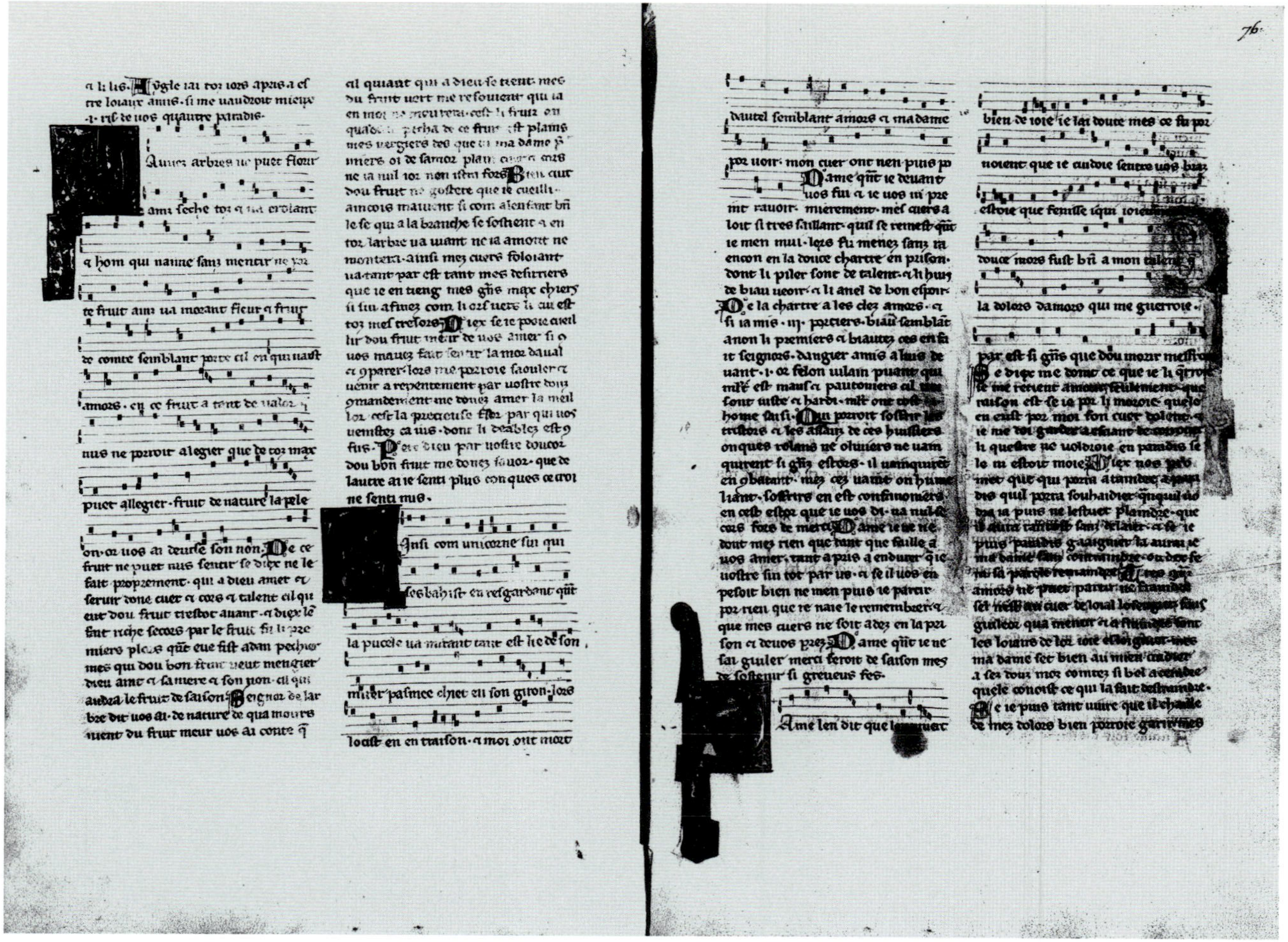

Pl. II. Thibaud, King of Navarre, *Aussi com l'unicorne*. Paris, BNF f. fr. 844, fos. 75ᵛ–76ʳ

PL. IV. Audefroy le Bastard, *Bele Ydoine se siet*. Paris, BNF f. fr. 844, fo. 148ᵛ

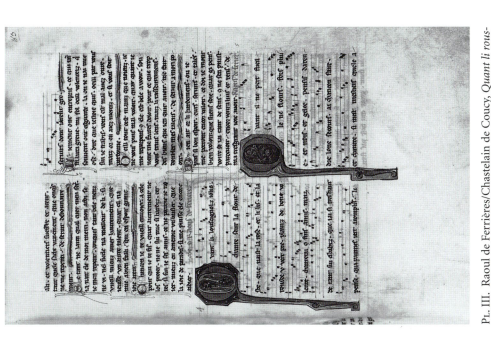

PL. III. Raoul de Ferrières/Chastelain de Coucy, *Quant li roussignol*. Paris, BNF f. fr. 844, fo. 83ʳ

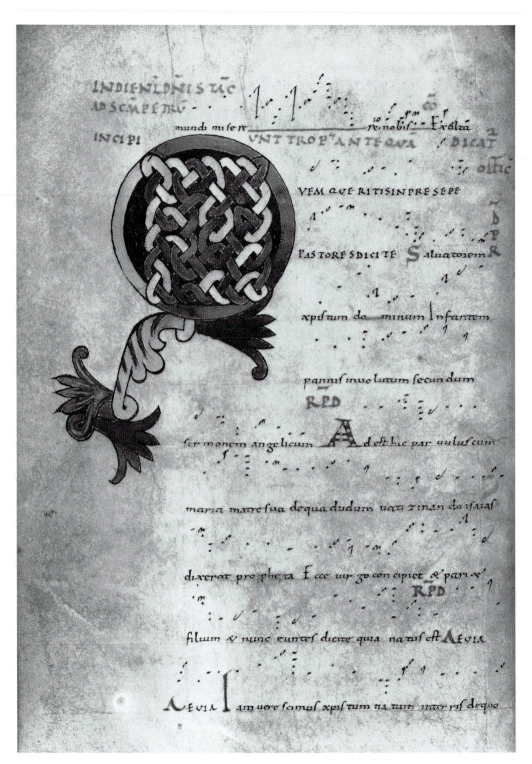

INDIENLDNISTAC
ADSCAPETRO · ·
INCIPI   mundi mifere   re nobif · · Exalta
                UNT TROP ANT EOVA   DICAT
                                              ostie
                VEM QVE RITIS INPRE SEPE

PASTORES DICITE Saluatorem

xpistum do   minum Infantem

pannif inuolutum secundum
RPD
sermonem angelicum Adest hic par aulus cum

maria matrefua dequa dudum uccti τ inan do ifaiaf

dixerat propheta Ecce uirgo concipiet & pariet
                                    RPD
filium & nunc euntef dicite quia natuf est AEVIA

AEVIA Iam uere scimus xpistum na tum inter rif dequo

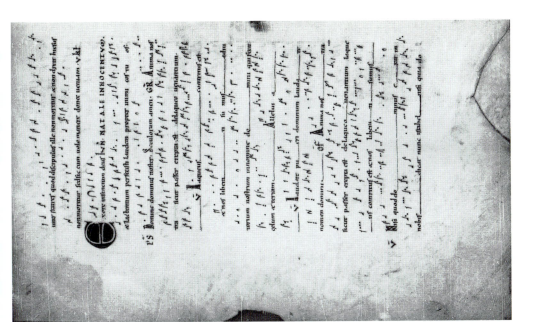

Pl. VI. (*above*) Lorraine notation. Laon, Bib. Municipale, MS 239, fo. 26ᵛ

Pl. VII. (*right*) North French notation. Paris, BNF lat. 1087, fo. 10ᵛ

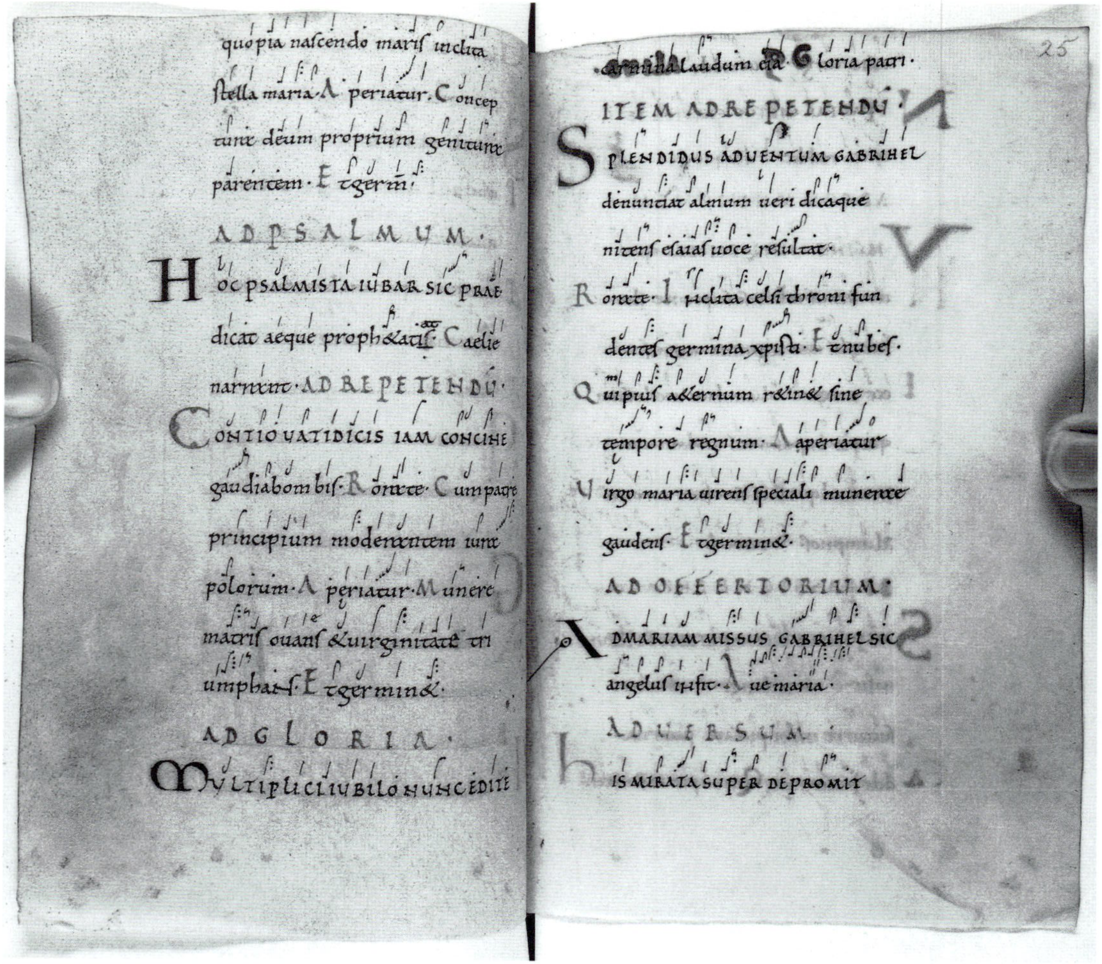

Pl. VIII. English notation. Cambridge, Corpus Christi College, MS 473, fos. 24ᵛ – 25ʳ

ine ter ter num Offerent

Diffusa est gra̅ria̅ in l̅a bus tuis ꝑptꝫ abenedixit te co̅

de us i n̅e ternum ... euouae ꝑ Eructauit

DO̅M . iij . de aduentu d̅n̅i

A̅ ICUDE ITSIN DOMINO SE̅M PERITARU̅M A̅N

dico gꝛu̅ d̅ote modestia uest̅ra nota̅ssit om̅

nibus homi ni bus dominus ꝓpe est Nihil solli ci

ti si tis sed in om̅ moratio̅ ne peticio̅ nes uestre̅ in̅otesca̅t

apud deum i . euouae ꝑ Benedixisti d̅ne terram

tuam auer tisti captiuitatem iacob ᵺ Er pax dei que exu

perat omnes sensum custodiat cor da uestra & intellege̅tias

uestras ᵺ Letemur angelica tur ba celoꝛ simul q ̇ ecclesie

chorus & omis̅ tur ba populoꝛ pariter Gaude te ℞

Qui sedes domine tu ꝓ cherubin excita

potentiam tuam ej uem

PL. XI. Spanish notation. London, British Library, Add. 30850, fo. 80ʳ

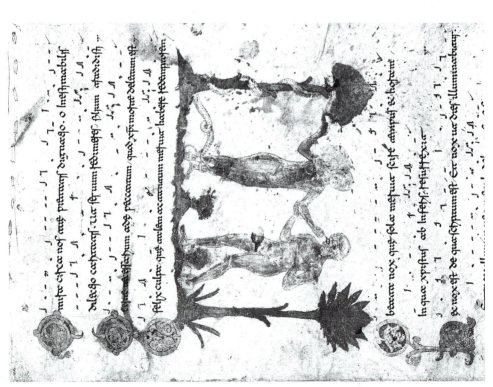

PL. X. Beneventan notation. London, British Library, Add. 30337, fo. 11ᵛ

of the longa. Since in the cantus coronatus a syllable is placed somewhat regularly at the interval of a perfect longa equivalent, the pacing is relatively slow. Further, if the performance of a cantus coronatus is to resemble the regular pace of Kyrie and Gloria, then the 'crowns' imply that each written note should be ornamented, but, as with the case described above in conjunction with Ex. 5.10(*a*), it does not mean that the notes are to be sustained an indefinite and irregular length of time. It would seem more reasonable to believe that the ornamentation takes place within the time allowed each note according to its durational value.

To continue along this line, Grocheio's point that the cantus coronatus is called by some a conductus simplex relates it to those conductus that were set almost completely syllabically, which may be the only similarity between those two forms. And he expands this relationship in another paragraph where he relates offertory, conductus, carol (*ductia*), and cantus coronatus (280; partially quoted in Ch. 2).[14] In this relationship he would seem to be connecting offertory to conductus not for its melodic simplicity, since offertory chants are usually highly ornate, but because of its modal conformity: 'according to the rules of the tones'. On the other hand it also may mean that the conductus simplex was regularly ornamented, or perhaps it too was sung at a slow and dignified pace, which may be the relationship the offertory has to the carol.[15] Elsewhere in the treatise Grocheio relates the cantus coronatus to hymns (241; partially quoted in Ch. 2), which allows us to approach the subject from a slightly different angle.

Johannes de Grocheio, 164:280. The offertory follows the Credo, and is constructed of many concords in the manner of a simple conductus, and it ascends and descends properly. It also begins, continues, and ends according to the rules of the tones, and is fully distributed among the eight modes. It is sung in the manner of carol (*ductia*) or cantus coronatus, so that the hearts of the faithful are awakened to devotion in sacrifice.

156:241. A hymn is an embellished song that has many verses. By embellished I mean in the manner of a cantus coronatus, which has concords that are beautiful and ornately arranged. The hymn is distinguished from the cantus coronatus because in the cantus coronatus the number of verses is limited to seven or thereabouts, but in hymns the number of verses is commonly found to be more or less than seven. A hymn is sung immediately after the Invitatory and the Venite in Matins, and after the Deus in adiutorium in the Hours, so that when Christ's faithful have been summoned it may rouse their hearts and souls to devotion and revive and fortify them to hear the psalms and gospels and to pray more heartily.

In this latter passage Grocheio seems to connect hymn and cantus coronatus on the basis of the 'ornate' melody (although, oddly, he does not make that connection with the offertory). He does not say that the hymn is made of perfect

---

[14] See above, Table 2.1, for a list of Grocheio's related compositions.
[15] On the nature of the carol (*ductia*) and Grocheio's description, see McGee, 'Medieval Dances'.

longas nor that it is 'crowned', although we might suspect a connection between 'ornate' and ornamented. On the other hand, ornamentation can only be performed successfully by a soloist, whereas hymns were performed by the entire schola in unison.[16] Therefore, I would not infer that Grocheio is recommending the addition of ornaments to hymns.[17] The one common element in all Grocheio's descriptions of cantus coronatus, Kyrie, Gloria, offertory, and hymn is a statement about the quality and purpose of their texts. The cantus coronatus text is to move souls to be 'daring and resolute, magnanimous and liberal, characteristics that all make for good rule', the Kyrie and Gloria are to 'move the hearts of those hearing them devoutly to praying', the offertory is sung so that 'the hearts of the faithful are awakened to devotion in sacrifice', and the purpose of the hymn is to 'rouse to devotion the hearts and souls of those faithful summoned by Christ, and fortify them to hear the psalms and gospels'. It is apparent, therefore, that in addition to certain formal, modal, and compositional elements, for Grocheio the nature of the text was an important factor in its composition and interpretation, and even the tempo of a composition was dictated by certain aesthetic elements (see Ch. 2, p. 34).

In terms of ornamentation of the forms discussed above by Grocheio, it would seem that he is proposing that only the cantus coronatus be given elaborate ornamentation throughout. And although he describes some aspects of Kyrie, Gloria, hymn, and offertory by analogy with the cantus coronatus, he does not suggest that ornamentation is applied to them in the same way he does when describing the performance of the cantus coronatus ('crowned around the sounds by masters and students'). Instead, it would seem that these other forms are in themselves ornate, and are to be performed with the slow tempo and dignified manner of the cantus coronatus.

PRELUDE, CAUDA, AND POSTLUDE

The clearest statement about the presence of a prelude in secular music is that by Johannes de Grocheio in reference to the abilities of a good vielle player (139).

---

[16] On strophic hymns and their use see Richard Crocker, 'Medieval Chant', in id. and David Hiley (eds.), *The Early Middle Ages to 1300* (New Oxford History of Music, rev. edn., ii; Oxford, 1990), 232–43.

[17] For further discussion see Warren, 'Punctus organi', 134–6. He believes (p. 135) that Grocheio also says that the Responsory and Alleluia are sung with fermatas. But Grocheio does not use the word 'fermata', nor does he say that these items are to be sung as if crowned: 'These three chants, that is, the Responsory, Alleluia, and Sequence, are sung immediately after the epistle and before the gospel, in mystery and reverence of the Trinity. The Responsory and Alleluia are frequently sung in the manner of an estampie (*stantipes*) or cantus coronatus, in order that they may impose devotion and humility in the hearts of the listeners. The Sequence is sung in the manner of a carol (*ductia*), in order that it may guide and gladden the listeners so that they can properly receive the words of the New Testament, for example the Holy Gospel, that are frequently sung immediately after' (Grocheio 276).

In addition to specifically including 'every song and cantilena', he also feels it necessary to add that this practice includes 'every musical form'. Since a musical instrument other than the organ is not usually acceptable in liturgical music, Grocheio is probably referring in this last phrase to all dance music and perhaps to all non-liturgical polyphony, forms that may not be included under the other headings.

Johannes de Grocheio, 134:139. A good musician generally preludes (*introducit*) every song and cantilena, and every musical form on the vielle.

Grocheio also describes a cauda or postlude in reference to certain mono-phonic compositions both sacred and secular (255 and 273). He speaks of the addition of such free improvisation to antiphons, evangelical psalms, the Alleluia, cantus coronatus, and estampie.

Johannes de Grocheio, 160:255. This chant [i.e. antiphon] is sung after the Psalms. Sometimes a *neupma* is added, for instance after the psalms and gospels. A neupma is like a coda or a finale following the antiphon, just as a coda is played on the vielle after the cantus coronatus or estampie, which the vielle players call a *modus*.

162:273. At the end of the verse the Alleluia is again taken up. And a kind of coda is added on to the Alleluia, just as the neupma is added on to the antiphons. Often, in place of the coda, a sequence is sung, as for instance when the Mass is celebrated with greater solemnity.

Although Grocheio does not give additional instructions as to the precise content of these caude or neupmae, we do have many surviving examples of chant as well as secular music in which short or long melismatic sections appear to be appended to the melody after a strong cadence. Such passages can be found in the monophonic conductus repertory and in a variety of polyphonic compo-sitions; the 'Amen' section to the Credo of the Machaut mass, for example, is written in a style completely different from that of the main text, and could be considered a polyphonic version of the type of coda or postlude that Grocheio describes. To take this concept a step further, one may look at certain melismas in various internal positions as well, in much of the sacred and secular mono-phonic and polyphonic music of the late Middle Ages, with the same thought in mind. After reading the above descriptions of how one improvises in exactly these places it is possible to regard certain of the written melismas as notated versions of the long-standing practice of adding diminutions—either sponta-neously or composed—to enhance and develop a basic melodic shape. Whether written or improvised, the placement and style of the diminutions would have been the same.

IMPROVISING AN ENTIRE UPPER PART IN POLYPHONY

The following discussion, improvisation of entire lines over a cantus firmus, is somewhat outside the limits of the present study, and is included here only in as much as it relates to the techniques of ornamentation. This follows on the preceding discussion and refers back to the point of view expressed in Chapter 1, that there was no clear line drawn between the practices of composition, ornamentation, and improvisation, and that in many respects the three were simply different ways of arriving at exactly the same result in performance.

In his treatise *Tractatus de discantu*, Anonymous II first introduces his motive for dealing with discantus (311), and then proceeds to give rules and examples for the composition of counterpoint that are the same as those found in other treatises. The value of this passage to the present study is the author's statement that by the thirteenth century improvised discant had been practised for 'a long time', and the fact that in describing it he simply presents the standard rules of counterpoint.

Anon. II, 311. Here follows the discussion of discant. Since hidden knowledge benefits no one and quickly passes away, but when shared it is of much benefit and is greatly augmented, for that reason I intend to elucidate for our special friends, according to my ability, the art of knowing how to compose and perform improvised discant, which for a long time was a secret among certain experienced musicians.

Anonymous I (C), writing in the mid-fourteenth century, after going through the standard rules of two-part counterpoint, describes a process of performing four-part discant that from the context also would seem to be improvised (361). The upper voices are to improvise over the tenor using both the perfect intervals and the imperfect consonances of third, sixth, and tenth according to the rules of counterpoint, a technique reported by many theorists. But most interestingly, Anonymous I states that the performers of the highest two parts are to fill their parts with diminutions, and that all the voices must sing these embellishments with a very light voice. In fact, the author has praise for the ornamental technique only when it is sung with a light sound. He also makes it clear that the singer of the cantus firmus is to sing his part in tempo and that the improvisers of the other parts are to observe those durational values. This is in agreement with the statements quoted above (p. 100) on the difference between discant and organum purum. As free as the singers were to improvise, with the exception of organum purum, they were to do it within the confines of the durational values written in the cantus firmus.[18]

---

[18] Page, 'A Treatise on Musicians', 17, interprets Arnulf's remarks about musicians in his first category as referring to unskilled singers who attempt to improvise over plainchant: 'The first [category of musician] is becoming notorious—as is fitting—in those who are utterly ignorant of the art of music, who do not profit from the benefit of any natural aptitude, who are not yet acquainted with plainchant, but who none the less try to gnaw—indeed to devour—musical consonances with a hungry bite as they lead the singing through the impetuous rashness of their ridiculous presumption. When they bray with the din of their brawling bark louder than an ass, and when they trumpet more terribly than the clamour of a wild animal, they spew out harsh-sounding

Anon. I (C), 361. Another mode of singing discant occurs, which, if it is well executed, strikes the listener as more skilful, although it is very light. In this method there will appear to be more than one singer of discant above the plainchant, although in reality there will be just the one, for the others will be singing the plainchant in various concords [i.e. on different pitches]. In this method let there be four or five men: the first begins by holding the plainchant; let the second prepare his voice at the fifth; the third at the octave; and let the fourth place his voice at the twelfth, if he should be present. When the concords have begun, all these singers will follow the plainchant to its conclusion. Those who sing at the twelfth and octave will do so together and in a continuous fashion; furthermore, they ought to subdivide and embellish the notes as much as is suitable for the tempo. Note well that the tenor [i.e. singer of the original chant] perform his notes entirely in tempo. The one who will sing the discant not only places his voice in perfect concords, but also in imperfect concords, that is [at the interval of] the third, sixth, and tenth. He should run to and fro through these concords, ascending and descending according to what will seem more expedient to himself and pleasing to the listener. Through this method, one who is experienced in discant, though he possess but a modest voice, is capable of producing a loud (*magnam*) melody when singing with others. If there is one who will discant continuously at the twelfth, this can be done with [only] four voices singing at the same time.[19]

While the passage quoted above deals with the invention of entire parts, in doing so it presents clear guidelines for embellishments of smaller sizes.[20] The difference is that with a written-out upper part the composer has seen to the problems of correct contrapuntal motion and consonance; the singer need only embellish the written notes with a light voice, taking care to remain in tempo. When improvising an entire part, each performer was responsible for the correct choice of contrapuntal intervals as well as the beauty of the embellishments. If the technique of improvised discant as described in the various treatises was known to and practised by the better singers, simply adding embellishments to an existing discant line must have seemed relatively easy.

things. Singing their parts in the reverse of the way in which they should, they produce barbarism in music contrary to rule; false blinded by a despicable delusion that arises from their presumption, they boast in their hearts that they can disregard excellent singers and surpass them, and they impudently offer themselves in the throng to give correction or leadership to these same [excellent singers] so that they who do not even know enough about music to be led, and who are always producing dissonance amongst those who are concordant, may give the appearance of being trained musicians. With their ineptitude they constantly pollute whatever is more correctly performed in the learned throng of musicians' (Arnulf, 15:4).

[19] This last phrase seems to suggest another possible method of performing this type of composition: two singers spelling one another on the highest part; this would explain the opening statement that 'let there be four or five men'.

[20] For a more extensive discussion of polyphonic improvisation over a cantus firmus see Ferand, 'The Howling in Seconds', and *Die Improvisation in Beispielen aus neun Jahrhunderten abendländischer Musik* (Cologne, 1956).

SPECIAL INSTRUMENTAL INSTRUCTIONS

Statements in a few of the theoretical treatises concerning ornamentation by instruments suggest that there are only small differences between vocal and instrumental embellishment, having to do mostly with speed and the lack of the possibility to vary pitches on some instruments. In fact, very few theorists discuss either the instruments or their performance practices. Giorgio Anselmi compares both wind and string instruments with voices and notes that once instrumentalists have set the strings correctly (he is probably referring to the tuning of the strings of a harp and both the tuning of strings and setting of frets on bowed and plucked strings), the instrument will stay within the correct mode, that is, it will continue to produce the correct distribution of whole- and half-steps (III:5).[21] Thus, an incorrect note from an instrument is easily recognized by the listener. By contrast, singers often stray from the correct mode, but are adept at covering it up. It would seem that much of this point revolves around the amount of pitch inflection available to singers versus that for instrumentalists. The vocal style included a large amount of pitch variation that would make it difficult for the casual listener to know the correct intervals, whereas the instruments were not as flexible. In the end, however, Giorgio points out that it was the voice that set the model for instruments to emulate.

Giorgio Anselmi, III:5. A lute string or a pipe, whenever it repeats a certain sound according as it has been struck will continue to resound with the same tone unless a lutenist, highly trained in the elements of his discipline, applies the plectrum more lightly or more energetically. But whereas even the unlearned will easily recognize the most infrequent errors of the musical instrument, even well-trained persons will scarcely recognize untuned, inappropriate, or dissonant sounds of a skilful singer. But certainly it becomes most difficult to keep the notes at the right pitch for a long time, even for one song: hence it happens that those who are experienced in song cannot easily be discovered from among them (especially when a trained singer is listening), but many hold their peace absolutely after the performance of a single song. For this reason the ancients placed all harmonic power in instruments. For they well knew, having tuned the strings in the proper proportions, how to preserve the rightful parts of the melody [i.e. stay in the correct mode], always, in every song, so that the pitches should remain correct, [all the while] aware that the human voice frequently falters or labours even though all musical instruments imitate it, and were made in its image.

Other than vielle-tuning instructions and a short reference to organ trills in Jerome's writing, what can be found is little more than the statements in the treatise of Johannes de Grocheio (135, 137 below, and 139 above), which briefly discuss instruments and their use, praising strings in general and the vielle in particular as suitable over all others for all kinds of music:

[21] By implication the correctly placed holes in a wind instrument will assure the same accuracy.

Johannes de Grocheio, 134:135. Here, however, we do not mean to discuss the disposition or classification of instruments, save for the purpose of presenting the variety of musical forms created on them. Among which, since stringed instruments possess pre-eminence . . .

134:137. Among all the stringed instruments that we have seen, the vielle seems to excell. Just as the intellective soul virtually embraces other natural forms in itself, as the square embraces the triangle, and as the greater number embraces the lesser, so the vielle virtually contains all other instruments in itself.

Anonymous IV states that instruments have wider ranges than voices (86:7), but the only mention of a difference in ornamentation practices appears at two different points in his discussion of the subdivision of note-values, where he points out that although vocalists cannot subdivide the breve by more than three semibreves, a good instrumentalist can subdivide further (39:8, 45:1):

Anon. IV, 86:7. There are nineteen notes (*cordarum*) [lit. strings] in the range of the diatonic genus, and fifteen concords, etc. Only rarely do some people progress further, to the third octave. This is commonly used, however, on the organ and other instruments, and among good musicians it is produced more completely with this number of strings or pipes [i.e. nineteen], as it is on well-tuned bells.

39:8. Customarily, we rarely subdivide notes further, that is, with the human voice we do not put four notes in place of a breve, although on instruments it is more often done, and done well. Among the discriminating, when this is done with respect to the first mode, (whether it is in the perfect mode or the imperfect), it can be done by completing [the temporal value] with a short or long rest, whichever is more appropriate.

45:1. Again there is a certain figure which is called *elmuahim* [= rhombus] or something similar. It is always written as an oblique shape, but it signifies different things. Sometimes it is called a semibreve if it should be before or after another note that is exactly the same. On the other hand, sometimes it is the third part of a breve, that is, when three notes are written in the manner of currentes, and thus there are three notes in place of a breve. If four currentes should be put in place of one breve, it is done in the same way, but this seldom happens. This subdivision cannot be done further with the human voice, but players are able to do it on stringed instruments.

That instrumentalists are capable of performing faster and therefore more ornate decorative passages than are singers may also be what Arnulf is saying in his description of the second category of musician (15:24), quoted more fully above, although the passage is somewhat ambiguous, depending on whether the words 'organicis instrumentis' are translated as referring to the organ or to vocal ornamentation applied to organum.

Arnulf, 15:32. We see among them some clerics who, on the instruments known as organs, perform the most difficult musical compositions, such as the human voice would scarcely undertake.

Jerome's instructions for the application of flowers to vocal music apply to instruments as well, with differences mostly in the execution on fixed-pitch instruments, as noted above (Ch. 4, p. 62). He devotes his chapter 28 to instruments, especially the tuning of the rubeba and viella, with elementary instructions about fingering,[22] but there is nothing to suggest that the ornamental practices are any different from those for singing, described at length in his chapter 25 and quoted extensively here in all chapters.

Grocheio's praise of the vielle includes the naming of three musical types usually performed on that instrument—cantus coronatus, carol, and estampie—but again, there is no suggestion that they perform these forms in a way significantly different from the voice in terms of ornamentation.[23] And his statement about the invention of instrumental caudae following a cantus coronatus and estampie, quoted above, again illustrates the similarity between vocal and instrumental practices, since he points out that the process of inventing caudae is the same in both instrumental and vocal forms, but given different names.

In summary, therefore, the performance instructions for instruments differ from those for the voice on only two points: Jerome's description of a trill on the organ, where the principal note is sustained and the trill note played intermittently; and the information that instrumental passaggi often include more subdivisions of the breve than those performed by singers. Otherwise, it would seem that instrumental practice, to the extent that was possible, followed that for the voice.

---

[22] For a discussion of Jerome's instructions for tuning the vielle see Christopher Page, 'Jerome of Moravia on the *rubeba* and *viella*', *Galpin Society Journal*, 32 (1979), 77–98, and 'Le Troisième Accord pour vièle de Jérome de Moravie—jongleurs et "anciens Pères" de France', in Christian Meyer (ed.), *Jérome de Moravie: un théoricien de la musique dans le milieu intellecteul parisien du XIII* siècle* (Paris, 1992), 83–96.

[23] Grocheio does describe the instrumental carol and estampie as formally different from the vocal forms of the same name, but this would not affect the performance technique in terms of ornamentation. See McGee, *Medieval Instrumental Dances* (Bloomington, Ind., 1989), 8–12.

6

Conclusions

THE theoretical treatises of the late Middle Ages describe an involved system of vocal practices and embellishment that extends to all types of music: sacred and secular, monophonic and polyphonic, vocal and instrumental. In order to present the breadth of the subject as well as the nature of the instructions, initially it was necessary to gather together as much information as possible on each subject area. This often meant pooling information from treatises written centuries apart and/or in widely separated locations, and without regard to the repertory to which any one theorist was referring. By reviewing and recombining the information in the theoretical statements now in terms of its application to music, the medieval performance tradition can be seen as a basically unified practice with some components that remained throughout the period and others that changed gradually over the centuries and that differed in some details from place to place. This approach will allow us to refine the singing and ornamentation instructions according to repertorial, geographical, and temporal boundaries, as discussed in Chapter 1.

MEDIEVAL SINGING STYLE

Vocal Sound

The most difficult of the medieval music traditions to bring into clear focus for the modern reader is that of vocal sound. Statements about the voice qualities of medieval singers have been presented in quantity in Chapter 2, and referred to constantly throughout the other chapters. To gain a correct historical image of medieval vocal style one of the obstacles the modern reader must overcome is the erroneous sound impression gained from the vast number of recordings of medieval music, especially of chant. With very few exceptions (and almost all those exceptions in recent recordings of secular music) they present a superimposition of modern Western conservatory vocal techniques and performance traditions on the early repertory. For the most part, the phrases on these recordings are smooth and long, the vocal colour is constant, the dynamic changes are limited and introduced very gradually, only diatonic pitches are sung, and nothing is added to the printed edition—the antithesis of what we have seen to be the medieval practice. Such performances are undoubtedly well-intentioned and they do acquaint the listening public with the vast and excellent repertory of medieval music, but the sound impression they convey is quite some distance from what the historical evidence indicates was actually heard in the Middle Ages.

From the instructions presented and discussed in Chapter 2, it becomes clear that there are some points of similarity between present-day singing ideals and those of the past. The desire for clarity of tone, enunciation, and articulation are values common to both eras, as are the directions to keep a steady tempo and to express the text. But the techniques to be employed in executing these shared basic principles are not the same for both time periods. Consideration of the demands on the voice required by the medieval ornaments themselves, viewed in conjunction with the instructions discussed earlier, will assist us to understand in what ways the medieval singing technique and vocal ideal were different.

In order to imagine the sound of the medieval voice one must realize that the rapid articulation, pulsating notes, sliding pitches, and non-diatonic tones were a part of the basic technique, and not just unusual and colourful sounds that were introduced into a vocal style that was otherwise similar to the modern practice. Looking back through the earlier chapters, it will be noticed that the performance of most of the ornaments includes some element that is foreign to the more standard modern Western practices. Based on that and the other evidence presented and discussed here, the obvious conclusion is that the entire medieval singing practice was a unified style in which flexible sounds and pitches had a basic and constant presence even outside the specific ornaments discussed in the treatises.

The descriptions of the performance practices to be employed for several of the standard neumes are useful in assisting us both to identify certain aspects of the required vocal sound and to realize how much these sounds were a part of the normal singing style: the pes normally employs a liquescent sound at the end of the second pitch, thus incorporating what might be thought of as an 'ornamental' gliding sound into the standard performance of a non-ornamental neume. The clivis requires a dark sound on the second of two pitches; the theorists even specify that the second sound should be formed in the epiglottis. If the second sound is to be recognized as dark, it follows that the usual sound is bright—bright enough that a sound difference between the first and second tones can be heard. This kind of flexible volume change is also mentioned by Guido when he describes the performance of a repeated note with alternating strong and weak stress. As Guido stated it, the change in volume between the two sounds was drastic enough that it gave the impression of higher and lower pitches. Rapid and extreme change of volume, therefore, was also a part of the standard technique. Along the same lines, we can probably infer that a good singer had a highly developed ability of quick throat articulation in order to separate every independently written note and neume, as recommended by several writers, including Guido and Jerome. It is also probable that many, if not most, medieval voices were clear and free of constant vibrato. The detailed instructions for the employment of trills, vibrato, glissando, reverberation, and pulsations would seem to support this conclusion. Even if Jerome had not excluded constant use of the vibrato from a particular French style, it is obvious that many of the ornaments he and the other theorists advocate are so subtle that a vibrato would render them inaudible and therefore useless. Certainly this would be true in the case of the use of non-diatonic pitches, which require a clearly defined pitch in order to be noticed by the listener.

Non-diatonic tones, indefinite and sliding pitches, and pulsing sounds mark the medieval vocal technique as definitely different from that of later centuries. Non-diatonic pitches are described in detail by many theorists, especially Jerome, Marchettus, and Bonaventura, as being regular choices in some traditions for dividing intervals in singing. Although theorists from some traditions dismissed it as being unsuitable as regular alternative choice in ecclesiastical chant (for example, Johannes de Muris and the *Summa musice*), non-diatonic pitch is a part of several of the standard ornaments. It is present in the trill/vibrato ornaments described in detail by Jerome, and as a part of the technique for filling in intervals from a half-step to a fifth. The sliding liquescent sound was applied regularly when singing certain syllables, and could be added as a grace to the end of most neumes.

Pulsation, with the notes either separated or connected, was employed in the performance of quilisma, pressus, morula, tremula, and the stropha neumes, and it was combined with the repercussion that begins several of the ornaments. The technique could involve the execution of one or more rapid reiterations at the beginning of a note, the middle, or the end, or sounding for its full length. The incorporation of this technique as a part of so many ornaments makes it plain that the ability to pulse the voice was a basic requirement for the execution of medieval music, and the number of subtle variations in its application indicates how refined the singers' command of that technique must have been.

Nowhere is the special nature of the technical demands of the medieval vocal style more evident than in the requirements for the execution of the stropha neumes and the filled-in interval. The stropha neumes combine both the repercussive and liquescent techniques, requiring the voice to execute rapid and separated pulsations of plicated notes (i.e. darkened and sliding from pitch). When we add to this the composite sounds involved in Jerome's description of a filled-in fourth, in which the voice moves rapidly from a set pitch to a plica-like sound followed by a reverberation and finally a vibrato on the last pitch, the amount of vocal flexibility required by medieval singing technique begins to come clear.

The way in which the medieval singing style differs from the present conservatory sound, therefore, lies both in the vocal technique and the repertory of sounds. The technique involves the ability to sing with a clear (vibratoless) voice, rapid throat articulation and pulsation, slow, fast, and accelerating vibrato at variable intervals, and voice placement that alternates between a bright sound made in the front of the mouth and a dark tone from the throat. The sounds include fixed and sliding tones, diatonic and non-diatonic pitches, aspirated, gargled, and sibilant sounds, and both clear and covered tone qualities.

Since the Western vocal sound of the present day does not resemble that of the Middle Ages, we might look elsewhere for a possible sound image that fits the above description. As mentioned earlier, the model that comes quickly to mind is that which is still common in the Eastern Mediterranean countries and in the music of India, where singers have extremely agile voices, use a light frontal sound with rapid throat articulation, and employ all the sound variations and colours described here and many more, as a part of the basic singing style.[1] An obvious additional similarity is that both Eastern music and medieval Western music are basically monophonic, and it is the embellishments discussed in these chapters that are the kind best suited to a monophonic tradition.[2]

The Eastern singing tradition is not a single style; there are numerous different style varieties among the various regions, but all have in common the basic techniques and sound images described in the medieval treatises quoted here. It is not possible to know with any degree of certainty which of the many present-day Eastern practices most closely resemble the sound of medieval Western music, but it is obvious from the above discussion that the basic vocal techniques and sound repertories used in all of the Eastern traditions have much in common with the vocal sound in medieval Europe. On the level of basic description, the ornaments, articulation demands, and the use of pitch and sound colour relate the two practices.[3] In the absence of a better model, therefore, any and all of the Eastern vocal practices can be used to assist the modern reader to conceptualize the kind of sound that would have resulted from applying what is described in the theoretical treatises and required by the ornaments.[4]

---

[1] Several writers have touched on this subject, but none has taken it up. See e.g. Solange Corbin, *Die Neumen* (Palaeographie der Musik, 1/3; Cologne, 1977), 196, 209; and Curt Sachs, 'Primitive and Medieval Music: A Parallel', *JAMS* 13 (1960), 43–9.

[2] For a discussion of the use of Eastern practices in European music see McGee, 'Eastern Influences in Medieval European Dances' in R. Falck and T. Rice (eds.), *Cross-Cultural Perspectives on Music* (Toronto, 1982), 79–100, and Shai Burstyn, 'The "Arabian Influence" Thesis Revisited', *Current Musicology*, 45–7 (1990), 119–46.

[3] In a recent dissertation the following characteristics are listed as features of the present-day classical Persian vocal style: 'vocal timbre is idiomatically bright, tense and somewhat nasal; several sorts of vibrato—oscillations around a primary tone or focusing on either an upper or lower neighbour note—are frequently but judiciously employed; a wide range of articulation and relative rhythmic weighting of notes'. See Robert Simms, 'Avaz in the Recordings of Mohammad Reza Shajarian' (Ph.D. diss., University of Toronto, 1996), 33–4.

[4] For discussions of the various Eastern singing styles see Judith Cohen, 'A Medieval Bulgarian Performance Style?', *International Society of Early Music Singers Newsletter*, 1 (1983), 6–8; ead., 'Oral

From some of the statements quoted in Chapter 2, we can see that this complex vocal style was not indigenous to all parts of Europe. I have argued elsewhere that the principal purpose of the graphic design of early notation was to transmit vocal nuances to the northern Europeans—the most difficult element in the style of singing imposed by Rome, and the one most unfamiliar to the people of northern Europe.[5] Indeed, it is believed that the early notation system originated in the north-west,[6] which suggests that the French may have developed the notation specifically in order to record the new Roman vocal style. We must ask, therefore, how this style was developed and when it spread through Europe. (I shall delay until later in this chapter the question of what the new style might have replaced.)

The criticisms of John the Deacon and Adhémar de Chabannes quoted in Chapter 2 are quite revealing in this regard; they provide a view of the changing vocal practices and suggest a time-frame for the introduction of the new style. Neither writer says that the northerners (who were the subject of both criticisms) cannot sing in tune or that they have not learnt the repertory—the type of criticism that one would expect to find levelled at incompetent or unwilling performers. Instead, what concerns both writers is the inability of the northerners to sing the necessary nuances: they are unable to perform the 'tremblings', 'subtleties', 'inflections', and 'repercussions'. In short, they could not adapt their voices to the style required for Roman chant. We may conclude from this that the performance style emanated from Rome, and that it was already fully adopted in northern Italy by the time of John's remarks in the ninth century, since he does not include the north Italians in his criticism. But according to him, no one north of the Alps could handle the technique.

Extant ninth-century notated manuscripts provide information that allows us to clarify John's statement and modify that of Adhémar. At least twenty surviving manuscripts from various locations north of the Alps give evidence

---

Tradition as a Clue to Ancient Practice' *Continuo*, 6 (1983), 16; Amnon Shiloah, 'La Voix et les techniques vocales chez les Arabes', *Cahiers de musiques traditionnelles*, 4 (1991), 85–101; and the discussion of a highly ornate folk style in Yugoslavia in Ankica Petrovic, 'Les Techniques du chant villageois dans les Alpes dinariques (Yougoslavie)', *Cahiers de musiques traditionnelles*, 4 (1991), 103–15.

[5] ' "Ornamental" Neumes and Early Notation'. Richard Crocker has pointed out that in 752 Pepin, King of the Franks, sent Archbishop Chrodegang of Metz to Rome in order to obtain the Roman chant texts and singing style; see 'Liturgical Materials of Roman Chant', in id. and Hiley (eds.), *The Early Middle Ages to 1300*, 111–45 at 112. As for a possible source for the Roman vocal style, Thomas H. Connolly has recently found evidence of the existence of Jewish Christian congregations in Rome in the early centuries that may have provided models for singing chant in the Middle Eastern style; 'Jewish Influence on Early Christian Chant: A New Model', paper delivered at the annual meeting of the American Musicological Society, 7 Nov. 1996.

[6] See Corbin, *Die Neumen*, 3.

that by the time of John's writing the Roman singing style was being promulgated in the northern areas. Although he may be correct with regard to the stylistic accuracy of the performances, the repertory was already being circulated in the north in notational forms that transmitted the vocal nuances.[7] Throughout the tenth century the notated manuscripts spread in increasing quantity throughout all parts of continental Europe and the British Isles. From this testimony and from what is known of the dissemination of liturgical practices, there is no doubt that by the end of the tenth century all European monastic and population centres were in possession of notation that transmitted both the Roman chant repertory and the nuances for its performance.[8] Theoretical sources of information for the interpretation of neumes and the ornamentation of chant quoted in the preceding chapters indicate that by the eleventh century the vocal tradition was widely known. Seen in that light, therefore, Adhémar's eleventh-century criticism of northern French vocal inabilities may be an exaggeration. It is more likely that he was noticing the kind of regional performance variations discussed below, and was comparing those of the northerners unfavourably with those of his own area.

What may be concluded from the above is that the style of singing described by the theorists and discussed in this book was common to chant performance in Italy at least by the ninth century. The style had come from Rome, and undoubtedly was spread to all parts of Europe along with the chant repertory as a part of the imposition of Roman liturgical practices.[9] No doubt, as proposed in many recent scholarly publications, the chant and its singing practices were adapted and adjusted according to various local practices,[10] but at the same time we must note that the notation in the manuscripts and the theoretical treatises reflects the European-wide adoption of a common basic vocal style, whatever the local variants may have been.

The question that naturally follows the above conclusion has to do with the dissolution of that vocal style: how, when, and why does the style described here

[7] A list of these manuscripts can be found in 'Notation', *New Grove*, xiii. 346. The earliest is Munich, Bayerische Staatsbibliothek, MS clm. 9543, originating from St Emmeram in Regensburg (South Germany) between 817 and 834.

[8] Exactly when and what chant was imported to northern Europe is an involved and still contested issue. For two recent views of the issue see Helmut Hucke, 'Toward a New Historical View of Gregorian Chant', *JAMS* 33 (1980), 437–67, and Kenneth J. Levy, 'On Gregorian Orality', *JAMS* 43 (1990), 185–227. Hucke contends that 'the standard version of Gregorian chant . . . was introduced into the Frankish Empire by King Pepin and Charlemagne' (p. 442), i.e. the late 8th and early 9th cc., and was adapted by the Franks. See above, n. 5.

[9] During a discussion of the adoption of the Roman liturgy by the Franks at the command of Charlemagne, Hucke asks 'What did the Franks really take over from the music of Roman chant?' and provides several answers, including the liturgical order, texts of chants, and church modes; 'Toward a New Historical View', 465–6. We may now add to that a new style of singing.

[10] Bibliography on this topic is vast. See e.g. the recent writings of Helmut Hucke, Leo Treitler, Kenneth Levy, James Grier, and Peter Jeffery, which set out the basic theories and provide extensive bibliographical notes.

begin to show elements that became the stylistic norm in later centuries? As was pointed out in Chapter 1, by the seventeenth century the medieval vocal style had evolved to what we know as 'bel canto' (although from what follows we may wish to adjust our concept of the elements of that style). The change must have been gradual, subtle, and nearly imperceptible during any one lifespan, and therefore it is not surprising that no writings have been found that chronicle the changes. Looking at the singing instructions as a whole and the changes in notational practices in conjunction with the repertory, however, we can obtain a general view of that change.

Beginning some time in the eleventh century, a change from unheighted neumes to staff-notation was brought about by a desire to standardize and control the melodic details of the chant as well as by the more practical consideration of communicating the repertory solely in written form. Guido, who is credited with the initial development of the staff, expressed in the early eleventh century the need for such a system by pointing out how impractical the tradition was of requiring the help of a teacher in order to learn even the simplest chant (34). The other motive for the change, that of standardization of the mode and melodic contour of each chant, was expressed at the end of that century by Johannes Affligemensis, in the context of advocating Guido's notational system (133).

Guido, *Aliae regulae*, 34. In our times singers are fools above all men. In every art there are very many more things that we learn from our perception than those we have learnt from a master. For in only reading through the psalter, little boys learn to read every book. Peasants immediately comprehend the science of agriculture. Whoever learns to prune one vine, graft one sapling, or burden one ass either will not hesitate to do the same, or even better, in all cases as he does in one. Extraordinary singers and singing students, however, although they should sing every day for a hundred years, will never sing one antiphon, not even a small one, through their own efforts without a master. The time they squander in singing is so great that they could have learnt the divine and secular writings in their entirety.

Johannes Affligemensis, 133. Since in the ordinary neumes [i.e. unheighted] the intervals cannot be ascertained, and the chants that are learnt from them cannot be securely committed to memory and therefore many inaccuracies creep into songs, but these neumes represent all the intervals clearly so that they prevent error and loss of memory in the singing once the neumes are perfectly learnt; is there anyone who cannot see the great advantage in them?

It can easily be seen how neumes without lines (*irregulares neumae*) promote error rather than knowledge, that *virgulae*, *clives*, and *podati* are all written on the same plane [lit: uniformly], and they do not indicate any manner [interval] of raising or lowering [of pitch].

The development of staff-notation also marked the beginning of a change in the shapes of neumes from the older forms that indicated vocal nuances to a new set that by and large did not. The change began in the eleventh century with Guido's two-line staff,[11] and proceeded over a period of less than a century to a standard four or five lines and more or less square notation. The new notation was not accepted in all locations immediately, and throughout the twelfth century manuscripts in unheighted neumes were still in use in most areas, although in ever decreasing numbers. Eventually all areas adopted the new notation system, although old-style unheighted neumes can be found in German manuscripts from as late as the fifteenth century.[12]

For the present subject it is important to know what is signified by the change in neume forms. It is obvious that the change of notation style indicated a change of values: exact pitch and specific duration were deemed to be more important to notate than nuances of performance. There is no reason why neumes on a staff cannot be shaped to indicate nuances of performance, but with a few notable exceptions, that kind of information was quickly abandoned in the new notation, which gravitated instead towards a relatively smaller number of neume shapes, most of which no longer contained nuance information. What remains in the new notation are a few graphically suggestive ornamental marks for quilisma, plica, and oriscus, and translations of other ornamental neumes (e.g. stropha, pressus) into square shapes that do not retain any indiction of the inflections that were a part of their shapes in the earlier notation (see above, Table 3.1). We are left to wonder if this means that the vocal inflections were no longer practised, or that the nuances were sufficiently ingrained in all areas that they no longer needed to be graphically notated. A complete answer to this question is not possible at this point, but there are some clear indications that nuances continued as part of the singing style for some time after the introduction of the new notation.

A comparison of the dates of the notational changes with those of the theoretical statements about neume performance yields interesting, although somewhat contradictory, information. As late as 1300, when nuance-free notation on a staff was widespread, treatises discussing and advocating performance with flexible pitch, sound inflection, pulsations, etc. were still being written in France, England, and Italy, by Jerome, Johannes de Garlandia, Walter Odington, and several others (see Ch. 1, Table 1.1). It is undeniable, therefore, that nuances were still being sung by the beginning of the fourteenth century, even though they were no longer written into the notation of the areas from which we have the bulk of the theoretical descriptions of ornamental singing. On the other hand, after the early fourteenth century very few statements about these practices can be found.

---

[11] On the development of the early stave see Joseph Smits van Waesberghe, 'The Musical Notation of Guido of Arezzo', *MD* 5 (1951), 15–63.

[12] See Solange Corbin, 'Neumatic Notation' (parts I–IV), *New Grove*, xiii. 128–54.

We have already seen that the Roman performance style was difficult for the northerners to learn, and there are indications that it may not have been fully adopted and accepted in all northern areas. As early as *c*.1030 Guido allowed for the performance of a full and focused pitch in place of a liquescent, stating that 'it is often more pleasing' (Guido, 177). Whatever the other vocal style—the one replaced by the new Roman practice—it obviously had made inroads to the point of being accepted as an equally valid choice in at least this one case. One might speculate, therefore, that the absence of nuance indications in the new notation forms does not reflect a significant change in the basic Roman vocal practices, but instead a lessening of the intensity with which it was being promoted. Or to state it differently, some of the regional vocal practices were being accepted into the Roman style.

A parallel situation that lends support to this last point can be found in the development of other facets of the Roman liturgy. Throughout its dissemination and promulgation during the sixth through the ninth centuries, the Roman liturgy was subject to a number of changes originating from the north. The powerful monastic centres in Metz and Cluny, for example, exerted influence over many details of the liturgy—reforms that were eventually adopted by Rome.[13] Helmut Hucke makes a case that the adoption of the system of eight church modes into Roman chant stems from the Franks.[14] His reference is to the repertory as a whole, but it is quite likely that as another facet of this same adjustment, the northern centres also instigated modifications in the style of singing—reforms that also would have been accepted by Rome. We have seen evidence that in the ninth century the northerners had difficulty learning to handle certain technical elements of the Roman style that was being pressed on them, and that they were still experiencing it as late as the eleventh; they had not completely changed over from their old singing style to the new Roman practices. It is not hard to imagine that in addition to the modifications introduced by singers who had difficulty with various details of the new vocal style, certain other changes in the performance of the Roman repertory would have taken place unintentionally as a natural result of the singers' lack of familiarity with the new technique, and that traditional local practices would have been incorporated both consciously and unconsciously into the new style.

---

[13] See Kenneth J. Levy, 'Latin Chant outside the Roman Tradition', in *The Early Middle Ages to 1300* (New Oxford History of Music, rev. edn.; Oxford, 1990), 69–110, for an overview of this process. He reports the possible influence of Gallican chant from the West Frankish area and Celtic chant through migrating Irish monks during the 8th and 9th cc. (p. 69).

[14] Hucke, 'Karolingische Renaissance und Gregorianischer Gesang', *Musikforschung*, 28 (1975), 4–18; and 'Die Herkunft der Kirchentonarten und die fränkische Überlieferung des Gregorianischen Gesangs', in *Bericht über den Internationalen Musikwissenschaftlichen Kongress Berlin 1975* (Kassel, 1980), 257–60. Further discussion is in his 'Toward a New Historical View', esp. 464–7.

The treatises demonstrate that the Roman technique was still being taught in the early fourteenth century. Perhaps, however, the relatively large number of treatises treating the matter from *c.*1300 are evidence of decline rather than strength—of a felt need to reinforce a tradition that was no longer as well known or well observed as it had been. It is at the turn of the fourteenth century that we find contradictory opinions in France concerning the suitability of applying the chromatic and enharmonic genera to ecclesiastical music: Jerome and Garlandia in favour, de Muris against. This may well be a sign of the decline of one aspect of the older practice in that region. The negative statements on the same subject from southern Germany in the twelfth century in Anonymous I (G) and the *Summa musice* suggest an earlier date for the lessening of this technique in the vocal practices of the north-east.

To continue along this line of speculation, it is possible to suggest what the gradual modifications to the full Roman vocal style might have been. We can be fairly sure that the neumes that were retained in graphic style in the later manuscripts (quilisma, oriscus, plica) were still performed in the earlier ornamental style. For those ornamental neumes that were translated into stable pitches (the stropha neumes, pressus, etc.) we cannot be sure. The newer notational form may be an accurate indication of performance practices at some point, but vocal traditions do not change quickly, and some aspects of the older vocal style undoubtedly lasted for many centuries after the notation no longer provided any indication. The problem is to identify which of the practices changed and which endured.

A small amount of help can be found by investigating the vocal practices of later centuries, where some techniques are clearly related to the earlier practices and probably descended from them. In this regard it is surprising to note that a number of medieval techniques were still a part of the vocal practices as late as the Baroque period. The traditions of individually articulating most notes and alternating strong–weak sounds in running passages were both standard techniques still practised in all European locations as late as the early eighteenth century.[15] The techniques of pulsation, both disconnected and connected, variable vibrato and trill, and indefinite pitch are all still discussed as parts of Italian vocal technique as late as Giulio Caccini and his followers in the early seventeenth century,[16] and in mid-seventeenth-century France, Jean Millet and

---

[15] On the details of these later performance techniques see McGee, *Medieval and Renaissance Music: A Performer's Guide* (Toronto, 1985), chs. 7, 8, and 9. The identification of so many elements of the medieval vocal style retained into the Baroque period suggests that our perception of Baroque vocal practices may be in need of adjustment.

[16] See Caccini, *Le Nuove Musiche, 1601*, ed. and trans. H. Wiley Hitchcock (Madison, Wis., 1970); and Christoph Bernhard, 'On the Art of Singing; or, Manier', *The Music Forum*, 3 (1973), 13–29.

Bénigne de Bacilly discuss repercussion, trill, vibrato, tone colouring, and plica-like sounds.[17] These Baroque writers discuss only secular music, but this still provides evidence of the continuation of techniques that have clear roots in the medieval sacred style discussed here. These later vocal practices probably can be accepted as evidence that once the Roman vocal style was learned, certain components of the performance technique were retained in all regions of Europe throughout the Renaissance and beyond, thus providing us with a general guide to what kinds of things remained and which were changed over the centuries.

Those vocal techniques that appear to be more limited in the later centuries are the elements of the Roman style that perhaps initially were the most foreign to the northerners' native technique: liquescent slides, non-diatonic intervals, pulsations, and darkened tones. This would seem to be what John the Deacon (ninth century) meant by the inability of the northerners to modulate the sounds, and Adhémar de Chabannes (eleventh century) when he criticized the French who could not correctly execute the 'tremulous or sinuous notes, or those that are to be elided or separated'. In this regard it is interesting that the earliest sources in Palaeo-Frankish notation from the north-west (ninth century) do not contain signs for most ornamental liquescent neumes (the other ornaments mentioned above—non-diatonic intervals, pulsations, and darkened tones—were not notated in any tradition).[18] The liquescent sound was also the first ornament mentioned as optional (Guido, eleventh century). There is continuing evidence, however, that not all liquescent sounds were eliminated—the quilisma's ornamental shape is retained in square-notated manuscripts from all regions—but the remainder of the evidence points to the abandonment or less frequent use of most other liquescent sounds in favour of stable pitch. As for the non-diatonic sounds, we saw above that the use of the chromatic and enharmonic genera was discouraged in the north-east as early as the twelfth century, and in the north-west by the end of the thirteenth. After 1300 it was promulgated only in treatises from northern Italy. In general, therefore, it would appear that the actual changes in vocal style through the centuries of the Middle Ages consisted only of the degree to which some sounds were employed. Table 6.1 presents some broad conjectures on the changes in singing style based on the above evidence and discussion. This, of course, does not fully address the subject of the individual regional characteristics of style. That topic, along with further

---

[17] Jean Millet, *La Belle Methode ou L'Art de Bien Chanter* (1666; repr. New York, 1973), and Bénigne de Bacilly, *Commentary upon the Art of Proper Singing*, trans. and ed. Austin B. Caswell (Brooklyn, 1968).

[18] Corbin, 'Neumatic Notation', 137. Her example is the 9th-c. missal Paris, Bibliothèque nationale de France, lat. 17305, from north-eastern France. See discussion of the Palaeo-Frankish notation in Jacques Hourlier and Michel Huglo, 'La Notation paléofranque', *EG* 2 (1957), 212–19.

TABLE 6.1. *Vocal techniques in the Middle Ages and Renaissance*

1. Quick throat articulation separating all notes not written in ligature.

2. Alternation of strong and weak sounds in moving passages.

3. Change of tone colour from bright to dark in a descending two-note ligature (clivis).

4. Lightening of the tone for the second note of an ascending two-note ligature (pes).

| | | Suggested time line of vocal techniques | | |
	Italy	*North-west Europe*	*Eastern Europe*	*Spain*
600	Roman	local styles	local styles	Spanish
700	Roman	——— Roman begins, more difficult ——— ornaments not fully developed		Arabic influence
1000	Roman	——— complete Roman, liquescents ——— not always used		Roman influence
1200	Roman	complete Roman, liquescents not always used	liquescents, non-diatonic often omitted	unchanged
1300	Roman	liquescents, non-diatonic notes often omitted	same	unchanged
1500	non-diatonic less used	——— no non-diatonic notes, ——— few liquescents		unchanged

discussion and refinement of the technical vocal changes, will be discussed below in conjunction with repertory.

As a final point in this section I would mention the special case of Spain. There is no theoretical information about Spanish singing practices from the late Middle Ages, but some idea of that style can be gained from other evidence and from treatises of later centuries. Spain was always in close contact with North African culture and was invaded and conquered by the Omayyad Arabs in 711, which formally exposed them to Arabic vocal style, theoretical writings, repertory, and a number of new musical instruments.[19] The Arabic musical style employs all the ornamental techniques discussed here, no doubt sharing a common basic origin with that promulgated by Rome. The Roman liturgy and

---

[19] Arabic theoretical writings were also known elsewhere in Europe. The treatise by Jerome of Moravia quotes from Al-Farabi.

vocal practices were not introduced in Spain until the Christian reconquest in the eleventh century, but there would not have been any difficulty in imposing those practices on a vocal style that employed the same techniques and was itself even more ornate; the evidence of the early Spanish notation is that the ornamental practices were far in excess of those found elsewhere in Europe.

Support for this speculation is found in a sixteenth-century Spanish treatise, *Arte de melodia sobre canto llano y canto d'organo*, that contains detailed instructions for chant ornamentation as practised in Toledo.[20] Although written well after the medieval treatises discussed above, it describes tremolo, trills, repercussion, diminution, mordents, appoggiaturas, and examples of filled-in intervals that are similar to those described by Jerome of Moravia and examined in Chapter 5. In his discussion of this treatise, Karl-Werner Gümpel relates these Spanish practices to the anonymous fourteenth-century treatise *Quatuor principalia*, and to the writings of the tenth-century Middle Eastern theorist Al-Farabi, and demonstrates a continuing tradition as described in other Spanish treatises of the sixteenth, seventeenth, and eighteenth centuries.[21] One may conclude, therefore, that the vocal practices discussed here, being closely allied with those already a part of Spanish culture, remained more or less intact in Spain throughout the Middle Ages and for several centuries afterward.

ORNAMENTS AND THEIR PLACEMENT

In Chapters 4 and 5 the ornaments were presented according to types, which is a useful way of classifying them in order to examine their individual techniques and application. In the section below I have reorganized them according to placement, function, and purpose in order to demonstrate their uses within a musical phrase.

Cadential Ornaments

The most important position for ornamentation in any phrase is the cadence. References quoted and discussed in the previous chapters establish the fact that cadential ornaments are usually somewhat different from those executed at other points of a phrase, and that it is at the cadence where ornaments provide a structural as well as a decorative function. According to the theorists, some type of ornamentation was to be applied to all cadences within a given composition. The amount and type of embellishment added to a particular cadence depended upon its type and function within the phrase; Guido tells us that the

---

[20] Barcelona, Biblioteca de Catalunya, MS 1325. Discussed and edited in Karl-Werner Gümpel, 'El canto melódico de Toledo: algunas reflexiones sobre su origen y estilo', *Recerca Musicológica*, 8 (1988), 25–45. I am indebted to Bonnie J. Blackburn for this reference.

[21] Ibid. 30–3.

more important cadences received the most elaborate embellishments, but it is clear that all points of melodic rest were to be accompanied by ornaments of some type.

Several of the theorists say that cadences are to be emphasized by retarding the last few notes and inserting particular types of embellishments. Guido states that this applies to all phrase endings, and he stresses that equal-length phrases are to be treated equally, by which he means that matching phrases should be made to balance one another both in terms of the amount of the retard and the quantity of ornamentation. He does not specify the type of chant to which he is referring, but the statement would seem to be most appropriate to poetic texts, although to a lesser extent it probably applies to all types.

Phrase endings are to receive some type of pulsating ornament while retarding. The various theorists use different words to describe the pulsation, but they are unanimous in recommending the use of this type of ornament to mark the last note of a phrase. Guido and his commentators recommend that the last note should receive either a pulsation of equal sounds separated by articulated silence (morula), or an alternation of loud and soft pulses (tremula). Jerome calls the cadential ornament a procellaris, and describes a very light trill/vibrato that is sung quickly and evenly. Jerome's procellaris ornament is different from the morula and tremula because it involves a slight change of pitch (although one of less than a semitone), whereas the morula and tremula do not. Statements by Walter Odington and in the treatise from St Emmeram also imply that in some traditions the pulsating ornament could be a vibrato as well as a morula or tremula as described above.

In addition to the ornament applied to the final note of the phrase, Jerome also recommends the application of a trill to the penultimate note of a complete phrase. When the last two notes involve an ascending half-step, a 'long' trill is to be applied (i.e. a slow trill of no more than a semitone, beginning—as do all trills—with a reverberation from above). The application of this ornament coincides with the beginning of the end-of-phrase retard, and thus it supports the distribution of the retard over the final two notes of the phrase and produces a sound that begins as a slow half-step trill of the penultimate note and dissolves into a quick and light pulsation of the final note (procellaris, morula, tremula, or vibrato). For the penultimate note in intervals other than an ascending half-step, Jerome advocates use of the 'open' trill (i.e. a slow trill of up to a full step). This would result in a cadential ornament similar in most aspects to that just described, with the exception of the size of the trill interval. The application of these ornaments to both the penultimate and final notes of a phrase while retarding would lend a very strong sense of cadence, and therefore this quantity of embellishment would probably be utilized only at section endings.

Jerome also discusses a type of ornament called *teleusis*, which he describes as a flourish at the end of a complete phrase and identifies as having the function of a period in grammar. He describes this ornament as an extension of a melody by two or more sounds, i.e. a melodic flourish. He also proposes the same treatment for the musical equivalents of the comma and colon, which he calls *systema* and *diastema*. These last two positions, both in grammar and music, are sub-phrases, and apparently are to be marked by a small retard and can be adorned with small melodic flourishes. In their internal phrase positions, the flourishes for systema and diastema serve both to mark the musical punctuation and to connect one sub-phrase with the next. The flourish at the phrase end (marked by a rest of some type), the *teleusis*, would serve only to heighten the sense of cadence. Anonymous IV mentions a similar practice of flourishes in conjunction with polyphonic cadences, in which several notes are added to the final note as an embellishment, but these are intended only to mark a break in the motion similar to Jerome's *teleusis*, and are not employed for sub-phrases or minor cadences. Anonymous IV does not discuss flourishes that serve to connect phrases, but he does mention that some singers add 'passages of organum purum . . . for a more noble ending'. This is a reference to an extended flourish at major polyphonic cadences, involving a sustained tenor note below a free cadential passaggio in the upper voice.

A further extension of cadential embellishments is the addition to a final cadence of caudae and postludes, which Grocheio describes as appropriate following certain antiphons, evangelical psalms, the Alleluia, cantus coronatus, and estampie. (This concept is hardly different from Anonymous IV's 'passages of organum purum' above.) The postludes that follow cantus coronatus and estampie are to be performed by the vielle, but apparently the others are sung. To this category of embellishment can also be added the two different kinds of flourishes marked by signs: the fermata flourish that begins on the written pitch, departs, and returns, and the signum congruentiae flourish that begins as an ornamental flourish and ends on the written pitch. In polyphony those two ornaments are treated differently in terms of their accompanying parts: for the fermata all voices sing the written pitches and sustain them throughout the embellishment; but for a signum congruentiae the accompanying voices are silent until the embellishing voice reaches the written pitch. These last two ornaments are not specifically reserved to cadences, but are most often found in that position.

Phrase Beginnings

The first note of a phrase does not receive as much ornamental attention as the cadential notes, but two specific kinds of embellishments are particular to that position. The 'long' trill, which may also be used on penultimate notes, is appropriate for the first note of a phrase when that note is a longa and when the interval between it and the following note is an ascending half-step. It is significant that Jerome reserves the 'long' ornament to only these two places and that its function in the two positions is somewhat different. A trill of a half-step is by its very nature harmonically tense (in both monophony and polyphony), and when it is performed slowly, that tension is increased. In its placement on the penulti-mate note of a phrase the tension of the 'long' trill is released by resolution to the final note of the phrase, thus strengthening the sense of cadence. But when sung on a longa that is the first note of the phrase, the harmonic tension of a trill adds necessary motion to what is otherwise a harmonically and melodically stagnant consonance. In advocating the use of the 'long' trill for initial longas, Jerome has provided instructions for the addition of exciting musical motion and direction in a position that otherwise would have very little.

The other embellishment specifically for the opening note of a phrase is a flourish to be added in that position in polyphonic settings. Anonymous IV describes two kinds of flourishes for the opening note, both of which are simi-lar to organum purum inasmuch as they are sung freely by the upper voice with-out temporal restrictions. One involves only a few notes and is sung while the tenor is holding the first note. It is obvious that the function of this ornament is the same as the 'long' trill: to provide motion to an otherwise stagnant long consonance at the beginning of the phrase. For that reason, although this type of flourish can be added to the first note of any phrase of polyphony regardless of the note that follows, it would seem most urgent when the first note is of a relatively long duration. The other opening flourish is called by Anonymous IV the *duplex longa florata*, which by its very name is to be an embellishment of some length. It can be begun either with or before the opening tenor note, but if the beginning of the added flourish would be discordant then the tenor must wait for a concordant note before entering.

If we look again at the directions for ornamenting the first note in a *mono-phonic* phrase, it is apparent that not enough information has been supplied by the treatises: the only specific directions given are for the application of the long trill, useful only on those occasions where a longa with an ascending half-step is concerned, which is not a frequent occurrence in the repertory. To add motion and tension to other melodic formations at the beginning of a phrase would require the employment of other embellishments that, unfortunately, are not clearly spelt out by Jerome or any other theorist. Given the above information concerning the function of an initial ornament, it is difficult to believe that only a single opening melodic formation would have need of such assistance. I would speculate, therefore, that other kinds of trills and flourishes would have been inserted when the first note of a passage was a longa followed by an interval other than an ascending half-step, the actual type of ornament being left to the creativity of the performer, who would make a selection according to the inter-val involved. It would seem that in singling out the 'long' trill for specific use, Jerome was simply noting the rather specialized use of a particular kind of orna-ment, rather than limiting first-note embellishments.

Internal Placements

This category is the largest. In general terms, nearly every type of ornament is appropriate in the midst of a phrase with the exception of those few discussed above that are specifically reserved for cadences and phrase beginnings (procellaris and the 'long' trill). For that reason this is also the least defined category of ornaments, allowing the greatest amount of discretionary selection on the part of the performer.

Available to the performer for internal placement are the graces described in Chapter 4: trills, morula, tremula, comminutio, appoggiaturas; and the passaggi of Chapter 5: diminutions, flourishes, filling-in of intervals—in addition to pitch variation, interval alteration, and all the vocal colours and sound variants associated with ornamental neumes (Ch. 3). Whereas the other two ornamental placements had quite specific roles—one to get the phrase under way, the other to bring it to a pause—the usual purpose of an internal ornament is to grace the melody, although it can also serve to fill in temporal gaps and bring additional harmonic motion. To do any of this properly (that is to say, musically), the performer must be aware of the function of each of the notes of the phrase so that the ornaments will not change those functions and destroy the basic shape of the phrase.[22] Within that limitation, however, there is much freedom of selection for the performer. Nevertheless, certain of the ornaments do seem to have both advantages and limitations that recommend them for specific use, as discussed below. The evidence derives from the nature of some of the ornaments themselves, hints in the theoretical treatises, and observations of written practices in the extant repertory.

Some ornaments have limitations by their very descriptions; for example, the comminutio requires notes that are on adjacent steps of the scale; the 'quick' trill requires a relatively long note in order to accelerate; the various filling-in patterns require specific intervals for their application; and the organum purum type of flourishes in polyphony require held notes in the tenor.

Graces tend to call attention to the notes they adorn, and thus one principle behind their use undoubtedly would have been placement on melodically important notes and those notes that set important words in the text. By melodically important notes I am referring to those that occupy structural positions within a phrase: long notes, those in important metrical positions (beginning of a metrical group, for example), highest and lowest notes in the phrase, and frequently those pitches that are modally functional (final, reciting tone, etc.). Most passaggi, on the other hand, tend to call attention to the note towards

---

[22] This last stated premiss is an ideal that most likely was not always observed. An overview of the embellished material from the late Middle Ages and Renaissance indicates that many ornaments were inserted without sensitivity to the original melodic line.

which they are directed, and therefore are best placed to introduce important notes and words. The exception to this last statement is flourishes; they are technically *passaggi* because they consist of many notes, but since they adorn a particular note, they actually function as graces.

Placement and Quantity

Even within the limits and purposes suggested above, it is easy to understand that the medieval performer had a wide range of choices in terms of type, placement, and quantity of ornament, and that the freedom and lack of specific detailed directions in the theoretical sources leaves a large number of unanswered questions for the modern reader as to exactly what would have been applied and how often. Unfortunately, there is probably no single answer to these questions since the spirit of freedom and personal choice that pervaded the artistic world of the Middle Ages undoubtedly would have spawned an enormous range of variation. And yet it would be quite helpful to our present-day understanding of the sound of medieval performances to have some idea of what would have been considered an 'average' amount of ornamentation in a given situation.

Analysis of the surviving repertory is a good source of information concerning certain types of ornamental placements. In order to learn about both *passaggi* and graces we can examine written phrases in order to determine where composers placed the embellishments and which ornaments they chose. This will not tell us about all ornaments, of course: no repertory contains written evidence for ornaments such as trills, vibrato, and change of sound colour.

We can begin with the moderately ornamented *Christus resurgens* (Ex. 6.1), a Communion verse for Wednesday of Easter week. The unheighted version is from the St Gall tradition and therefore contains a high ratio of ornamental

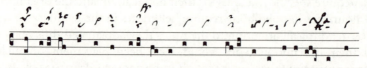

Chri-stus re - sur-gens ex mor - tu - is, iam non mo - ri - tur, al-le-lu - ia, mors

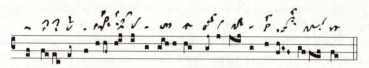

il - li   ul-tra non do-mi-na-bi - tur, al-le-lu - ia, al-le - lu - ia.

Ex. 6.1. *Christus resurgens* (*LU* 795), with unheighted neumes from Einsiedeln, Benediktinerkloster, MS 121, p. 217

sounds. In a basic form each syllable would need only one note, so we can see that the composer has ornamented nearly every syllable. Very few syllables are left with only a single neume; the most common setting is two notes, most of which are marked for liquescent sound. Some of the liquescents are retained in the square notation, but many more are marked in the unheighted version. Stepwise elaboration is the most common, but several skips of a third are present and two fourths. Most of these are marked for liquescent treatment, but it would also be possible to substitute a filling-in ornament as described in Chapter 5.

Those syllables left unornamented are usually in a structural position—the beginning or end of a sub-phrase. The final syllable of each of the sub-phrases is left unadorned: 'mortu*is*', 'morit*ur*', and the first and second 'allelu*ia*' receive only a single note. As we have seen above, these are places for standard impro-vised ornaments—a retard and an interpolated procellaris or a slight flourish. The other two cadential positions, the final text word, 'dominabi*tur*', and the last 'allelu*ia*', which have a stronger cadential placement, are given two notes in a descending order, allowing for an open trill on the penultimate note, proceeding to a procellaris and/or a flourish on the final.

In a number of the written flourishes the composer has combined grace-type ornaments with passaggi: over the first 'allel*uia*', for example, he has written three neumes: a tractulus, followed by a porrectus with a liquescent third sound, followed by a pressus. In the two repetitions of the same word, that same sylla-ble receives similarly elaborate treatment. The grammatical role of a word is not always taken into consideration: most syllables of nouns, verbs, and adjectives are given more than one note, but the treatment is not fully consistent: the word 'non' receives only a single note the first time, but a two-note neume later in the phrase.

In addition, the St Gall version makes use of the expressive letters to augment the ornamental marks. The opening neume for first word, 'Christus', is marked 'i' ˙ and 's' ſ, indicating a lowered and heavy note that rises with a sibilant sound that is to continue ('e' = equal) for the second syllable. The first syllable of the next word, 'resurgens', is marked 'l' for loud, as well as 'c' (quick perfor-mance), and the second syllable is marked to begin with a sibilant sound. The first syllable of 'mortuis' has a three-note neume (salicus) in which the third note is curved to indicate a liquescent sound, and both the first and third notes are marked 's' for a sibilant sound. The second 'non' is only a two-note neume, a pes, but it has three expressive letters: it is to begin with a sibilant sound while the upper note, which has a writen liquescent loop, is first to be proclaimed ('p'), and then lowered with a heavy sound ('i').

For comparison with the secular repertory, we can analyse the ornaments in a song by the trouvère Audefroy le Bastard, which shows similar ornamental practices. In *Bele Ydoine se siet* (Pl. IV), all initial and final phrase syllables are set to only a single note (allowing for the types of opening and closing graces

(a)

Ex. 6.2. Ornamented lines. (a) and (b) *Missus Gabriel de caelis*, opening and closing sections, from B. Gillingham, *The Polyphonic Sequences*, pp. 57, 59; (c) *Homo gaude*,

opening section. From T. Karp, *The polyphony of Saint Martial and Santiago de Compostela*, 1992, Vol. 2, p. 149. By permission of Oxford University Press.

described above), but all other syllables can receive embellishments of up to four notes, mostly stepwise. Several plicas are marked, including one over '*verde*' (second line) that would seem to be a pressus.

The polyphonic repertory provides similar opportunities to observe practices of melodic elaboration, although the notation does not include many indications of nuance. In the florid lines shown in Ex. 6.2(*a*) and (*b*) I have distinguished the written ornaments by numbers and the notes where other ornaments might be interpolated by letters. Ex. 6.2(*c*) is less ornate, and following both the instructions in the treatises and my summary of ornamental functions, I have marked where certain of the passaggi and graces might be added. A glance back at the vocal nuances in the unheighted version of Ex. 6.1 will suggest the kinds and quantity of pitch and sound inflection that would have been appropriate. In the light of the quantity of ornaments in that example, my markings in Ex. 6.2(*c*) do not seem to be excessive. Even chromatic and enharmonic divisions of the scale would be acceptable in the polyphonic examples as long as they are sung in the passaggi and return to diatonic pitches for those notes sung against changes in the tenor part.

A somewhat different way of looking at the same process is to compare variant readings. An example of comparative analysis within a rather limited range has been done by James Grier, demonstrating the variety of ornamentation applied to specific compositions within the eleventh- and twelfth-century Aquitanian repertory.[23] Ex. 6.3 shows the type of variation that can be found in the transmission of specific phrases of the same chant.[24] It is one of Grier's conclusions that the variants are ornamental, and that they reflect the musical personalities of specific cantors.

The chant *Justus ut palma* demonstrates another aspect of variety in ornamental applications. Ex. 6.4 shows three samples from the many available in the third volume of *Paléographie musicale*; these show much similarity in the placement of ornaments, but differing applications of performance nuances such as liquescent sounds and articulation. The flourish over the word 'libani', for example, shows many more liquescent signs in the Rome version, including a quilisma in that version in place of what is a pes in both other sources.

Many more examples could be adduced throughout the medieval repertory to illustrate the same point, and a reader wishing to obtain a more practical grasp of the tradition of ornamentation would find the time spent in collection and analysis rewarding. It is true that all such comparisons are limited and somewhat suspect because of the implied difference between written and extem-

---

[23] See Grier, 'Transmission in the Aquitanian Versaria of the Eleventh and Twelfth Centuries' (Ph.D. diss., University of Toronto, 1985).

[24] Examples taken from James Grier, 'Scribal Practices in the Aquitanian Versaria of the Twelfth Century: Towards a Typology of Error and Variant', *JAMS* 45 (1992), 373–427 (pp. 402, 405).

(a)

(b)

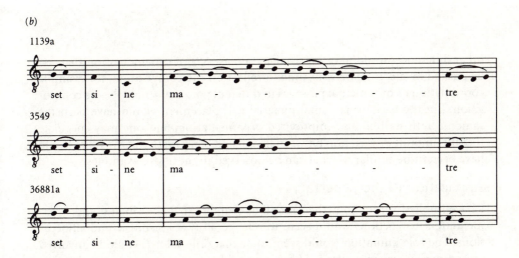

Ex. 6.3. Ornamented lines. (*a*) *Veri solis radius*, (*b*) Sanctus *Qui deus est vere*. From James Grier, 'Scribal Practices', *JAMS* 45, pp. 402–3, 405. University of Chicago Press.

porized ornamentation, but it is our only source of information on this matter. As we can see from the treatises, extemporized ornamentation would not have followed instructions or procedures different from those for composition, except that certain kinds of vocal and pitch inflections may not be notated. The only

(a)

(b)

(c)

Ju - stus ut pal - ma flo - re - - bit si - cut ce - drus

(a)

(b)

(c)

li - ba - ni   mul - ti - pli - ca -

Ex. 6.4. *Justus ut palma*: (*a*) Troyes, Bibliothèque de la Ville, MS 1047, fo. 93ʳ; (*b*) Paris, BNF, n. acq. 1235, fo. 23ᵛ; (*c*) Rome, Biblioteca Barberini, no. XII, fo. 23ʳ. From *Paléographie musicale*, 3

other difference would have involved certain aspects of ornamentation that can be created by a composer with time to reflect on the composition, for example coordination of ornamental passages in different voices of a polyphonic composition. But the basic ornamental material and placement would have been the same in both written and improvised ornamentation, and one may speculate that the amount of variation between liberal and conservative performers would have been quite similar to what can be observed in the above examples.

Application to the Repertory

I have implied throughout the preceding chapters that the singing and ornamentation instructions would seem to refer to all types of music and all occasions. The sole limitation would seem to be that only soloists could be involved in improvised ornamentation. There is no evidence that any singing style other than that described here was applied to any repertory whatsoever, nor that any soloist repertory was exempt from the addition of improvised ornaments. Certain ornaments would appear to be more appropriate to particular types of compositions, as discussed below, but the practice of soloist embellishment of music would seem to be without exclusions. Jerome does state that tempo and ornamentation must be adjusted according to the solemnity of the liturgical occasion, with the most elaborate practices reserved for Sundays and special feasts, but the passage does not say that the ornamentation is to be omitted on ferial days, only that it is limited. This would seem to exclude only the more elaborate vocal inflections on ferial days—perhaps because of the more rapid tempo to be taken on those occasions.

There is no question that the ornamentation practices cited here should be applied to chant; all the treatises discuss them in terms of chant, and many of them mention that repertory exclusively, but references to secular music do exist, especially in the treatises from France at the end of the thirteenth century. When Anonymous IV points out that instruments can subdivide music into smaller values than can voices, the reference must be to secular music since that is the major repertory for instrumental music.

In dismissing the use of chromatic and enharmonic genera for ecclesiastical music, Johannes de Muris mentions a wide spectrum of compositional types. According to him, only the diatonic genera is used for 'all ecclesiastical chant . . . all chant measured by specific time-value as in conductus, notas, organum, and the remaining types of song—and all secular chant sung by men or women, young or old—and all music for instruments'. What is important to the present discussion is first, that he includes various types of secular song types along with sacred song as if there were no differences in their performance practices, and second, that he acknowledges that intervals from the other genera were possible on instruments, although difficult. Since the one instrument known to be used regularly with sacred music—the organ—did not have this capacity, he must be referring to the other instruments—those that played secular music—as the ones that employed the non-diatonic intervals. Thus, in a somewhat convoluted way, de Muris unites the performance practices of sacred and secular music in terms of this particular technique.

Johannes de Grocheio's treatise constantly mixes references to sacred and secular music, including statements about ornamentation, without any indication that the two types of compositions differ other than in matters of modal consideration. When Johannes de Garlandia suggests the interpolation of melodies from well-known works for the embellishment (colouring) of upper parts in polyphony, he cites secular forms—instrumental phrases, a phrase from a *lai*—but there is no hint that this practice should be limited to secular compositions. These statements, especially those by de Muris, Grocheio, and Garlandia, are significant in that they intermix discussion of both sacred and secular music without differentiation. This strongly implies that the same ornamental approach is valid for both repertories, and also that they are sung with the same vocal style. If either of these points were not true, discussion of the two repertories could not be intermixed.

The preceding discussion involves evidence from theorists who were writing near the year 1300. No references to secular music are found from earlier centuries and thus we cannot know how early Roman vocal practices were adopted for the secular repertory. What we do know is that the earliest extant secular music was performed in the same basic style as the sacred repertory. All the above evidence points to the conclusion that once the new style of singing Roman chant was imposed upon and finally accepted by the nations north of the Alps and south of the Pyrenees, that style became all-pervasive in Western Europe, and that the tradition of ornamentation that was a part of that style was also applied to all repertories. For the repertory up to the end of the thirteenth century the performance practices described above do not need much qualification since it would seem that medieval performance practice basically remained stable and intact throughout Europe from *c.*1000 to 1300. The repertory during those centuries, both sacred and secular, was mainly monophonic, and there is no evidence of substantial changes in either compositional techniques or style of performance.

Modifications would have come about slowly with the advent of polyphony. Polyphony, even in its simpler forms, involves harmonic compatibility, and thus the most serious restriction polyphony would have imposed on the singing and ornamental practices would have been in reference to pitch colouring. In performing twelfth- and thirteenth-century organum and discant, either written or improvised, the performer would not be as free to alter the diatonic pitches by a semitone or quarter-tone for decorative purposes. When improvising a passage of organum purum the soloist would be able to add all the vocal colorations at will within the moving passage, but when the sustained lower voice changed pitch, the upper voice would be restricted by the requirement to sing harmonically compatible notes that were uninflected in terms of pitch (i.e. no non-diatonic sounds or liquescent movement away from pitch), although coloration of the sound *quality* would not have been restricted. Discant and the more complex polyphonic compositions of the fourteenth and fifteenth centuries would have further reduced this freedom to alter the pitch, relegating that technique to ornamental situations (e.g. as a grace of the written note) or those places without simultaneous motion in other voices.

Polyphony would not have altered other improvised ornamental practices very much; none of those described in Chapters 4 and 5 would interfere with the polyphonic texture, but the quantity probably was affected. The polyphonic music written in France and England beginning in the fourteenth century more and more involved the interaction of the parts harmonically, melodically, and rhythmically. The complexity of many of these compositions is itself ornamental, and thus the need—and the opportunity—for improvised linear ornamentation would have lessened. Exactly how much ornamentation could be added to any polyphonic composition is subject to the same limitations as in a monophonic work: relatively simple compositions could receive a large quantity of ornaments of all types; complex and ornate works would probably allow only for small graces and sound colouring. As we learnt in conjunction with instructions for the ornamentation of organum purum, only the top voices would be ornamented in a polyphonic composition; the tenor adds nothing other than vibrato at cadential points.[25]

We are limited in our investigation of ornamentation in the fourteenth and fifteenth centuries because of the lack of statements in theoretical treatises and the elimination of most indications of nuance from the notation. The only types of ornaments visible in compositions from the fourteenth and fifteenth centuries are of the passaggi type; with a single exception, graces are not marked.[26] Nevertheless, evidence does exist that the ornamentation practices—and therefore at least some of the vocal practices—remained intact throughout the remainder of the Middle Ages and into the Renaissance. First of all, we must remember that monophonic music remained the most commonly performed repertory throughout the Middle Ages and well into the Renaissance, providing the basis for a continuing tradition throughout that time period. Second, in addition to many examples of passaggi found in compositions and described in performance instruction manuals beginning in the mid-sixteenth century, there also is evidence that graces remained in practice, although by their vary nature they were not written into the music.[27] And third, throughout the decades of the Renaissance, chant notation retained nuance markings for plica, quilisma, and oriscus, along with fixed-pitch neumes for pressus and the stropha neumes, indicating that these too were probably preserved in some fashion.

Vocal and instrumental instructions from the sixteenth and seventeenth centuries describe the addition of a number of graces that are identical with those included in the earlier medieval treatises: trill/vibrato, pulsation (both morula and tremula), mordent types, repercussion, appoggiatura, and sound colouring. There is no evidence that different vocal techniques and styles were employed for sacred and secular music in the fourteenth through sixteenth centuries, and therefore the presence of nearly all the medieval graces in the late Renaissance can be taken as strong evidence of a continuous and unbroken performance tradition. Adding these bits of evidence to the fact that ornaments were a basic ingredient of medieval vocal style, and that much of that basic style remained intact throughout the fourteenth and fifteenth centuries, I would conclude that, similar to the vocal style as a whole, with only minor modifica-

---

[25] As can be seen in the elaborations of secular and sacred music of the Faenza and Robertsbridge codices. See McGee, *Medieval and Renaissance Music*, 156–60.

[26] The only examples of marked graces known to me are those in the Buxheim MS from approximately 1460. The conjecture by Willi Apel, that circles in the Robertsbridge Codex are indications of ornaments, has not been proved. See Apel, *The Notation of Polyphonic Music, 900–1600* (Cambridge, Mass., 1953) 38–40.

[27] For details see Brown, *Embellishing 16th-Century Music*, and McGee, *Medieval and Renaissance Music*, ch. 7.

tions the ornamentation practices of the Middle Ages described above continued as an unbroken tradition beyond the medieval time period.[28]

GEOGRAPHICAL STYLISTIC DIFFERENCES

At this point we can return to the subject of regional style preferences with an
eye to refining the information on performance practice.

That different geographical areas developed individual cultural traits during
the Middle Ages is obvious in language, art, costume, and so forth, and was
undoubtedly true in music. Such differences have already been established in
conjunction with the music of later periods. It is possible to discuss geographical stylistic differences in the Baroque era with some degree of sophistication: we
are aware of the extreme stylistic differences between the practices of, for example, Roman monodic song of the seventeenth century and the Parisian *air de
cour* of the same time. Unfortunately, the same stylistic differentiation has not
yet been made clear for Renaissance performance practices, although there is
little doubt that it existed.

The presence of geographical stylistic differences in medieval ornamentation
and vocal practices has been established above during the discussion of chrono-
logical changes. A rather general acknowledgement of regional differences can
be seen in the treatise of Guilielmus Monachus, an Italian writing in the fifteenth
century, who describes various styles of counterpoint that could follow the practices of the English or the French, or 'according to us' (*apud nos*), that is in the
Italian style.[29] And the well-travelled mid-fourteenth-century Dutch theorist
Johannes Boen, after specifically mentioning English harmonic preferences,
alludes to a much wider range of regional musical differences:

Johannes Boen, 76. The second consideration relates to region or time. For different
regions demand different music, as is demonstrated by my experience in England. When
I lived in the schools at Oxford, a region which the sea alone divides from the county of

---

[28] At the same time I draw the reader's attention to a recent article by David Fallows, in which
he quotes a statement attributed to Josquin that would bring into question the appropriateness of
embellishing polyphonic music of the mid- to late 15th c.; see Fallows, 'Embellishment and Urtext
in the Fifteenth-Century Song Repertories', *Basler Jahrbuch für historische Musikpraxis*, 14 (1990),
59–85. Given the amount of information presented above for the embellishment of both monophonic and polyphonic medieval music, coupled with information presented by Howard Brown
concerning 16th-c. embellishments (*Embellishing Sixteenth-Century Music*), and the 15th-c. manuscripts that would appear to me to be examples of written-out ornamentation, the conclusion that
a fairly solid—and even consistent—tradition of ornamenting *all* music would seem to be justified.
Yet Fallows's case is well put, and the reader should consider his evidence and conclusions as a
possible refinement of the statements presented here.

[29] See the statement in sect. VI of his treatise, in which he introduces counterpoint 'tam secundum modum Francigenorum quam Anglicorum' (ed. Seay, 33), followed by 'Modus autem istius
faulxbordon aliter posset assumi apud nos' (38).

Holland—the place of my birth—there I saw that the laymen, clerks, old men, and youths, and all without distinction bestowed so great a love on thirds and sixths and, preferring them to octaves and fifths, that they spoke only of these very intervals, as if to revere them. I was very much astonished all the time at the different nature of so close a region, and I wonder at it still.

There are overlapping boundaries and categories of information and influences that help define a regional musical style: various elements of a particular culture derive from and permeate the society and are expressed in all its artistic creations. Many of these elements are lost to us, but evidence still exits that can help us establish some of the regional stylistic traits. One of the most accessible clues is that of vernacular language, which has a profound influence on vocal tone colour. Certain vocal sounds are more easily formed in conjunction with particular vowel and consonant pronunciations. Nasal vowels and diphthongs, for example, have completely different sounds than do pure vowels; the pronunciation of soft and hard consonants also facilitates different kinds of sound colours. Languages with pronunciation practices as different from one another as French and Italian, therefore, would result in very different kinds of vocal colouring. These sounds, learnt in the vernacular, would carry over unconsciously into the performance of Latin texts.[30]

The influence of regional chant traditions as well as local 'folk' singing traditions—they were probably quite similar—would be another element of local culture that, when added to the influence of vernacular language pronunciation, would give a regional cast to a performance.[31] There is very little evidence of the details of various local singing practices, but I would speculate that their influence on the imported Roman style may be present in the early written neumes. In Chapter 3 I pointed to the relationship between the shape of early neumes and their performance. If we look at the neume shapes from different regions we see that the same neumes were given different graphic details—in some cases, substantially different. My speculation, therefore, is that these shapes reflect regional performance styles. There are no theoretical statements that directly support this conclusion, but one can see that the scribal differences in the neume forms are far more extreme than those found in the letter shapes of the texts of the same manuscripts, thus suggesting that the variants in neume forms are the result of some influence other than local scribal traditions. If, as I have concluded, the main purpose of the neume forms was to impart details of nuance, then we can speculate that their shapes relate directly to local vocal practices, and that these differences are evidence of regional performance variations

---

[30] On the pronunciation of European languages in the Middle Ages see McGee (ed.), with David N. Klausner and A. G. Rigg, *Singing Early Music: A Guide to the Pronunciation of European Languages in the Middle Ages and Renaissance* (Bloomington, Ind., 1996).

[31] For a discussion of regional chant traditions see Hiley, *Western Plainchant*, ch. 8.

in terms of articulation and vocal colouring. To cite two specific examples: first, the graphic sign for the tractulus/punctum in Lorraine notation may indicate a waving sound as the norm for the performance of separate notes, rather than a focused pitch that is indicated by a dot or straight dash in other traditions. Second, the presence of so many curves in the neumes of the St Gall manuscripts would represent a sound that was quite fluid.

Although the evidence is strong that a relationship exists between neume shape and sound, it is not possible to tell exactly how or to what extent notational shapes reflect local singing style. The presence of a particular element—the wavy tractulus in Lorraine, for example—probably represents a local performance preference, but the absence of a sign does not necessarily signify the absence of a practice. The use of so many letter symbols in the St Gall manuscripts probably is evidence of an extremely expressive performance tradition, but we cannot be sure that the lack of letters in other traditions signifies a lack of expression. It will be seen below that the positive evidence of the neumes is supported by other factors, and therefore is useful in that context as an aid in defining the various regional singing practices.

The following descriptions of regional stylistic characteristics are a distillation of the evidence of notational practices as they relate to an analysis of performance style.[32] Further understanding of the different regional nuances can be gained by attempting to sing chant passages in the fashion represented by the graphic shapes of the neumes.[33]

(i) Aquitaine (Pl. V). Heighted from very early. Most neumes are made up of puncti; a virga usually ends with a punctum. There is very little use of ligature. All ornamental neumes are present in the notation but they are not used frequently.

Performance implications: a detached singing style with most notes sung on focused pitch; occasional use of ornamental sounds.

(ii) Lorraine (Pl. VI). The wavy tractulus is the most frequently used single note form; there are very few straight lines—most are wavy or curved. There is some use of puncti. A full set of ornamental neume shapes is used frequently. A variety of articulations is present in composite neumes, and there is some use of expressive letters.

Performance implications: a wavy single pitch is the norm. There is much use of liquescent sound, and the style in general is expressive.

---

[32] Some of this information is based on Hiley, *Western Plainchant*, 346–56.

[33] There are a number of sub-groups within many of the notational traditions described here. For a more complete list as well as descriptions of the characteristic notational forms see Corbin, *Die Neumen*, and Hiley, *Western Plainchant*.

(iii) Northern French (Pl. VII). In general, a combination of Lorraine and Aquitaine practices. Neumes are often heighted, with a mixture of wavy tractulus and punctum. All ornamental neumes are used frequently, and there is a high proportion of detached marks within combination neumes.

Performance implications: less detached than Aquitaine, not as connected as Lorraine; frequent ornaments but not as much use of liquescence as Lorraine.

(iv) St Gall and Germany (Pl. I). Ornamental shapes for all standard neume forms, and all ornamental neumes are frequently used. A diverse set of articulations is found for each neume. There is a high proportion of liquescents. The St Gall tradition makes frequent use of expressive letters.

Performance implications: liquescent sounds are the norm; very smooth motion from one note group to the next; heavily ornamented; extremely expressive and ornate.

(v) English (Pl. VIII). The virga is more frequent than the punctum. All ornamental neumes are used, with a low proportion of liquescent symbols.

Performance implications: much use of separate notes within neumes but less detached articulation than Aquitaine; as connected as Lorraine but with less use of liquescents; ornamentation less frequent than Lorraine.

(vi) Northern Italian and Beneventan (Pll. IX and X). There is frequent use of 'tractulus' rather than punctum, and a high proportion of ligatures. Tractulus has both straight and curved forms. The proportion of ornamental signs is high.

Performance implications: very connected line; much use of liquescent sound in all neumes; highly ornate.

(vii) Spanish (Pl. XI). The characteristics are combinations of detached passages interspersed with groups of ligated neumes; more use of tractulus than punctum; and frequent use of liquescent forms. Ornamental forms occur that are not found in any other notation, and some passages are extremely ornate. Ornamental and non-ornamental neumes are not as intermixed as in St Gall and Lorraine.

Performance implications: much use of varied articulation; high contrast of florid and syllabic passages; ornamental passages extreme, diverse, and highly concentrated, making much use of liquescents.

DISTRIBUTION OF STYLES

In addition to the above information, other factors must be considered when attempting to identify regional stylistic characteristics. The similarities and differences in notational practices attest to the fact that neume shapes—and thus vocal practices—were sometimes a reflection of geographical location and at

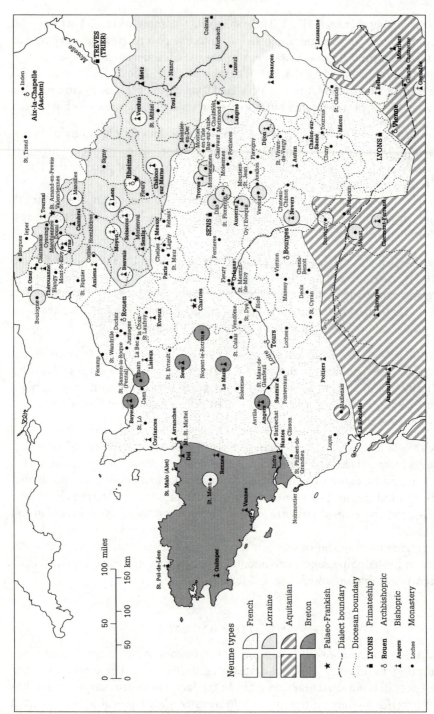

MAP 1. Distribution of neume types in northern Europe *c.*900–1200

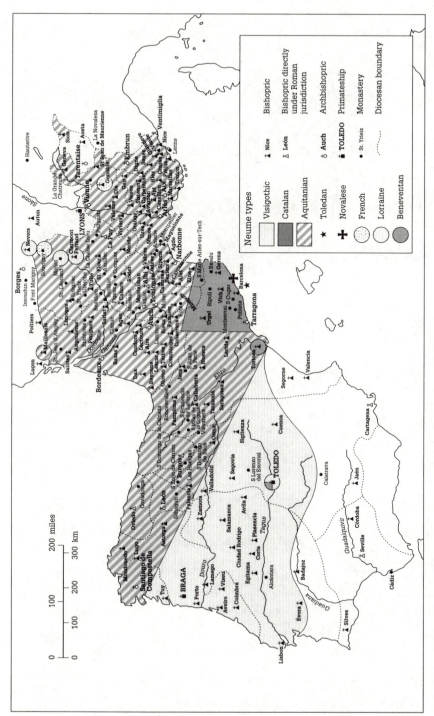

MAP 2. Distribution of neume types in southern France and Spain *c*.900–1200

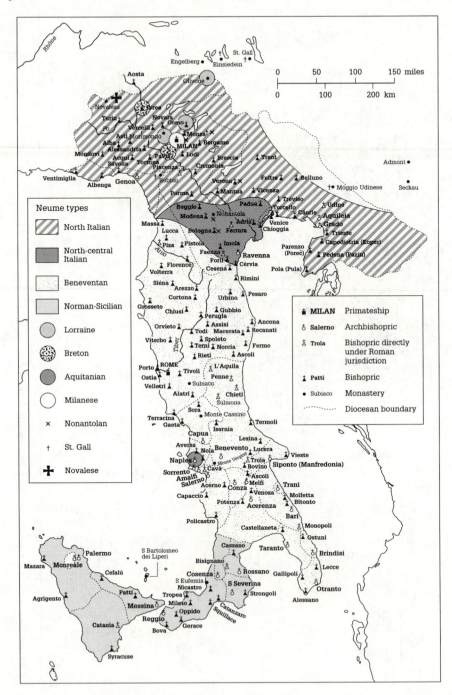

MAP 3. Distribution of neume types in Italy *c.*900–1200

other times a product of monastic affiliations that were not confined by political boundaries or areas of vernacular languages. Maps 1, 2, and 3 chart the distribution of neume types in Western Europe *c*.900–1200, indicating both these types of relationships. Each region shows preference for a particular style of notation, although pockets can be found in each region where a monastic house uses a style that is quite removed from the area in which it is situated.

The fact that the neume traditions cut across language boundaries complicates the issue a bit, but fortunately it also allows us to refine some of this stylistic information even further: once the nuances symbolized by a set of neumes is interpreted, that sound can be further adjusted according to the influence of the local vernacular pronunciation. The combination of influences can be somewhat extreme: for example, the chant from Tortosa would have a combination of Beneventan singing practices (evident in the notation), adjusted by the influence of Spanish-Latin pronunciation and the Spanish tradition of extremely ornate singing. What will result from considering the combination of these criteria should be a more accurate—although still incomplete—identification of regional chant practices.

A last element in the delineation of local styles and their gradual changes is provided by the repertory and its evolution during the final centuries of the Middle Ages. Since the basic vocal and ornamental style we have been discussing contains elements that do not necessarily suit polyphonic performance, the popularity of polyphony undoubtedly had an influence on ornamentation. The new compositional forms did not gain acceptance at the same rate in all regions, and therefore the interest of any region in polyphony can serve as a guide to particular changes in vocal delivery. By adding to our criteria the element of preference in compositional style—which has a fairly broad regional aspect to it—we can develop additional guidelines for the evolving vocal practices.

Italy

In comparison with the French, Italians seem to have written very little polyphonic music in the fourteenth and fifteenth centuries, preferring the monophonic repertory, including an improvised secular tradition that lasted beyond the Renaissance.[34] No doubt Italy, where the vocal style originated, retained more elements of both the vocal and ornamental practices for a longer period of time than many of the other regions.

Giulio Caccini's 'bent' and shaded pitches suggest a continuing interest in sound colouring and pitch inflection that continued past the Renaissance, and

---

[34] Although additional sources of polyphonic music from Italy continue to come to light, there is other evidence of the Italian preference for monophony; see Nino Pirrotta, 'Music and Cultural Tendencies in Fifteenth-Century Italy', in *Music and Culture in Italy from the Middle Ages to the Baroque* (Cambridge, Mass., 1984), 80–112.

both the Faenza Codex (early fifteenth century) and much of extant Italian poly-phonic music from the fourteenth and early fifteenth centuries reflects an inter-est in a free-flowing upper line with dense ornamentation.[35] Italian practice, therefore, throughout the Middle Ages would have remained as close as possible to the vocal and ornamental style disseminated from Rome as early as the eighth and ninth centuries and probably in practice there from much earlier.

Spain

Spain, similar to Italy, retained an interest in monophonic music all through the fourteenth and fifteenth centuries. The Spanish vocal tradition was heavily influ-enced by the North African style, which is basically the same as that promoted by Rome. Spanish singers, therefore, would have had little trouble adopting the Roman practices, which suggests that the ornamental elements were preserved longer there than in the northern regions of Europe, a fact documented by state-ments in theoretical treatises of the sixteenth, seventeenth, and eighteenth centuries.[36] Many elements of that vocal style are still in practice today.

France and England

France would seem to have been the earliest area to compromise the Roman singing style. After developing the nuance-rich unheighted notation in order to learn the new style, they converted to the new heighted form early in the twelfth century, suggesting that they welcomed the tacet permission to modify the Roman style with elements of their own. The north-western regions of France, Belgium, Switzerland, and England were the earliest to adopt polyphony in noticeable quantity, and that compositional style grew quite complex in those regions by the mid-fourteenth century. The north-western area of Europe, therefore, would probably have been more conservative in terms of Roman vocal practices. Although Jerome, writing in Paris around 1300, advocated the use of all types of vocal ornaments, he admitted that not everyone agreed, and Johannes de Muris, writing in Paris shortly afterwards, suggested a more conser-vative approach to pitch inflection. The same equivocation can be found in England in the treatise by Walter Odington (c. 1300), who advocated the more colourful style, as contrasted with the slightly later treatise by Anonymous I (C), which is more conservative.

Germany

Germany retained the staffless neumes longer than the other northern regions and did not develop polyphony until the fifteenth century, suggesting that much

---

[35] For a study of stylistic features in ornamentation in the early 15th c. see McGee, 'Ornamentation, National Styles, and the Faenza Codex', *Early Music New Zealand*, 3 (1987), 3–14.
[36] See Gümpel, 'El canto melódico'.

of the Roman style was retained into the fifteenth century. The author of the *Summa musice*, writing in 1200, rejected the chromatic and enharmonic genera as being both difficult to sing and unpleasant to hear (478; see p. 84), and in the passage on p. 86 expressed the thought that all singers north of the Alps sang differently from the Italians. There is evidence from other writers that this was an exaggeration (Jerome, Garlandia), and that as late as 1300 some French still sang in the Roman manner. We can probably assume, however, that the *Summa musice* writer was accurate in terms of the practices in his own south German area. This probably indicates that the north-eastern practices were conservative in terms of pitch inflection, but there is no evidence that they rejected any of the other tenets of the Roman style. Conservatism is also suggested in that the St Gall notation forms were adopted in German regions, but without the 'Notker' letters.

This is as close as I can come to a description of medieval vocal and ornamental style. It is evident that tightly focused studies of the evolving performance style are needed if we are to refine this type of information further, and I believe that this book has laid the foundation for such an approach by providing the broad lines of connection between medieval practices and those of the centuries that followed. The principal objective has been to establish the medieval vocal and ornamental traditions, and I believe this has been accomplished. In clarifying medieval practices this study has also sought to connect performance practices of the Renaissance and Baroque periods with the sources of their techniques and traditions along a continuum of gradual change beginning before the year 900. With this as a base we can now set about to refine that information, ideally to the point where each century and each location has its own identifiable practices, enlarging our concept of the sound of early music to one that encompasses many varieties of those sounds.

Appendix:
Excerpts from Theoretical Sources

LATIN citations are by page (6), by page and sentence or line number (1:6), or by book and sentence number (I:6). The pages on which the English translation can be found are indicated at the end of each paragraph.

1. Adhémar de Chabannes. From Angoulême, active at Limoges, first half of the 11th c. Latin citation from Handschin, 'Eine alte Neumenschrift', 72.

Omnes Franciae cantores didicerunt notam Romanam quam nunc vocant Franciscam, excepto quod tremulas vel vinnolas sive collisibiles vel secabiles voces in cantu non poterant perfecte exprimere Franci, naturali voce barbarica frangentes in gutture voces potius quam exprimentes.   17

2. Ailred (Ethelred) of Rievaulx, *Speculum charitatis*. Born in Northumberland, *c.*1110 and joined Cistercians at Rievaulx (near York). Elected abbot 1147, d. 1167. Latin citation from Ailred of Rievaulx, *Opera omnia*, 97–9.

Book II, cap. XXIII, *De uana aurium uoluptate*
Sed quia aperte malos ab hac consideratione putauimus remouendos, de his nunc sermo sit, qui sub specie religionis negotium uoluptatis obpalliant: qui ea, quae antiqui patres in typis futurorum salubriter exercebant, in usum suae uanitatis usurpant. Vnde, quaeso, cessantibus iam typis et figuris, unde in Ecclesia tot organa, tot cymbala? Ad quid, rogo, terribilis ille follium flatus, tonitrui potius fragorem, quam uocis exprimens suauitatem? Ad quid illa uocis contractio et infractio? Hic succinit, ille discinit, alter supercinit, alter medias quasdam notas diuidit et incidit. Nunc vox stringitur, nunc frangitur, nunc impingitur, nunc diffusiori sonitu dilatatur. Aliquando, quod pudet dicere, in equinos hinnitus cogitur, aliquando virili vigore deposito in femineae vocis gracilitates acuitur, nonnunquam artificiosa quadam circumuolutione torquetur et retorquetur. Videas aliquando hominem aperto ore quasi intercluso halitu exspirare, non cantare, ac ridiculosa quadam vocis interceptione quasi minitari silentium; nunc agones morientium vel extasim patientium imitari. Interim histrionicis quibusdam gestibus totum corpus agitatur, torquentur labia, rotant oculi, ludunt humeri, et ad singulas quasque notas digitorum flexus respondet. Et haec ridiculosa dissolutio vocatur religio; et ubi haec frequentius agitantur, ibi Deo honorabilius seruiri clamatur. Stans interea uulgus sonitum follium, crepitum cymbalorum, harmoniam fistularum tremens attonitusque miratur; sed lasciuas cantantium gesticulationes, meretricias uocum alternationes et infractiones non sine cachinno risuque intuetur, ut eos non ad oratorium, sed ad theatrum, nec ad orandum, sed ad spectandum aestimes conuenisse. . . .

    Ideoque talis debet esse sonus, tam moderatus, tam grauis, ut non totum animum ad sui rapiat oblectationem, sed sensui maiorem relinquat portionem. Ait nempe beatissimus Augustinus: Mouetur animus ad affectum pietatis diuino cantico audito: sed si magis sonum quam sensum libido audiendi desideret, improbatur. Et alias: cum me, inquit, magis cantus quam uerba delectant, poenaliter me peccasse confiteor, et mallem non audire cantantem. Cum igitur aliquis, spreta ridiculosa illa et damnosa uanitate, antiquae Patrum moderationi sese contulerit, si ad memoriam nugarum theatricarum prurientibus auribus immane fastidium grauitas honesta intulerit, sicque totam Patrum serietatem quasi rusticitatem contemnat ac iudicet, modo cantandi, quem Spiritus sanctus per sanctissimos Patres quasi per organa sua, Augustinum uidelicet, Ambrosium, maximeque Gregorium, instituit: hiberas, ut dicitur, naenias, uel nescio quorum scholasticorum nugas uanissimas, anteponens. Si ergo hinc crucietur, hinc doleat, hinc ad ea quae euomuerat anxius anhelet, quae rogo huius laboris origo, iugum caritatis, an onus concupiscentiae mundialis?   23–24

3. Anonymous I (C), *De musica antiqua et nova.* From England (probably Bury St Edmunds), mid-14th c. This material is also found as the fourth book of the *Quatuor principalia*, and some quotations in Franco of Cologne. Latin citation after Coussemaker, *Scriptores*, iii.

361. Alius modus discantandi invenitur, quoniam, si bene pronuntiatur, artificiosius auditur et apparet, cum tamen valde levis sit. In isto modo plures super planum cantum discantare apparebunt, cum tamen in rei veritate unus tantum discantabit, alii vero planum cantum in diversis concordantiis modulantur. Hoc modo sint quatuor vel quinque homines: primus incipit planum cantum in tenore; secundus paret vocem suam in quinta voce; tertius vero in octava voce, et quartus, si fuerit, ponat vocem suam in duodecima voce. Hi omnes, concordantiis inceptis, continuabunt planum cantum usque in finem. Qui vero in duodecima et in octava voce simul et continue cantant, frangere debent et florere notas prout magis decet mensura. Sed nota bene, tenor quippe integre notas pronunciet in mensura. Is vero qui discantabit, vocem suam non modo ponet in concordantia perfecta, sed etiam in concordantiis imperfectis videlicet in tertia, sexta et decima. Per istas enim concordantias discurrat ascendendo et descendendo secundum quod magis sibi videbitur expedire et auditori placere; sicque unus in discantu expertus, habens etiam vocis humilitatem, potest cum aliis sic canentibus magnam facere melodiam. Sufficit enim quod sint quatuor simul canentes, si unus fuerit qui discantet continue duodecimam notam.   113

4. Anonymous I (G), *Duo semisphaeria quas magadas vocant.* The two manuscript sources of this treatise are both from Austrian libraries. One, possibly dating from the 10th c. in the monastery of St Blasien, was lost in a fire. The other, now in Vienna, is ascribed to the 12th-c. Abbot Berno. Latin citation from Gerbert, *Scriptores*, i. 331.

331. *Diatonicum* enim dicitur, quod tonorum dimensione & compositione exquiritur: quod reliqua non obtinent, dum haec per semitonia, illud per dieses, quod in sequentibus patefiet, exaratur. Hoc genus fortius et durius comprobatur. Et ne animi audientium vel canentium dulcedine cantus emolliantur, ecclesiastico usui eligitur. Musica enim suavitate vel morositate animos commutari, & quilibet in se ipso potest experiri, & sapientium scripta novimus attestari. *Chromaticum* quasi coloratum dicitur, quod a

diatonico primum discedens alterius sit quasi coloris; chroma enim color dicitur. Hoc genus mollissimum comprobatur, quocirca ecclesiastico usui non applicatur. *Enarmonicum* autem, quod ex utrisque his modeste compactum & temperatum sit, nomen accepit ab harmonia, quae est diversarum rerum concordabilis convenientia. Hoc genus quasi medietatis locum possedit, ut nec durum nec molle sit, sed ex utrisque compositum dulcescit. 81

5. Anonymous II, *Tractatus de discantu*. Probably Parisian, 13th c. Latin citations from Coussemaker, *Scriptores*, i. English translation: Anonymous 2, *Tractatus de discantu*.

307. Quid est organum? Organum est [cantus] armonicus diversis troporum consonantiis dulci concordia prolatus, symphoniis variisque metrorum coloribus adornatus. 99

311. Sequitur de discantu. Quoniam latens scientia nulli prodest et cito labitur, distributa vero multum prodest et magnum recipit incrementum. Idcirco artem sciendi componere et proferre discantum ex improviso qui diu latuit apud quosdam peritos musicos pro posse nostro nostris specialibus proponimus enodare. 5, 112

6. Anonymous IV, *De mensuris et discantu*. Probably an Englishman writing in the last decades of the 13th c. Latin citations from Reckow, *Der Musiktraktat*. English translations: Yudkin, *The Music Treatise of Anonymous* IV, and Dittmer, *Anonymous* IV.

39:8. Et ulterius per consuetudinem raro frangimus, videlicet non ponimus quatuor pro brevi in voce humana; sed in instrumentis saepius bene fit, et sic quoad primum modum inter subtiles, sive fuerit in modo perfecto sive imperfecto, reducendo ad integra cum brevi pausatione vel longa, prout melius competit. 115

45:1. Iterato est quaedam figura, quae dicitur elmuahim vel simil<e> sibi. Et semper iacet obliquo modo quodammodo, sed diversimode significat. Quandoque dicitur semibrevis, si sit ante alteram consimilem vel post. Aliter quandoque est tertia pars brevis, et hoc est, quando tres per modum currentium ponuntur. Et sic sunt tres pro brevi. Consimili modo si quatuor currentes pro una brevi ordinentur, sed hoc raro solebat contingere. Ulterius vero non in voce humana, sed in instrumentis cordarum possunt ordinari. 115

46:12. Ipse vero magister Perotinus fecit quadrupla optima sicut *Viderunt*, *Sederunt* cum habundantia colorum armonicae artis. 10

84:4. Et cum talibus quidam addunt punctum puri organi post praedicta loco nobilioris finis, et simili modo addunt per modum organizandi in principio duo puncta vel tria bene concordabilia et propter convenientiam inceptionis nobilioris, et ea ponunt ante longam pausationem florificando, prout mos est in puro organo et in talibus etc. 98

86:7. Et sunt numero decem et novem cordarum in distantia diatonici generis, et in numero concordantiarum quindecim etc. Ulteriori quidem processu quidam raro procedunt usque ad triplex diapason, quamvis in communi usu se habeat in instrumento

organorum et ulterius aliorum instrumentorum, et hoc numero cordarum vel fistularum vel prout in cimbalis benesonantibus apud bonos musicos plenius habetur.   115

87:10. Item duo puncta in eodem sono, sive fuerint in concordantia sive non, pro longa
florata ponuntur.   90

88:3. Item sunt quandoque longae plurimae ratione coloris vel pulcritudinis melodiae,
sive fuerint concordantes sive non, quod quidem per se patet in operando.   96

88:6. Item quaedam est duplex longa florata. Et illa ponitur in principio in nomine sanc-
tissimi alpha, et dicitur principium ante principium; et semper erit concordans. Item
sunt quidam ponentes duo vel tria loco unius; sed prima potest esse concordans vel
discordans, et semper incipit ante tenorem breviter, et tenor incipit cum secundo, si
fuerit concordans, vel cum tertio. Et ille tertius punctus habet elongationem, ut praedix-
imus, florificandam. Et quidam possunt ponere ante inceptionem tenoris tres ligatas vel
quatuor; si ultima fuerit concordans, secum erit tenor incipiens; quae si fuerit discordans, ad primam sequentem concordantem erit inceptio. Et hoc unum est, si fuerit
modulatio meli <ratione> alicuius pulcritudinis <vel> convenientis coloris etc. similia,
quae pertinent ad inceptionem ante principium.   96, 98

7. Anonymous, *Ars musicae mensurabilis secundum Franconem*. From France,
late 13th, early 14th c. The treatise is based on Franco of Cologne's *Ars cantus
mensurabilis*. Latin citations from Anonymous, *Ars musicae mensurabilis*.

44. De plicis in figuris simplicibus. Plica est nota divisionis eiusdem soni in gravem vel
in acutam, et debet formari in gutture cum epygloto.   51

8. Anonymous, *Breviarium regulare musicae* (Willelmus). From England, *c*.1400.
Latin citations from Anonymous, *Breviarium regulare*.

26. Secundo de notis solitariis plicatis est dicendum. Unde notandum est quid sit plica
secundum magistrum Franconem, capitulo secundo musicae suae: plica est nota divisionis
eiusdem soni in grave et acutum. Et secundum Walterum Odyngton, libro sexto, capitulo
secundo: plica est inflexio vocis a voce sub una figura. Ex hiis diffinitionibus pono eis quartam conclusionem. Conclusio. Omnis nota praeter simplam est plicabilis.   51

27. Pono igitur regulas. Prima regula. Propter plicam nec augmentatur nec minuatur
tempus alicuius notae a tempore eiusdem non plicatae. Secunda regula. Omnis plica vel
ascendens est vel descendens, ascendens vero significat sonum in fine acuendum,
descendens vero significat sonum in fine deprimendum.   51

9. Anonymous, *Commentarius in Micrologum Guidonis Aretini*. Writer possibly
from Bavaria. The treatise was written in Liège between *c*.1070 and 1100. Latin
citations from van Waesberghe, *Expositiones in Micrologum*, 93–172.

149:21. Et non solum morula morulae conferatur, sed etiam tremulae et connexis vocibus
et e converso, quocumque modo disponantur in cantu. Tremula est similiter vox reper-
cussa sicut morula, sed illud interest, quia in morula voces eaedem aequali impulsu vocis

proferuntur, in tremula vero eaedem nunc maiori, nunc minori impulsu vocis efferuntur quasi tremendo.   54, 73–4

149:24. Unde liber in sequentibus easdem voces repercussas dicit videri has elevatas, has depositas. Et hic vero varium tenorem vocat eas quantum ad visum, cum in rei veritate sit idem tenor, quia tenent se in eadem voce.   30

150:27. Tenor alius repercussus, alius non repercussus ut ille per quem distinctionem syllabasque et neumas discernimus, quando in fine aliquarum vocum aliquamdiu immoramur.   76

150:28. Repercussio alius morula, alius tremula, et hoc est: aut habeant morulam, aut tremulam, id est varium tenorem per varium impulsum, non per variam vocem. 54, 74

153:59. Morula dupliciter longior est aut brevior, si silentium inter voces duplum est ad aliud silentium inter duas voces. Eodem modo morula dupliciter est brevior, si taciturnitas inter duas voces simplum est ad aliam taciturnitatem inter duas voces.   54, 74

153:61. Quod dicit: aut tremulam habeant, puto intelligendum sic esse: Tremula est neuma quam gradatam vel quilisma dicimus, quae longitudinem, de qua dicit 'duplo longiorem', cum subiecta plana virgula denotat, sine qua brevitatem, quae intimatur per hoc quod dicit 'vel duplo breviorem', insinuat.   54

10. Anonymous, *Instituta Patrum de modo psallendi sive cantandi*. From St Gall, *c.*1200. It has been attributed to Ekkehard V. Van Dijk, 'Saint Bernard and the Instituta Patrum', makes a case for it being a semi-official document from St Gall, based on an earlier text ascribed to St Bernard. Latin citations from Gerbert, *Scriptores*, i.

6. Tres ordines melodiae in tribus distinctionibus temporum habeamus, verbi gratia, in praecipuis Solempnitatibus, toto corde & ore omnique affectu devotionis; in Dominicis diebus & maioribus Festivitatibus sive Natalitiis Sanctorum (in quibus plebes laborant partim vel totaliter) multo remissius; privatis autem diebus ita psalmodia moduletur nocturnis horis, & cantus de die, ut omnes possint devote psallere & intente cantare sine strepitu vocis, cum affectu absque defectu.   39–40

8. Histrioneas voces, garrulas, alpinas, sive montanas, tonitruantes, vel sibilantes, hinnientes velut vocalis asina, mugientes, seu balantes quasi pecora; sive foemineas, omnemque vocum falsitatem, iactantiam seu novitatem detestemur, & prohibeamus in Choris nostris; quia plus redolent vanitatem & stultitiam quam religionem; & non decent inter spiritales homines huiusmodi voces in praesentia Dei & Angelorum eius in terra sancta Sanctorum. Tales enim qui eiusmodi voces habent, & carent modo naturali, quia nec aliquando exercitati alicuius instrumenti musicalis artificio; & ideo aptam flexibilitatem vocis non valent habere ad Neumas. Ergo isti, cum sint incompositi moribus & voce, tamen sub obtentu Religionis praesumunt esse & videri Cantores & Rectores in Choris, cum non sciant, nec scire velint; propterea interdum subministrant discordiam & dissolutionem in Choris, & sustollunt ceteros: cum aut levitate nimia praecipitant cantum, aut gravitate inepta syllabas fantur, quasi qui trahat molarem lapidem ad montem sursum, & tamen in praeceps ruat semper deorsum; ideoque nullo moderamine

contenti, non percipiunt subtilem dulcedinem intellectus, & raro perveniunt ad delectationem virtutum; multo magis nunquam aspirant ad speculandum divina mysteria, & ad rimandum secreta coelestia. Talium utique hominum vocibus, cum non sint bonae, Musica tamen scit eis bene uti in locis opportunis, quod illi ignorant, qui eas habent in arca sui pectoris.   19

11. Anonymous, *Metrologus*. A commentary on eleven chapters of the *Micrologus*, probably from England in the 13th c. Latin citations from van Waesberghe, *Expositiones in Micrologum*, 59–92. Commentary on Guido's ch. 15. Guido's words are italicized.

89. *Liquescunt autem in multis voces more litterarum*, id est consonantiarum, *ita ut inceptus modus unius ad alteram limpide transiens nec finiri videatur. Porro liquescenti voci* descendendo *punctum quasi maculando supponimus*, aliquando super consonantias ut reg, dig, leg, ag, vim, vem, tum, tem et super consimiles sonando usque ad proximam vocem vel notam iuxta se vel supra se hoc modo: [example] ascendendo vero hoc modo: [example] Et si proxima nota subsequens inferior se fuerit, tunc non est liquescens, sed duae notae sunt post hanc liquescentem hoc modo: [example] Aliquando sequitur alia nota inferior se similiter fiet et post has notas.

Super vocales vero non faciat liquescentem vel strictionem nisi tantum super au, eu, luy, ley, et ey. Quando vero super a e i o vel u, sic formatur: [example] Tunc vero ultima pro duabus reputatur vocibus.

Et si eam, scilicet liquescentem *plenius vis proferre non liquefaciens nihil nocet, saepe autem magis placet. Et omnia quaecumque diximus nec nimis raro nec continue facias, sed cum discretione.*   48

12. Anonymous, *Quatuor principalia*. Probably from England, *c*.1300–50, formerly attributed to Simon Tunstede. Latin citation from Coussemaker, *Scriptores*, iv, with corrections from Warren, 'Punctus organi', 131.[1]

297. Praeterea sciendum est quod organum purum non potest haberi nisi super solum tenorem et sine mensura, hoc modo: pronuntians tenorem in aliquibus locis fingere se debet, videlicet quando per consonantiam sentit concordantiam aliquam perfectam imminere, et specialiter in penultima, tunc enim se ad concordantiam debet signare. Cantans vero organum super tenorem tali modo habet modulari, ut quamdiu organum purum durat, discurrere per notas oportet <sine> mensura usque ad concordantiam. Sed cum ad concordantiam perfectam pervenerit, moram ibidem trahet, et specialiter super penultimam, ut hic. [example]   100

13. Anonymous of St Emmeram, *De musica mensurata*. Probably written in Paris in the late 13th c. and acquired for St Emmeram in Regensburg by the mid-14th c. Latin citation from Yudkin, *De musica mensurata*.[2] English translation: Yudkin.

[1] This passage also appears in Anon. I (C): CS iii. 363
[2] Another edition in Sowa, *Ein anonymer glossierter Mensuraltraktat 1279*.

102. Tempus igitur, prout hic sumitur, est morula, ubicumque recta brevis habet fieri. Et recta brevis est illa que unum solum tempus continet, et illud est indivisibile secundum illud praedictum, id est quo ad rectam brevem. Et nota, quod tempus potest tripliciter considerari et hoc proportionaliter, quoniam aut per vocem rectam aut cassam aut omissam. Vox recta est vox instrumentis naturalibus procreata. Vox cassa idem est quod sonus, non vox, artificialiter procreatus, sicut patet in musicis instrumentis, in quibus sonus nunc proportionaliter accipitur et habetur; vel vox quassa a quassa dicta, est idem quod vox imperfecta aut etiam semiplena, per sonos varios diminuta. Vox omissa fit per recreationem spirituum et per pausationem aliquam praedictae voci aequipollentem. Illud sequidem tempus per vocem quassam, ut dictum est, divisibile est et imperfectum quoad semibreves, quae de semus, sema, semum, quod est imperfectus, imperfecta, imperfectum, dicuntur, quasi imperfectae breves. 77–8

14. Anonymous, *Summa musice*. Probably written *c.*1200, from the Cathedral of St Kilian in Würzburg. According to Page, it was intended as a practical manual directed at pupils. Latin citations from Page, *The* Summa Musice. English translation: Page. Citations are by line numbers.

478–88. Et huiusmodi triplicem cantum diatonicum appellabant quasi de proprietate tonorum. Cantum autem qui est gravi gravior postponebant propter sui molliciem parum et nihil valentem, et hunc organicum appellabant eo quod organum vocis est deficiens in illo. Similiter illum qui est acuto acutior non curabant propter intolerabilem eius laborem–in ipso etiam nulla dilectio invenitur–et cantum huiusmodi enharmonicum appellabant eo quod extra diatonici cantus harmoniam positus et cantorem et auditorem fatigat et ledit, per nullam recreationem delectationis oblectans. 84

523–40. Punctus ad modum puncti formatur et adiungitur quandoque virge, quandoque plice, quandoque podatu, quandoque unum solum, quandoque plura pariter, precipue in sonorum descensu. Virga est nota simplex ad modum virge oblonga. Clivis dicitur a cleo, quod est 'inclino', et componitur ex nota et seminota, et signat quod vox debet inflecti. Plica dicitur a plicando et continet notas duas, unam superiorem et aliam inferiorem. Podatus continet notas duas quarum una est inferior et alia superior ascendendo. Quilisma dicitur 'curvatio', et continet notulas tres vel plures quandoque ascendens et iterum descendens, quandoque e contrario. Pressus dicitur a premendo, et minor continet duas notas, maior vero tres et semper debet equaliter et cito proferri. Sed cantus adhuc per hec signa minus perfecte cognoscitur, nec per se quisquam eum potest addiscere, sed oportet ut aliunde audiatur et longo usu discatur, et propter hoc huius cantus nomen usus accepit. 44

540–54. Olim cantores cantu sic complacuere

Heredesque suos voluerunt scita docere.

Contigit ergo novas hos ingeniare figuras

Ut possent varias vocum figurare tenuras

Quas dixere notas certus quod ab inde vocatur

Cursus cantandi qui vocali sociatur.

Clives, plice, virga, quilismata, puncta, podati

Nomina sunt harum; sint pressi consociati.

Pes notulis binis vult sursum tendere crescens;

Deficit illa tamen quam signat acuta liquescens.

Vult notulis binis semper descendere clivis

Obscurumque sonum notat illius nota finis.

Precedit pausam vel stat pausantis in ore,

Ac si perfecte notule fungatur honore.   44

573–81. Hiis nominibus note, ut dictum est, appellantur a Gallicis, Anglicis, Teutonicis, Hungariis, Slavis et Dacis, et ceteris Cisalpinis. Itali autem alias notas et nomina dicuntur habere, quod qui scire voluerit querat ab ipsis.   86

2055–65. Si enim materia dictaminis in cantu fuerit gaudiosa, notam decet esse levem et letam, sicut est cantus de Sancta Maria, de Sancto Iohanne Baptista, de Epiphania, de Resurrectione et de similibus. Si vero dictamen rem laboriosam vel secundum virtutem vel secundum apparentiam significat, nota debet esse gravis et transire de b molli in ♮ durum et e contrario. . . . Dum vero materia medio modo se habet et cantus medio modo se debet habere, quod stulti putant ratione carere.   40

15. Aribo Scholasticus, *De musica*. Dedicated in 1078 to Bishop Ellenhad of Freising. The author probably spent some time in Liège. Latin citations from Aribo, *De musica*.

66:34. Morula dupliciter longior est vel brevior, si silentium inter duas voces duplum est ad aliud silentium inter duas voces. Eodem modo morula dupliciter est brevior, si taciturnitas inter duas simpla est ad aliam taciturnitatem inter duas voces. Quod dicit 'aut tremulam habeant', puto intelligendum sic esse. Tremula est neuma quam gradatam vel quilisma dicimus quae longitudinem, de qua dicit duplo longiorem cum subiecta virgula denotat, sine qua brevitatem, quae intimatur per hoc quod dicit vel duplo breviorem insinuat.   54, 74

16. Arnulf of St-Ghislain, *Tractatulus de differentiis et gradibus cantorum*. Possibly from Hainaut, *c*.1400. Latin citations from Page, 'A Treatise on Musicians'. English translation: Page.

15:4. Prima plebescit in illis, ut convenit, qui artem musice prorsus ignari, nullo etiam naturalis dispositionis suffragante beneficio, per fatue sue presumptionis ausum temerarium, planam nundum gnari musicam, musicales actamen consonantias avido morsu rodere et verius devorare precentando satagunt, et in sue corrixationis latratu dum clamore rudiunt altius asino et brutali clangore terribilius intubant, cachephaton evomunt, organizantesque per antifrasin faciunt in musica irregulariter barbarismum atque execrabili sue presumptionis falso cecati putamine se ipsos in se iactitant cantores posse postponere seu preire precipuos, ipsosque in turba quasi corrigere vel dirigere se impudenter offerunt ut apud homines musici videantur qui nec tantum de musica sapiunt ut ducantur, semper cum consonantibus nichilominus dissonantes et soloestico fedantes vicio in scolata musicorum turba quidquid profertur regularius adeo cantoribus intollerabiles et nocivi . . . 19, Ch. 5 n. 18

15:24. Secunda vero differentia patet in illis laycalibus qui, licet sint totius artis musicalis expertes, zelo tamen ducti dulcedinis delicatas aures suas ad quevis musicalia prebent, attentius adamantes et associantes musicos et, veluti panthera boni odoris quevis insequntur animalia et apis ob dulcorem mellis argumentat, in studium propositos studiosius prosecuntur, florum et spicarum musicalium messis manipulos colligentes quos possunt, ut in plerisque cum cantoribus gratius garriendo concordent et frequentius usitando in multis musicalibus quodammodo habilitentur et reddantur experti ut quod artis in eis deficit usus suppleat et industria naturalis. 88–89

15:32. Ex istis nonnullos videmus clericos qui in organicis instrumentis difficilimos musicales modulos quos exprimere vix presumeret vox humana adinveniunt atque tradunt per miraculosum quoddam innate in eis inventive Musice prodigium, reliquos autem qui que sic gesta sunt et tradita paulo minus laudabiliter recordantur, et interdum inventoris laudem convenit gracialis industria recordantis. 88, 115

15:41. Tertia est et aperte comprobatur in illis qui in suorum sacrariis pectorum gloriosos possident artis et discipline musicalis thesauros virtute studii laudabiliter acquisitos, qui licet defectum patiantur in organo ad alta digne proferenda que sapiunt, verumptamen vivax artis scientia supplet in ipsis impotentiam naturalem ut quod per se promere notaliter consonando nequeunt per discipulos fieri procurant, propositos regulariter edocendo ipsisque musicales communicando divitias et margaritas, Musice digne dignis revelando secreta. De eorum namque pectoribus nedum fluunt theorica musicalis doctrine fluenta; verumptamen practizantes in illa facto pandunt et opere unde auris sapientis et oculus practicum musicum indicant laude dignum, nam quod habet in habitu exhibet audiendum et speculandum in facto. Tales non sophisticantur in musica sed realem musicam profitentur, et quamvis in cantando fastidiant auditores hunc defectum in ipsis redimit eorum facundia dum per doctrinam verbalem artis regulas eloquntur. 21

16:56. Quarta ordine, dignitate prior, attenditur clarere glorianter in illis quos naturalis instinctus, suffragante mellice vocis organo, figuraliter reddit philomenicos, meliores tamen multo Nature munere philomenis et laude non inferiores alaudis, in quibus nobilis acquisitio artis cantorie organum naturale dirigit regulariter in modo, mensura, numero et colore, miro modulamine in consonantiis vicissitudines variando, et varietate pluriformi modorum novelle recreationis adducit materiam in animo auditoris, qui etiam, intercedente prolationis gracia melioris, inculta queque et m[i]nus decenter exhibita musicalia, ad incudem sui gutturis reportata, quasi remonetando gratiorem reducit in formam. Quis enim non mirare poterit quo proferendi magisterio proportio musicalis artis, primaria traditione dissona, eorum super artificiali docescat [*sic*] et ad consonantie gratiam reducatur? 9

16:75. E quibus pars altera, favorosi videlicet sexus feminei, que quanto rarior tanto preciosior, dum in dulcinomi gutturis epigloto tonos librate dividit in semitonia, et semitonia in athomos indivisibiles garritat, ineffabili lascivit melodiomate quod magis putares angelicum quam humanum. 25, 89

17. Aurelian of Réôme, *Musica disciplina*. From Autun, 840–9. Written for Bernard, abbot of Saint-Jean-de-Réôme, near Langres in eastern France. Latin citations from Aurelian of Réôme, *Musica disciplina*, ed. Gushee. English translation: Ponte, Aurelian of Réôme, *The Discipline of Music*.

97:15. Versus istarum novissimarum partium tremulam adclivemque emittunt vocem.   53

122:45. Sagax cantor, sagaciter intende, ut si laus nomino trino integra canitur, duobus in locis scilicet in XVI syllaba, et post in quarta decima, trina ad instar manus verberantis facias celerum ictum.   57

18. Bernard of Clairvaux, *Ad Guidonem abbatem et monachos Arremarenses* (letter to Guy, Abbot of Montier-Ramey). Bernard was born in 1090 at Fontaines-lès-Dijon, became abbot of the Cistercian monastery at Clairvaux (east-central France), and died in 1153. Latin citation from Bernard of Clairvaux, *Sämtliche Werke*, ed. Winkler, iii. 780–2. English translation: Bruno S. James, *The Letters of St. Bernard of Clairvaux* (London, 1953), 502.

Epistola CCCXCVIII. Ad Guidonem Abbatem et Monachos Arremarenses.
Venerabili Guidoni, abbati Arremarensi, et sanctis qui cum eo sunt fratribus, Bernardus, servus sanctitatis eorum: servire Domino in sanctitate.
Cantus ipse, si fuerit, plenus sit gravitate: nec lasciviam resonet, nec rusticitatem. Sic suavis, ut non sit levis: sic mulceat aures, ut moveat corda. Tristitiam levet, iram mitiget; sensum litterae non evacuet, sed fecundet. Non est levis iactura gratiae spiritualis, levitate cantus abduci a sensuum utilitate, et plus sinuandis intendere vocibus quam insinuandis rebus.   22

19. Bonaventura da Brescia, *Regula musice plane*. From Brescia, end of the 15th c. Latin citations from facs. edn. in Monuments of Music and Music Literature in Facsimile, 77 (New York, 1975). English translation: Bonaventura da Brescia, *Rules of Plain Music*, trans. Seay. Citations are to chapter number (the original is not paginated).

12. Item nota che sono tre specie de semitonio: cioe semitonio enarmonico: semitonio diatonico: & semitonio cromatico. vel sic. semitonio menore. semitonio mazore. & semitonio excellente &c. Il semitonio enarmonico: cioe menore: e per tutto doue se troua .mi. fa. in ascensu. & fa mi in descensu: ut supra patet in figura. Item semitonio diatonico siue mazore per tutto doue se troua .fa mi. in ascensu. & .mi fa. in descensu. e de questi se ne troua doi ne la mane: quo ad ordinem naturalem. scilicet doue sono li b.fa. ♮mi. e questo semitonio se troua dal primo b. al secondo: ut hic [example]. Item el semitonio cromatico siue excellente se fa per musica ficta. s. quando de tono per musica plana faciamo semitonium. per ficta musica. & questi tali semitoni cromatici: siue collorati se fanno in descensu. s. quando de fa. uel de ut naturalis: facimus mi. accidentalis. ut hic patet [example].   83

42. De modo cantandi secundum Guidonem. Item nota del modo del intonare in choro: ut ait Guido in tertio sue musice: che li responsi nocturni se voleno intonare viva voce

per dismiscidare li somnolenti. Ne le antiphone cum dolce voce e suave. Ne li introiti come voce preconicha per incitare il populo aldiuino officio. Ne li alleluya suauemente se debeno intonare. Ne li tracti e graduali cum la voce morigerata e pausata se debe continuare. Ne li offertorii & communione moderatamente quanto sia possibile se debeno cantare: & in questo modo le nostre conscientie apresso el vero e superno idio e a la zente del mondo saranno excusati.   39

20. Canonical Rule of the Council of Basle, 1435. Latin citations from Harrán, *In Defense of Music*, App. I, 107–14. English translation: Harrán.

108. Laudes divine per singulas horas: non cursim ac festinanter, sed tractim et cum pausa decenti: presertim in medio cuiuslibet versiculi psalmorum: debitam faciendo inter solenne et feriale officium differentiam.   34

110. Quoscumque etiam alibi beneficiatos seu in sacris constitutos cum ad horas canonicas teneantur: ammonet hec sancta sinodus: ut si orationes suas deo acceptas fore cupiunt: non in gutture vel inter dentes: seu deglutiendo aut sincopando dictiones vel colloquia vel risus intermiscendo: sed sive soli sive associati diurnum nocturnumque officium reverenter verbisque distinctis peragant. ac tali in loco unde a devotione non retrahantur.   22

21. Elias Salomonis, *Scientia artis musicae*. Writer was French. Treatise was written in Rome in 1274, and dedicated to Pope Gregory X. Latin citations from Gerbert, *Scriptores*, iii.

17. Quod execrabilius est, cantum planum, & bene ordinatum per angelos, & per sanctos prophetas, & per beatum Gregorium, deridendo, assumendo aliquoties naturam cantus scientiae organizandi, quae totaliter supra scientiam cantus plani est reperta. Et etiam vix dignantur aliquotiens pedem suum facere de cantu plano, anticipando, festinando, retardando, & male copulando punctos, ex quibus effectus scientiae organizandi completur: quia fortassis vident punctos taliter paratos. Hoc autem factum est ad decorem & honestatem positionis punctorum, & notae libri, non ad cantandum, ut videntur. Hoc sciant pro certo, non quaerentes, quae nostra sunt quae vident, nec Dei, nec debitum artis musicae, quia illam ignorant; sed speculando dicentes in aere miau minau, ut appareat & audiat hospes; & fortassis, quod damnabilius est, ut magis frequenter oblationes afferantur, forte ad illicitos usus convertendae, & in marsupiis recludendae.   26

21. Bene caveatur, non debemus ponere falcem nostram in messem alienam assumendo naturam organizandi, punctos properando: nam qui ad utrumque festinat, utrumque destruendo neutrum bene peragit. Regula infallibilis, omnis cantus planus in aliqua parte sui nullam festinationem in uno loco patitur plusquam in alio, quam [*sic*] est de natura sui: ideo dicitur cantus planus, quia omnino planissime appetit cantari.   31, 101

60. Sed quare voces non distant aequali numero punctorum? Respondeo: consonantia vocum, neque natura cantus artificialis nec naturalis hoc permittit; & si fieret, turpem sonoritatem generaret. Et ita artificialiter & ordinabiliter positum est in figura, & habet veritatem, aliter non haberet. Et est sciendum, quod cantus laicorum a natura infixus

eisdem ut in pluribus, & instrumentorum ligneorum appetit illud idem, non tamen cantus Lombardorum, qui ululant ad modum luporum. Quod manifeste patet; nam si unus laicus audiret alium laicum cantare in prima bassa voce, bene saliret recta in tertia, non autem aliquo modo in secunda; vel e contrario de tertia in prima, sed nunquam in secunda.   18

22. Franco of Cologne, *Ars cantus mensurabilis*. Possibly from Germany, he was papal chaplain and preceptor of the Knights Hospitallers of St John in Cologne. He may have taught at the University of Paris. The treatise, written in France between 1260 and 1280, was important in establishing the notational system used for the next 200 years. Latin citations from Franco of Cologne, *Ars cantus mensurabilis*, ed. Reaney and Gilles. English translation: Strunk, *Source Readings*, 139–59.

75:1. Copula est velox discantus adinvicem copulatus. Copula alia ligata, alia non ligata. Ligata copula est quae incipit a simplici longa et prosequitur per binariam ligaturam cum proprietate et perfectione ad similitudinem secundi modi; ab ipso tamen secundo modo differt dupliciter, scilicet in notando et proferendo: in notando quia secundus modus in principio simplicem longam non habet; copula vero habet, ut hic patet: [Ex. 2.2(*a*)]. Sed si inter primam simplicem et ligaturam divisio modi apponatur, tunc non est copula, sed de secundo modo appellatur, ut hic: [Ex. 2.2(*b*)]. In proferendo etiam differt copula a secundo modo, quia secundus profertur ex recta brevi et longa imperfecta, sed copula ista velociter profertur quasi semibrevis et brevis usque ad finem.

Copula non ligata ad similitudinem quinti modi fit; differt tamen a quinto dupliciter, in notando et proferendo. In notando differt a quinto quia quintus sine littera ubique ligabilis est, sed copula ista nunquam super litteram accipitur, et tamen non ligatur, ut hic patet: [Ex. 2.2(*c*)]. In proferendo differt etiam a quinto, quia quintus ex rectis brevibus profertur; copula vero velocius proferendo copulatur.   41

80:1. Organum proprie sumptum est cantus non in omni parte sua mensuratus. Sciendum quod purum organum haberi non potest, nisi supra tenorem ubi sola nota est in unisono, ita quod, quando tenor accipit plures notas simul, statim est discantus, ut hic: [example]

Ipsius organi longae et breves tribus regulis cognoscuntur. Prima est: quicquid notatur in longa simplici nota longum est, et in brevi breve, et in semibrevi semibreve. Secunda regula est: quicquid est longum indiget concordantia respectu tenoris; sed si in discordantia venerit, tenor taceat vel se in concordantiam fingat, ut hic patet: [example]. Tertia regula est: quicquid accipitur immediate ante pausationem quae finis punctorum dicitur, est longum, quia omnis penultima longa est.   79, 98–9

81:7. Item notandum quod quotienscumque in organo puro plures figurae simul in unisono evenerint, sola prima debet percuti, reliquae vero omnes in floratura teneantur, ut hic [example].   30, 90

23. Giorgio Anselmi da Parma, *De Musica*. Written in Parma in 1434. Latin citations from Giorgio Anselmi da Parma, *De Musica*, ed. Massera.

III:4. Cum certe sit humana vox cantabilis, quotiens in se apta fuerit et arte composita, nulli instrumento musico compar, omnia excedens mirum in modum ut sonus illi nullus equari valeat in demulcendo humanas aures, in sedando corporis passiones et anime languores, tanta mensura tanta equalitate tanto ordine tantaque sonoritate mellita cantor doctus cantabiles profert voces, . . . superat siquidem animantium cunctorum voces et instrumentorum sonitus vocis inflexione et mensura, novit enim eandem quantitate vocem exasperare, remollire et quosvis arte pro arbitrio quodlibet ad genus cantus convertere.   16

III:5. At cordula cithare, aut fistula, quotiens quendam pro modo sonitum pulsa reddiderit semper deinceps eundem servat nisi quantum citharedus perdoctus partibus plectrum lenius aut incitatius attulerit. Sed et indocti perfacile cognoscunt errores instrumenti musici rarissimos, quod et benedocti vix apti cantoris distinguunt voces ecmeles, ineptas et dissonas. Sed certe difficilissimum fit diu vel pro cantilena una costantes quantitate sua voces continere: hinc fit ut ex eis ad cantum experti non facile producuntur auditore presertim docto cantore, sed et unica pro modo cantilena decantata prorsus taceant. Eapropter antiqui omnem vim harmonicam in instrumentis posuerunt. Noverunt siquidem, quotiens dedissent rationes congruentes cordulis, semper in omni cantilena debitas melodie partes conservare tamquam infatigabiles ut certi starent sonitus, experti etenim humanam vocem plerumque deficere et defatigari etsi instrumenta omnia musica emulentur illam, et illius ad instar facta sint.   114

III:229. Quemadmodum enim defatigatum auditorem sepius ioco quodam lenit orator et gratum reddit, sic auditorem cantus doctus cantor moras quasdam cantabilibus intermiscens vocibus avidum magis et intentum ad reliquas cantilene partes iniciendas facit. Moras has sive quietes a cantu pausas nominant.   78

24. Guido of Arezzo, (1) *Micrologus*, written *c.*1026–8, in Arezzo; (2) *Aliae regulae de ignoto cantu*, possibly begun in Pomposa, but perhaps not finished until *c.*1030. Guido may have been born and educated in France in the late 10th c. (according to Strunk, *Source Readings*, 117). It is known with more certainty that he spent some time in the north Italian abbey of Pomposa (near Ferrara) early in the 11th c., visited Rome *c.*1032, and settled in a Camaldulese monastery near Arezzo shortly thereafter. Latin citations from Guido of Arezzo, *Micrologus*, ed. van Waesberghe (English translation: *Hucbald, Guido, and John*, 49–83), and Gerbert, *Scriptores*, ii. 34–5 (English translation: Strunk, *Source Readings*, 117).

Micrologus

162. Igitur quemadmodum in metris sunt litterae et syllabae, partes et pedes ac versus, ita in harmonia sunt phtongi, id est soni, quorum unus, duo vel tres aptantur in syllabas; ipsaeque solae vel duplicatae neumam, id est partem constituunt cantilenae; et pars una vel plures distinctionem faciunt, id est congruum respirationis locum. De quibus illud est notandum quod tota pars compresse et notanda et exprimenda est, syllaba vero compressius.   29

163. Tenor vero, id est mora ultimae vocis, qui in syllaba quantuluscumque est, amplior in parte, diutissimus vero in distinctione, signum in his divisionis existit. Sicque opus est

ut quasi metricis pedibus cantilena plaudatur, et aliae voces ab aliis morulam duplo longiorem vel duplo breviorem, aut tremulam habeant, id est varium tenorem, quem longum aliquotiens apposita litterae virgula plana significat. 73

165. Ac summopere caveatur talis neumarum distributio, ut cum neumae tum eiusdem soni repercussione, tum duorum aut plurium connexione fiant, semper tamen aut in numero vocum aut in ratione tenorum neumae alterutrum conferantur, atque respondeant nunc aequae aequis, nunc duplae vel triplae simplicibus, atque alias collatione sesquialtera vel sesquitertia. 75

174a. Item saepe vocibus gravem et acutum accentum superponimus, quia saepe aut maiori impulsu aut minori efferimus, adeo ut eiusdem saepe vocis repetitio elevatio vel depositio esse videatur. 30

174b. Item ut rerum eventus sic cantionis imitetur effectus, ut in tristibus rebus graves sint neumae, in tranquillis iocundae, in prosperis exultantes et reliqua. 37

175a. Item ut in modum currentis equi semper in finem distinctionum rarius voces ad locum respirationis accedant, ut quasi gravi more ad repausandum lassae perveniant. Spissim autem et raro prout oportet, notae compositae huius saepe rei poterunt indicium dare. 31, 75

175b. Liquescunt vero in multis voces more litterarum, ita ut inceptus modus unius ad alteram limpide transiens nec finiri videatur. Porro liquescenti voci punctum quasi maculando supponimus hoc modo: [Example]. Si eam plenius vis proferre non liquefaciens nihil nocet, saepe autem magis placet. Et omnia quae diximus, nec nimis raro nec nimis continue facias, sed cum discretione. 46

Aliae regulae de ignoto cantu

34. Temporibus nostris super omnes homines fatui sunt cantores; in omni enim arte valde plura sunt, quae nostro sensu cognoscimus, quam ea, quae a magistro didicimus. Perlecto enim solo psalterio omnium librorum lectiones cognoscunt pueruli, & agriculturae scientiam subito intelligunt rustici. Qui enim unam vineam putare, unam arbusculam inserere, unum asinum onerare cognoverit, sicut in uno facit, in omnibus similiter, aut etiam melius facere non dubitabit. Mirabiles autem cantores & cantorum discipuli etiamsi per centum annos quotidie cantent, numquam per se sine magistro unam vel saltem parvulam antiphonam cantabunt, tantum tempus in cantando perdentes, in quanto & divinam & secularem scripturam potuissent plene cognoscere. 123

25. Guilielmus Monachus, *De preceptis artis musicae*. An Italian writing probably c.1480–90. This is his only known work and is important for its discussion of the English practices of gymel and faulxbordon. See discussion in Seay's Introduction, 7–12, and text, 38–43. Ch. 6 n. 29

26. Hucbald, *De harmonica institutione*. Hucbald was born c.840 and died 930. He joined the Benedictine monastery of Saint-Amand in the diocese of Tournai in Flanders, where he spent most of his life and eventually became director of the school. He was also educated in Nevers and Saint-Germain-d'Auxerre, and taught in several places in northern France, including Reims, where he possibly wrote the treatise *c.*893. Latin citation from Gerbert, *Scriptores*, i. 118. English translation: *Hucbald, Guido, and John*, 37.

Hae autem consuetudinariae notae non omnino habentur non necessariae; quippe cum et tarditatem cantilenae et ubi tremulam sonus contineat vocem, vel qualiter ipsi soni iungantur in unum vel distinguantur ab invicem, ubi quoque claudantur inferius vel superius pro ratione quarundam litterarum, quorum nihil omnino hae artificiales notae valent ostendere, admodum censentur proficuae.   59

27. Isidore of Seville, *Etymologiarum sive originum libri xx.* Isidore was born *c.*559 and died in 636. He was archbishop of Seville and was canonized in 1598. Latin citation from *Etymologiarum sive originum libri xx*, ed. W. M. Lindsay (Oxford Classical Texts; Oxford, 1911), 3. 22. 14.

Perfecta autem vox est alta, suavis et clara: alta, ut in sublime sufficiat; clara, ut aures adinpleat; suavis, ut animos audientium blandiat. Si ex his aliquid defuerit, vox perfecta non est.   20

28. Jacobus of Liège, *Speculum musicae, liber septimus.* From Liège, *c.*1330. Latin citations from *Speculum musicae*, vii, ed. Bragard.

7. Haec et alia multa ars requirit mensurabilis, sicut supra tactum est libro primo, capitulo XVI, et propterea cantus hic dicitur quia in eo distinctae voces simul sub aliqua temporis morula certa vel incerta proferuntur. Dico autem 'incerta' propter organum duplum quod ubique non est certa temporis mensura mensuratum ut, in floraturis in penultimis, ubi supra vocem unam tenoris in discantu multae sonantur voces. Reponitur autem talis cantus sub mensurabili quia in eo locum habet discantus et requirit distinctas voces simul prolatas quae ab uno et eodem simul proferri non possent.   100

29. Jerome of Moravia, *Tractatus de musica.* Originally from Moravia. A member of the Dominican order, he is believed to have spent some years in Paris. Treatise written between 1272 and 1304. Latin citations from Cserba, *Hieronymus de Moravia*.

59:3. Unisonus est plurium notarum in spatio vel in linea in eodem sono geminatio. Et dicitur unisonus quasi unus sonus eo, secundum Johannem, quod cum sit una vox, continue repercutitur.   68

153:34. Quod autem grammatici colon, comma et periodum dicunt, hoc in cantu quidam diastema, systema et teleusim nominant, per diastema distinctum ornatum cantus significantes, qui fit, quando cantus non in finali, sed in alia decenter pausat, per systema vero conjunctum ornatum indicantes, quotiens scilicet in finali decens fit pausatio, per teleusim autem finem cantus denotantes.

Diastema autem proprie est vocis spatium vel duobus vel tribus vel pluribus sonis mutuatum intervallum, vel diastema, certi tractatus pronuntiationis. Systemata vero proprie sunt principales partes musicorum. Sistere est interdum resistere vel prohiberi, id est aliquam rem in aliquo loco stare facit, assistere, in medio adesse, consistere, habitare vel stare. 103

181:8. Nota longa in cantu ecclesiastico sumpta habet et habere debet duo tempora modernorum, resolvendo vero VI tempora antiquorum, longior tria tempora modernorum, sed IX tempora antiquorum, longissima vero IIII tempora modernorum, sed XII tempora antiquorum. 64

181:13. Item nota brevis sumpta in cantu ecclesiastico habet et habere debet unum tempus modernorum, resolvendo vero tria tempora antiquorum, brevior duas instantias modernorum vel duo tempora antiquorum, brevissima vero unam instantiam modernorum, quae quidem secundum modernos et antiquos indivisibilis est vel unum tempus antiquorum. 65

181:19. De quibus omnibus tales dantur regulae:

Omnis cantus planus et ecclesiasticus notas primo et principaliter aequales habet, unius scilicet temporis modernorum, sed trium temporum antiquorum, id est breves, exceptis V. 65

181:24. Prima omnium est, a qua unusquisque cantus incipit. Quae et principalis dicitur, quae semper est longa, si tamen in finali cantus existit; alias brevis est ut ceterae. 65

181:27. Secunda est, quae etiam secunda syllabae dicitur, quando videlicet aliqua syllaba plures habet notas quam unam. Tunc enim secunda post primam est longa, si tamen aliqua ex praedictis V notis ipsam non praecedit vel non subsequitur immediate; alias brevis est ut ceterae. 65

181:32. Tertia nota est quadrata quidem, sed ex utraque parte caudata, et est duplex: quando enim cauda dextra longior est sinistra, sive ascendendo sive descendendo, plica longa dicitur, ut hic: ↲ ◸ . Haec autem est duplex, scilicet simplex et ligata. De simplicibus jam patuit. Ligatae vero sunt, cum dictis longioribus caudulis, sive in ascendendo sive in descendendo, tamen de tertia in tertiam ad minus et etiam ultra, quae longae plicae et ligatae dicuntur, ut hic: ◿ ◺ . 65–6

182:8. Quando vero e converso cauda sinistra longior est dextra, plica brevis dicitur, et hoc sive ascendendo sive etiam descendendo, ut hic: ◿ .

Quare brevis est ut ceterae. Haec similiter duplex, scilicet simplex, ut jam patuit, et ligata, cum scilicet duae notae descendentes tamen et non plus quam ad tonum et semitonium in ecclesiastico cantu ligantur, ut hic: ◿ ◿ . 66

182:15. Nam prima brevis est ut ceterae, secunda longa, si tamen locum obtinet dictarum V notarum; alias brevis est ut ceterae. 66

182:18. Quarta nota de quinque notis est paenultima. 66

182:19. Quinta est ultima uniuscujusque pausae, quae est longa non semper. Nam solum in pausa imperfectae dictionis, quae brevis est, ultima nota est longa, id est duorum temporum. In pausa vero perfectae dictionis, quae est longa duorum scilicet temporum, est longior, scilicet trium temporum. In pausa autem orationis perfectae, quae longior est, trium scilicet temporum, est longissima, temporum scilicet quatuor. 66

183:21. Secundo, quod notae in figura conjunctae conjungantur [= *conjungentur*] in cantu, sed disjunctae solvantur [= *solventur*]. Quae quidem disjunctio non pausa, sed suspirium dicitur, et nihil aliud est quam apparentia pausationis sive existentia unius scilicet instantis.   29, 59, 70

183:26. Tertio, quod nulla nota brevis cum reverberatione sumatur, nisi dictae V notae, quae singulariter mensurantur. Quae tamen diversimode sumuntur. Nam aliquae ex eis cum reverberatione sub specie semitonii, aliquae sub specie toni, aliquae vero cum reverberatione omnium aliorum modorum.   70

183:32. Est autem reverberatio brevissimae notae ante canendam notam celerrima anticipatio, qua scilicet mediante sequens assumitur.   70

184:4. Est autem flos harmonicus decora vocis sive soni et celerrima procellarisque vibratio. Florum autem alii longi, alii aperti, alii vero existunt subiti.   63

184:7. Longi flores sunt, quorum vibratio est morosa metasque semitonii non excedit. 64

184:9. Aperti autem sunt, quorum vibratio est morosa metasque toni non excedit. 64

184:11. Subiti vero sunt, quorum quidem vibratio in principio est morosa, in medio autem et in fine est celerrima metasque semitonii non excedit.   64

184:14. Horum autem florum qualitas simul et diversitas in organis ostenditur hoc modo: quando enim aliquem cantum tangimus in organis, si aliquam notam ejusdem cantus florizare volumus, puta G in gravibus, tunc ipsa aperta immobiliterque detenta non sui inferiorem inmediate, puta F grave, sed potius superiorem, a scilicet, vibramus acutum. Ex quo pulcherrima harmonia decoraque consurgit, quam quidem florem harmonicum appellamus.   62

184:22. Quando igitur clavis immobilis cum vibranda semitonium constituunt et ipsa vibratio est morosa, tunc est flos, qui dicitur longus. Quando autem includunt tonum et vibratio nec est morosa nec subita, sed media inter ista, est flos apertus. Quando vero constituunt quidem semitonium, sed vibratio in aggressu sit morosa, in progressu autem et egressu sit celerrima, tunc est flos, qui subitus appellatur.   62

184:30. Quinto igitur est notandum, quod dicti flores non debent fieri in aliis notis praeterquam in V singulariter mensuratis, sed differenter. Nam longi flores fieri debent in prima, paenultima et ultima nota in ascensu semitonium intendente. Si vero aliquem aliorum modorum in descensu, constituunt flores apertos, quos et nota secunda syllabae debet habere. Sed flores subitos non alia quam plica longa, inter quam et immediate sequentem notae brevissimae ponuntur ob harmoniae decorem.   64, 66, 67

185:4. Sexto, quod ipsos flores reverberatio praecedere debet sub specie toni vel semitonii sive cujuscumque modi in omnibus quidem V notis excepta ultima, quae sub specie semitonii reverberationem assumit. Sed in nota procellari finitur, quae quidem nihil aliud est, quam vocis sive soni sub specie semitonii lenta vibratio. Quare manat de longorum genere florum. Procellaris autem dicitur eo, quod sicut procella fluminis aura levi agitata movetur sine aquae interruptione, sic nota procellaris in cantu fieri debet cum apparentia quidem motus absque tamen soni vel vocis interruptione.   68–9

185:15. Hunc cantandi modum non quidem in omnibus, sed in aliquibus quidam Gallicorum observant, in quo quidem cum plures delectentur nationes eo quod solidus sit, de eodem quaedam substantiliora non piget exprimere. Non videtur autem alias bene nec sufficienter fore dictum, nisi de modis omnibus ex quibus omnis cantilena contexitur, singulariter specialiterque diceretur. De unisono igitur primo et principaliter est dicendum. 90

185:23. Unisonus si plures quam duas habeat notas, omnes sunt semibreves excepta paenultima et ultima, quae cum reverberatione sumitur ab ipsis. Quod etiam cum duae notae sunt unisonae servatur unius syllabae vel plurium unius vel plurium dictionum. 90

185:28. Item cum per semitonium vel tonum duae notae distant, sive ligatae sive sint solutae, mediante tertia secundae conjuncta junguntur. Quae etiam nota dicitur mediata. Semibrevis est ut frequenter primaeque unisona, aliquando tamen est brevis, scilicet cum resolvitur in tres instantias, ex quo quidam descensus sensui apparet inter dictas duas notas celerius. Aliquando etiam de prima nota solutarum, descendentium tamen, faciunt plicam longam sursum mediatis interjectis ut prius. In ascensu vero reverberationem faciunt supra secundam. 92–3

186:4. Item cum per semiditonum vel ditonum distant ligatae vel solutae duae notae, secundam mediante semibrevi vel etiam brevi, cum in tres resolvitur instantias, conjungunt in cantu. Aliquando tamen in descensu de prima fit plica longa deorsum usque ad mediam, a qua reverberatio sumitur ad tertiam, ut prius, et e converso in ascensu, vel, quod communius est, fit reverberatio supra tertiam. 94

186:11. Item cum distant per diatessaron in descensu, de prima fit plica longa deorsum usque ad secundam, a tertia vero reverberatio fit ad quartam. In ascensu vero fit reverberatio supra quartam. 94

186:15. De diapente apud quosdam idem fit quod et diatessaron, tam scilicet in ascensu quam in descensu, sed communius in descensu fit reverberatio toni supra quintam. Nulla vero fit in ascensu, quod et de omnibus fit modis qui sequuntur. 95

187:8. Gaudent insuper, cum modum organicum notis ecclesiasticis admiscent, quod etiam non abjicit primus modus, necnon et de admixtione modorum duorum generum relictorum. Nam diesim enharmonicam et trihemitonium chromaticum generi diatonico associant. Semitonium loco toni et e converso commutant, in quo quidem a cunctis nationibus in cantu discordant. 80

187:15. Notas procellares communiter abjiciunt, unde et omnes nationes eisdem utentes voces tremulas dicunt habere. In quibus quidem dictis finaliter dictorum modus cantandi et formandi notas et pausas cantus ecclesiastici concluditur. 69

187:20. Hic autem uterque modus cantandi scilicet et formandi notas et pausas ecclesiastici cantus magis et minus pro tempore observetur. Si quis enim indifferenter utitur ipso, non discernens vocum imbecillitates et ipsos dies feriales, non uti, sed potius abuti dictis modis diceretur. Solum igitur in dominicis diebus et festis praecipuis modi, quos diximus, sunt tenendi. In profestis vero diebus modus quidem omnino idem, quantum scilicet ad V notas speciales, formaliter commutatis tamen longis notis in semibreves et semibrevibus in brevissimas, necnon et commutatis temporibus modernorum in tempora antiquorum est tenendus. 34

187:31. Ut igitur tam ordinate simul et debite a duobus vel etiam a pluribus cantetur cantus ecclesiasticus, quinque sunt cantantibus necessaria: 27

188:1. Primum est, ut cantus cantandus diligenter simul ab omnibus praevideatur et in ipsa qualitate sive quantitate harmonici temporis vel secundum antiquos vel etiam secundum modernos unanimiter conveniant.   27

188:5. Secundum est, ut quantumcumque sint omnes aequaliter boni cantores, unum tamen praecentorem et directorem sui constituant, ad quem diligentissime attendant, et non aliud quam ipse sive in notis sive etiam in pausis dicant. Hoc enim est pulcherrimum.   27

188:10. Tertium est, ut voces dissimiles in tali cantu non misceant, cum non naturaliter sed vulgariter loquendo quaedam voces sint pectoris, quaedam gutturis, quaedam vero sint ipsius capitis. Voces dicimus pectoris, quae formant notas in pectore, gutturis, quae in gutture, capitis autem, quae formant notas in capite. Voces pectoris valent in gravibus, gutturis in acutis, capitis autem in superacutis. Nam communiter voces grossae et bassae sunt pectoris, voces subtiles et altissimae sunt capitis, voces vero inter has mediae sunt ipsius gutturis. Nulla igitur ex his alteri jungatur in cantu, sed vox pectoris pectorali, gutturis gutturali, capitis autem capitali.   27

188:22. Quoniam autem omnes voces vigorem consequuntur ex pectore, ideo quarto necessarium est, ut nunquam adeo cantus alte incipiatur, praecipue ab habentibus voces capitis, quin ad minus unam notam ceteris bassiorem pro fundamento suae vocis statuant in pectore, et nec nimis basse, quod est ululare, nec nimis alte, quod est clamare, sed mediocriter, quod est cantare, ita scilicet, ut non cantus voci, sed vox cantui dominetur, semper incipiant. Alias pulchrae notae formari non possunt.   28

188:31. Si quis autem plures pulchras notas scire desiderat, hoc pro regula teneat, ut nullius etiam rudissimi cantum despiciat, sed ad cantum omnium diligenter attendat, quia cum molaris rota discretum aliquando reddat stridorem ipsa quid agat nesciens, impossibile est, quod animal rationale cupiens omnes suos actus in debitum finem dirigere, quin aliquando saltem a casu et a fortuna debitam et pulchram notam faciat. Cumque sibi placentem notam audierit, ut ipsam in habitu habeat, diligenter retineat.   28

189:3. Praecipuum autem impedimentum faciendi pulchras notas est cordis tristitia, eo quod nulla nota valet nec valere potest, quae non procedit ex cordis hilaritate. Propter quod melancholici pulchras quidem voces habere possunt, pulchre vero cantare non possunt.   28

30. Johannes Affligemensis, *De musica cum tonario*. He is often referred to as John Cotton or Cotto, and some modern writers believe he was from England. Most probably he was from the monastery of Afflighem (near Brussels). The treatise was probably written *c*.1100, in southern Germany, between St Gall and Bamberg. Latin citation from Johannes Affligemensis, *De musica cum tonario*. English translation: *Hucbald, Guido, and John on Music*, 147.

133. Cum enim in usualibus neumis intervalla discerni non valeant, cantusque, qui per eas discuntur, stabili memoriae commendari nequeant, ideoque in cantibus plurimae falsitates subrepant. Hae autem omnia intervalla distincte demonstrent, usque adeo, ut et errorem penitus excludant, et oblivionem canendi, si semel perfecte sint cognitae, non admittant: quis non magnam in eis utilitatem esse videat?

Qualiter autem irregulares neumae errorem potius quam scientiam generent in virgulis et clinibus atque podatis considerari perfacile est, quoniam quidem et aequaliter omnes disponuntur, et nullus elevationis vel depositionis modus per eas exprimitur.   123

138. Solent autem nonnulli neumas illas quibusdam notis resarcire, per quas cantorem videntur non docere, sed duplicato errore impedire. Nam cum in neumis nulla sit certitudo, notae suprascriptae non minorem praetendunt dubitationem, praesertim cum per eas multae dictiones diversarum significationum incipiant, ideoque ignoretur quid significent. Sed et si eis tribuatur aliqua certa significatio, non tamen per hoc extirpatur omnis dubitatio, dum cantor adhuc manet incertus de modo intensionis et remissionis; siquidem .c. diversarum dictionum principium est, veluti cito, caute, clamose; similiter .l. ut leva leniter, lascive, lugubriter; simili modo .s. quemadmodum sursum, suaviter, subito, sustenta, similiter, etc.   33–4

31. Johannes Boen [Boon], *Musica*. A Dutch priest and music theorist who attended Oxford and the University of Paris and died in Rijnsburg in 1367. He wrote two music treatises, *Ars musicae, c.*1350, which comments on the teachings of Johannes de Muris, and *Musica, c.*1355–7, which is the source of the excerpts given here. Latin citations from Frobenius, *Johannes Boens Musica und seine Konsonanzenlehre*.

45. Nam secundum diversitatem temporis et regionum multa nova et inaudita poterunt suboriri, sicut forte pronuntiatio commatis et trium semitoniorum minorum ac multorum similium, que, licet hactenus non audita sunt, forte tractu temporis per nova instrumenta et vocum habilitates posterius audientur, sicut nec ante Pitagoram fuit tanta subtilitas in cantu, quanta hodiernis temporibus est in usu, nec talem nos, qualem Anglici, G<alli>ci vel Lumbardi in cantu facimus fracturam.   85, 89

63. Sed ne dicta conclusio lateat indiscussa, est subtilius advertendum, quod modernus usus dictas litteras in clavibus extra naturam monocordi manualis admittit solum propter consonantias vel lasciviam ipsius cantus—non enim tantis olim quantis nunc in prolatione practica alicuius cantilene lasciviis homines inhyarunt—; et ut hec lasciva iocunditas absque omnimoda novi monocordi compositione signari possit in scriptis, sicut habet fieri in sonis, ut signum signato respondeat, rationabiliter eas litteras et earum effectus in diversis clavibus usus admisit.   85

76. Secunda forte ratio stat in regione vel tempore. Diverse namque regiones diversos cantus exigunt, ut in hoc experimento—dum scolas Oxonienses in Anglia colui, quam regionem a Comitatu Hollandie, loco mee nativitatis, solum mare discriminat—audito, quod layci ibidem et clerici, senes, iuvenes et indifferenter omnes tertiis et sextis tantam atribuebant affectionem quodque, duplis et quintis postpositis, ipsas solas invocantes quasi adorare videbam; vehementer attonitus de tam vicine regionis diversa natura continue ammirabar.   144–5

32. Johannes de Garlandia, *De mensurabili musica*. From Paris, late 13th c.[3] Latin citations from *De mensurabili musica*, ed. Reimer, i. English translations: Antley,

---

[3] According to Reimer, ii. 39–42, chs. 14–16, on three- and four-voice discant writing, from which most of the Garlandia excerpts here are taken, is considered to be an unauthentic appendix to Garlandia's treatise, added when Jerome of Moravia included the revised edition with his own treatise. See Ch. 4 n. 10.

'The Rhythm of Medieval Music'; and Johannes de Garlandia, *Concerning Measured Music*, trans. Birnbaum.

95:10. Color est pulchritudo soni vel obiectum auditus per quod auditus suscipit placentiam. Et fit multis modis: aut sono ordinato, aut in florificatione soni, aut in repetitione eiusdem vocis vel diversae. In sono ordinato fit dupliciter: aut respectu unius secundum proportionem infra diapente, ut hic: [example] aut respectu plurium infra diapason proprie, ut patet in exemplo, et per abundantiam usque ad triplum. Et tali ordinatione utimur in instrumentis triplicibus et quadruplicibus. 　　　　　　　　　　9, 71

95:14. In florificatione vocis fit color, ut comminutio in conductis simplicibus. Et fit semper ista commixtio in sonis coniunctis et non disjunctis, ut hic apparet: [example]. Repetitio eiusdem vocis est color faciens ignotum sonum esse notum, per quam notitiam auditus suscipit placentiam. Et isto modo utimur in rondellis et cantilenis vulgaribus. 　　　73

96:22. Nobilitatio soni est augmentatio eiusdem vel diminutio per modum superbiae, in augmentatione, ut melius videatur, in grossitudine, ut bene audiatur, in fictione, ut melius appetatur, in dimissione, ut spiritus recurventur. 　　　　　　　　　　　　8

97:16. Tertia regula est: pone colores loco sonorum proportionator\<um\> ignotorum, et quanto magis colores, tanto sonus erit magis notus, et si fuerit notus, erit placens. Item loco coloris in regione cuiuslibet pone cantilenam notam copulam vel punctum vel descensum vel ascensum alicuius instrumenti vel clausam lay. 　　　　　　　　9

33. Johannes de Grocheio, *De musica*. From Paris, end of the 13th c. Latin citations from Rohloff, *Die Quellenhandschriften*, with corrections by Christopher Page, 'Johannes de Grocheio on Secular Music: A Corrected Text and a New Translation', *Plainsong and Medieval Music*, 2 (1993), 17–41.[4] English translations: Seay, *Johannes de Grocheo*, and (partial trans.) Page, 'Johannes de Grocheio'.

130:112. Cantus coronatus ab aliquibus simplex conductus dictus est. Qui propter eius bonitatem in dictamine et cantu a magistris et studentibus circa sonos coronatur, sicut gallice *Ausi com l'unicorne* vel *Quant li roussignol*. Qui etiam a regibus et nobilibus solet componi et etiam coram regibus et principibus terrae decantari, ut eorum animos ad audaciam et fortitudinem, magnanimitatem et liberalitatem commoveat, quae omnia faciunt ad bonum regimen. Est enim cantus iste de delectabili materia et ardua, sicut de amicitia et caritate, et ex omnibus longis et perfectis efficitur. 　　　　35, 107–8

132:120. Cantilena, quae dicitur stantipes, est illa, in qua est diversitas in partibus et refractu tam in consonantia dictaminis quam in cantu . . . Haec autem facit animos iuvenum et puellarum propter sui difficultatem circa hanc stare et eos a prava cogitatione divertit. 　　　　　　　　　　　　　　　　　　　　　　　　　　　　35

132:121. Ductia vero est cantilena levis et velox in ascensu et decensu, quae in choreis a iuvenibus et puellis decantatur . . . Haec enim ducit corda puellarum et iuvenum et a vanitate removet, et contra passionem, quae dicitur amor vel ἔρως, valere dicitur.[5] 　　35

---

[4] For speculation as to his possible family name and place of origin see p. 18.

[5] Page, 'Johannes de Grocheio', 27 n. 39, points out that the manuscripts transmit *amor heros* ('erotic love'), which Rohloff has edited to '*amor vel eros*', using Greek for the last word.

134:135. Nos autem hic non intendimus instrumentorum compositionem vel divisionem nisi propter diversitatem formarum musicalium, quae in eis generantur. Inter quae instrumenta cum chordis principatum obtinent . . . 115

134:137. Et adhuc inter omnia instrumenta chordosa, visa a nobis, viella videtur praevalere. Quemadmodum enim anima intellectiva alias formas naturales in se virtualiter includit et ut tetragonum trigonum et maior numerus minorem, ita viella in se virtualiter alia continet instrumenta. 115

134:139. Bonum autem artifex in viella omnem cantum et cantilenam et omnem formam musicalem generaliter introducit. 111

134:140. Est autem ductia sonus illitteratus, cum decenti percussione mensuratus . . . eo quod ictus eam mensurant et motum facientis et excitant animum hominis ad ornate movendum secundum artem, quam ballare vocant, et eius motum mensurant in ductiis et choreis. 36

134:141. Stantipes vero est sonus illitteratus, habens difficilem concordantiarum discretionem, per puncta determinatus . . . Propter enim eius difficultatem facit animum facientis circa eam stare et etiam animum advertentis et multoties animos divitum a prava cogitatione divertit. 35

142:176. Et ulterius, cum cantus aliquoties sit sine dictamine et discretione syllabarum, ut signum signato responderet, oportuit haec ligatione figurarum repraesentare. 29

142:179. Istis autem figuris diversimode significantionem tribuerunt. Unde sciens cantare et exprimere cantum secundum quosdam, secundum alios non est sciens. Omnium autem istorum diversitas apparebit diversos tractatus aliorum intuenti. 29

156:241. Hymnus est cantus ornatus, plures habens versus. Dico autem ornatus ad modum cantus coronati, qui habet concordantias pulchras et ornate ordinatas. Sed ab eo differt, eo quod in cantu coronato est numerus <versuum> determinatus ad septem vel eo circa, in hymnis vero ad plus <vel> ad minus ut plurimum est inventus. Et cantus iste immediate post invitatorium et Venite in matutinis et post Deus, in adiutorium in horis decantatur, ut Christi fidelibus invitatis eorum corda et animos excitet ad devotionem et extollat ad psalmos et legendas audiendum. Et iterum post legendas resumitur, ut eos revigilet et revigoret ad psalmos evangelistas et vigorosius exorandum. 36, 109

160:255. Cantus autem iste post psalmos decantatur. Et aliquoties neupma additur, puta post psalmos evangelistas. Est autem neupma quasi cauda vel exitus sequens antiphonam, quemadmodum in viella post cantum coronatum vel stantipedem exitus, quem modum viellatores appellant. 111

162:270. Sed <Gloria> sine Kyrie eleison numquam invenitur. Isti autem cantus cantantur tractim et ex longis et perfectis ad modum cantus coronati, ut corda audientium ad devote orandum promoveantur et ad devote audiendum orationem, quam immediate dicit sacerdos vel ad hoc ordinatus. 36, 108

162:273. In fine autem versus resumitur Alleluia. Et <in> alleluia additur cauda quaedam, sicut neupma in antiphonis. Et multoties loco caudae cantatur sequentia, puta cum missa celebratur cum maiori sollemnitate. 111

164:276. Isti autem tres cantus, puta responsorium, alleluia et sequentia, cantantur immediate post epistolam et ante evangelium in mysterio et reverentia trinitatis.

Responsorium autem et alleluia decantantur ad modum stantipedis vel cantus coronati, ut devotionem et humilitatem in cordibus auditorum imponant. Sed sequentia cantatur ad modum ductiae, ut ea ducat et laetificet, ut recte recipiant verba novi testamenti, puta sacrum evangelium, quod statim postea decantatur.   34–5

164:280. Hunc autem cantum sequitur offertorium, quod est cantus ex pluribus concordantiis compositus ad modum simplicis conductus et ascendit et descendit recte. Et etiam incipit et mediatur et finitur secundum regulas tonorum, et secundum octo modos plenarie variatur. Et cantatur ad modum ductiae vel cantus coronati, ut corda fidelium excitet ad devote offerendum.   36, 109

34. Johannes de Muris, *Musica speculativa*. Written in 1323. Author was born in Lisieux *c*.1300 and died in 1350. He was a mathematician, astronomer, and music theorist, and taught at the University of Paris as *magister artium*. His writings on proportion and mensural notation were more widely circulated than any other for over a hundred years after his death. Latin citation from *Die* Musica speculativa *des Johannes de Muris*, ed. Falkenroth, 262, 264, 266. Another edition of the treatise *Musica speculativa*, ed. Fast. The English translation is by Andrew Hughes.

Sed miror multum et nescio, quod in partibus nostris, ubi viget religio katholica fidelium in orbe terrarum, numquam in usu ceciderunt illa duo genera melodiarum, 'chromaticum' et 'enarmonicum', sed in genere diatonico omnis cantus ecclesiasticus, quem invenerunt sancti patres et doctores et homines bonae mentis et dignae memoriae <est>. Omnis cantus mensuratus per tempora certa, ut in conductis, modulis, cantilenis caeterisque modis, omnisque cantus laicorum virorum et mulierum, iuvenum et senum, omnisque cantus cunctorum nostrorum instrumentorum—nescio quo spiritu, nisi divino quodam nutu et spontanea voluntate—naturaliter incidit et sonetur per diatonicum; in qua parte orbis terrarum, in quibus angulis regionum, sub qua parte caeli modo latitant alia duo genera, nescio. Nihil plus opinor nisi quod quasi contra naturalem inclinationem humanarum vocum ad cantus divisa sunt. Scio enim, quod aut vix aut numquam humana vox in his generibus concordaret nec umquam de seipsa certa esset; in instrumento tamen possibile est multum. Tamen non dubito, <quin> dura et aspera iniocundaque esset illa musica istorum duorum modorum hominibus imbutis in tertio genere diatonico, ut nos sumus: hoc autem non ignoro, quin posset diatesseron etiam dividi in quinque semitonia per maiora et minora, per commata. Sed ex hoc esset excedere tetrachordum in figuris et chordis; verbi gratia de praedictis patet in figura.   84–5

35. Johannes Tinctoris, *Liber de arte contrapuncti*. The author taught at cathedrals of Orléans and Chartres. Treatise dated 1477. Latin citation from Tinctoris, *Opera theoretica*, ii. 107. English translation: Johannes Tinctoris, *The Art of Counterpoint*.

107. Porro tam simplex quam diminutus contrapunctus dupliciter fit, hoc est aut scripto aut mente.

   Contrapunctus qui scripto fit communiter res facta nominatur. At istum quem mentaliter conficimus absolute contrapunctum vocamus, et hunc qui faciunt super librum cantare vulgariter dicuntur.   5

36. John the Deacon. Rome, 9th c. Cited from Müller-Heuser, *Vox Humana*, 89 n. 131.

Alpina siquidem corpora vocum suarum tonitruis altisonae perstrepentia susceptae modulationis dulcedinem proprie non resultant, quia bibuli gutturis grossitas dum inflexionibus et repercussionibus et diaphoniarum diphthongis mitem nititur edere cantilenam, naturali quodam fragore quasi plaustra per gradus confuse sonantia rigidas voces iactat.   17

37. John of Salisbury, *Policraticus*. Born near Salisbury *c*.1115–25, studied in Paris with Peter Abelard. He was secretary and counsellor to Theobald, archbishop of Canterbury, but left England in 1164 to stay for a few years in Reims. He was bishop of Chartres from 1176 until his death in 1180. Latin citation from *Policraticus* –IV, ed. Keats-Rohan, 48–9. English translation: Dalglish, 'The Origin of the Hocket'.

48. Ipsum quoque cultum religionis incestat quod ante conspectum Domini . . . lasciuientis uocis luxu, quadam ostentatione sui, muliebribus modis notularum articulorumque caesuris, stupentes animulas emollire nituntur. Cum praecinentium et succinentium, concinentium et decinentium, intercinentium et occinentium praemolles modulationes audieris, Sirenarum concentus credas esse non hominum . . . Ea siquidem est ascendendi descendendique facilitas, ea sectio uel geminatio notularum, ea replicatio articulorum singulorumque consolidatio, sic acuta uel acutissima grauibus et subgrauibus temperantur ut auribus sui iudicii fere subtrahatur auctoritas, et animus quem tantae suauitatis demulsit gratia, auditorum merita examinare non sufficiat. Cum haec quidem modum excesserint, lumborum pruriginem quam deuotionem mentis poterunt citius excitare.   23, 45–6

38. Lambertus (Pseudo-Aristotle), *Tractatus de musica*. End of the 13th c., perhaps from France. Latin citation from Coussemaker, *Scriptores*, i.

273. Prima differentia plice perfecte descendendo, est quedam figura duos habens tractus, quorum ultimus longior est primo, ut patet hic: ⌐
Ascendendo vero unum solum retinet tractum, ut patet: ♩

Habet autem omnem potestatem, regulam et naturam quam habet perfecta longa, nisi quod in corpore duo tempora tenet et unum in membris. Fit autem plica in voce per compositionem epiglotti cum repercussione gutturis subtiliter inclusa.

Seconda differentia est plica imperfecta, in forma perfecte similis, sed regulam imperfecte tenet et naturam, et continet unum tempus in corpore et reliquum in membris:
⌐ ∟   51

39. Marchettus of Padua, *Lucidarium*. Written in 1317–18. Latin citation from Herlinger, *The Lucidarium*. English translation: Herlinger.

2.8.9–10. Hec enim bipartitio toni debet fieri cum colore ficticio, ut qui eam profert fingat in primo descensu, qui est dyesis, ac si vellet post talem descensum sursum redire; post hec cromaticum descendat, et sic consonantia, licet minus naturaliter et proprie, subsequitur.   82

40. Notker, *Litterae significativae.* (Sometimes known as Notker 'Balbulus'.) From St Gall, d. 912. This is a letter addressed to Lantbert explaining the meaning of the letters used in St Gall notation. Latin citation from Froger, 'L' Épître de Notker', 23–72.

Notker Lantberto fratri salutem
Quid singulae litterae in superscriptione significent cantilenae, prout potui iuxta tuam petitionem explanare curavi.

A. Ut altius elevetur, admonet.

B. Secundum litteras quibus adiungitur, ut bene id est multum extollatur vel gravetur sive teneatur, belgicat.

C. Ut cito vel celeriter dicatur certificat.

D. Ut deprimatur demonstrat.

E. Ut equaliter sonetur eloquitur.

F. Ut cum fragore seu frendore feriatur efflagitat.

G. Ut in gutture gradatim garruletur genuine gratulatur.

H. Ut tantum in scriptura aspirat, ita et in nota idipsum habitat.

I. Iusum vel inferius insinuat, gravitudinemque pro g interdum indicat.

K. Licet apud latinos nihil valeat, apud nos tamen alemannos pro [χ] graeca positum, klenche id est clange clamitat.

L. Levare laetatur.

M. Mediocriter melodiam moderari mendicando memorat.

N. Notare hoc est noscitare notificat.

O. Figuram sui in ore cantantis ordinat.

P. Pressionem vel prensionem praedicat.

Q. In significationibus notarum cur quaeratur? cum etiam in verbis ad nihil aliud scribatur nisi ut sequens V vim suam amittere queratur.

R. Rectitudinem vel rasuram non abolitionis sed crispationis rogitat.

S. Susum vel sursum scandere sibilat.

T. Trahere vel tenere debere testatur.

V. Licet amissa vi sua valde veluti vau greca vel hebrea velificat.

X. Quamvis latina per se verba non inchoet, tamen expectare expetit.

Y. Apud Latinos nihil hymnizat.

Z. Vero licet et ipsa mere greca, et ob id haut necessaria romanis, propter praedictam tamen r litterae occupationem, ad alia requirere, in sua lingua zitîse [final verb supplied in another hand: require]

Ubicumque autem due vel tres aut plures litterae ponuntur in uno loco, ex superiori interpretatione, maximeque illa quam de b dixi, quid sibi velint facile poterit adverti. 32–3

41. Petrus dictus Palma ociosa, *Compendium de discantu mensurabili*. A member of the Cistercian order in the Cherchamps cloister in the diocese of Amiens. Treatise written in 1336. Latin citation from Wolf, 'Ein Beitrag', 516–17.

Dicunt enim flores musicae mensurabilis, quando plures voces seu notulae, quod idem est, diversimode figuratae secundum uniuscuiusque qualitatem ad unam vocem seu notulam simplicem tantum quantitatem illarum vocum continentem iusta proportione reducuntur. Quamvis autem nonnulli dicant et affirment flores scientiae musicalis fore innumerabiles secundum diversos modos discantus, et de innumerabilibus non valet haberi certitudo, volentes ob hanc causam de floribus huiusmodi aliquam artem componere. Tamen ne iuvenes et alii cupientes in dicta scientia proficere aliquam artem de eadem non habentes ob hoc fiant tepidi et remissi istam scilicet addiscendo, idcirco ego circa capacitatem ingenioli mei XII modos seu maneries de discantu mensurabili floribus adornato compilavi. 10, 88

42. Regino of Prüm, *Epistola de armonica institutione*. Treatise addressed to Archbishop Rathbod of Trier in early 10th c. Author was abbot of the monastery of Prüm in western Germany from 882 to 899. He died in Trier in 915. Latin citation from Gerbert, *Scriptores*, i. English translation: Bower, 'Natural and Artificial Music', 18–19.

230. Cum frequenter in ecclesiae vestrae dioecesibus chorus psallentium psalmorum melodiam confusis resonaret vocibus, propter dissonantiam toni, & pro huiuscemodi re vestram venerationem saepe commotam vidissem; arripui Antiphonarium, & eum a principio usque in finem per ordinem diligenter revolvens, antiphonas, quas in illo adnotatas reperi, propriis, ut reor distribui tonis. 21

43. Rudolf of St Trond (possible author), *Questiones in musica*. Rudolf was abbot of St Truiden (near Liège). Treatise written *c.*1120. Latin citation from Steglich, *Die Quaestiones in Musica*. This section of the treatise is taken from the *Musica enchiriadis*, written *c.*900.

60. Numerose igitur canere est, ut adtendatur, ubi productioribus, ubi brevioribus morulis utendum sit. Quatinus uti, quae sillabae breves, quaeque sint longae, adtenditur, ita, qui soni producti quique correpti esse debent, adtendatur, ut ea, quae diu, ad ea, quae non diu, legitime concurrant ac veluti metricis pedibus cantilena plaudatur. Age canamus exercitii usu. Plaudam pedes ego in praecinendo, tu sequendo imitabere. Solae in tribus membris ultimae longae, reliquae breves sunt [musical example missing]. Sic itaque numerose est canere, longis brevibusque sonis morulas ratas metiri nec per loca contrahere vel protrahere magis quam oportet, sed infra scandendi legem vocem continere, ut possit melum finiri mora, qua caepit. Vel si aliquociens moram mutare velis, id est circa initium et finem protensiorem vel incitatiorem cursum facere, duplo id feceris, id est ut productam moram duplo correptiore seu correptam immutes duplo

longiore. Sumamus quodvis canere melum nunc correptius nunc productius, ita ut morulae, quae nunc sunt productae correptis suis, nunc item fiant pro correptis ad eas, quae fuerint productiores se. Canamus modo: [text examples].[6] Prima sit mora correptior, subiungatur producta, tunc correpta iterum. Haec igitur numerositatis ratio doctam semper cantionem docet et hac maxima sua dignitate ornatur seu ab uno, seu a pluribus, seu tractim seu cursim canatur. Fitque, ut, dum numerose canendo alius alio nec plus nec minus protrahit aut contrahit, quasi ex uno ore vox multitudinis audiatur. Item in alternando seu praecinendo et respondendo per eandem numerositatem non minus morae concordia servanda est quam sonorum.

Morarum ergo concordia fit, si id, quod subiungendum est, aut aequali mora repondeat sive pro conpetenti causa duplo longiore aut duplo breviore.   76–7

44. *Statuta antiqua* of the Carthusian Order, *c.*1250. This was a compilation of statutes in England. Latin citation from Gerbert, *De cantu et musica sacra*, ii. 97.

Quia boni monachi officium est plangere potius, quam cantare, sic cantemus voce, ut planctus, non cantus delectatio sit in corde: quod . . . poterit fieri, si ea, quae cantando delectationem afferunt, amputentur, ut est fractio & inundatio vocis, & geminatio puncti, & similia, quae potius ad curiositatem attinent, quam ad simplicem cantum.   25

45. Walter Odington, *Summa de speculatione musice*. Author from Evesham (near Worcester); treatise written between 1280 and 1320. Latin citations from Walter Odington, *Summa de speculatione musice*, ed. Hammond. English translation: Walter Odington, *De speculatione musicae*, trans. Huff.

94. Apostropha est species accentus quae tollit ultimam vocalem dictionis cum sequens dictio inchoat a vocali cuius figura est haec: . . . Semivocalis medietatem sui temporis transfert ad aliam vocem. Quae dicitur semivocalis descendens semitonus dicitur ascendo. Gutturalis dicitur quia cillenti gutture formatur. Sinuosa dicta quia recurvatur ad similitudinem baculi pastoralis.   52, 57, Ch. 3 n. 12

95. Pes quassus dictus quia voce tremula et multum mota formatur, quassum enim violenter motum est. Quilissimi dicti ad similitudinem, quilos enim graece humor et mus terra, quasi humida terra a receptione aquarum.   53, 78

129. Plica est inflexio vocis a voce sub una figura. Solae longae et breves sunt plicabiles. Plicarum alia ascendens, alia descendens, quae in plano <cantu> vocantur semitonus et semivocalis.   51

140. Est et alia species, quae procedit per binariam ligaturam sicut secundus modus, sed velocior est et longam immensuratam accipit in principio, quae Copula dicitur, nomen habens a re. Est et alia copula quae singulos habet punctos per se morosior quam sextus modus, dicta per contrarium quia non copulatur.   41

141. Fit igitur organum purum hoc modo. Accepto uno puncto vel duobus aut tribus de plano cantu certo <modo> disponitur tenor, et superius proceditur per concordias et

---

[6] See Ch. 4 n. 15.

concordes discordias quantumlibet. Incipit autem superior cantus in diapason supra tenorem vel diapente vel diatessaron et desinit in diapason vel diapente vel unisono. Et est cantandum leniter et subtiliter, descensus vero cito et aequaliter, tenor autem tremule teneatur et cum discordo offendit. [Ex. 4.9]   78–9

146. Acutiorem cantum cantaturus incipiat et sicut copulae sufficiat isto utens puncto qui diu teneatur cui omnes alii succedant qui distincte canant et aequaliter secundum commensurationem temporum leniter sed ascultando et plane desinant cum paenultimo puncto producto. Alii vero sunt ornatus psallendi qui non verbisque sed voce tenui exprimi possunt.   42

Bibliography

AGUSTONI, LUIGI, 'I neumi liquescenti', *Musica sacra* (Milan), 83 (1953), 34–42.

AILRED OF RIEVAULX, *Aelredi Rievallensis Opera omnia*, ed. Dom A. Hoste and C. H. Talbot (Corpus Christianorum, Continuatio mediaeualis, 1; 1971).

ALBAROSA, NINO, 'Un elemento liquescente nelle notazione nonantolana', *Rivista internazionale di musica sacra*, 1 (1980), 171–89.

——'La notazione neumatica di Nonantola', *Rivista italiana di musicologia*, 14 (1979), 225–310.

ANDERSON, GORDON A. (ed.), *The Las Huelgas Manuscript* (CMM 79; American Institute of Musicology, 1982).

ANONYMOUS, *Ars musicae mensurabilis secundum Franconem*, ed. Gilbert Reaney and Andreas Gilles (CSM 15; Rome, 1971).

ANONYMOUS, *Breviarium regulare musicae* (Willelmus), ed. Gilbert Reaney (CSM 12; American Institute of Musicology, 1966).

ANONYMOUS 2, *Tractatus de discantu*, trans. Albert Seay (Critical Texts and Translations, 1; Colorado Springs, 1977).

ANSELMI, GIORGIO, *De Musica*, ed. Giuseppe Massera (Florence, 1961).

ANTLEY, BOB RICHARD, 'The Rhythm of Medieval Music: A Study in the Relationship of Stress and Quantity and a Theory of Reconstruction with a Translation of John of Garland's De Mensurabili Musica' (Ph.D. diss., Florida State University, 1977).

APEL, WILLI, *Gregorian Chant* (Bloomington, Ind., 1958).

—— *The Notation of Polyphonic Music, 900–1600* (Cambridge, Mass., 1953).

ARIBO, *De musica*, ed. Joseph Smits van Waesberghe (CSM 2; Rome, 1951).

AURELIAN OF RÉÔME, *The Discipline of Music (Musica Disciplina)*, trans. Joseph Ponte (Colorado College Music Press Translations, 3; Colorado Springs, 1968).

—— *Musica disciplina*, ed. Lawrence Gushee (CSM 21; American Institute of Musicology, 1975).

BACILLY, BÉNIGNE DE, *A Commentary upon the Art of Proper Singing*, trans. and ed. Austin B. Caswell (Brooklyn, 1968).

BARALLI, D. RAFFAELLO, AND TORRI, LUIGI, 'Il *Trattato* di Prosdocimo de' Beldomandi contra il *Lucidario* di Marchetto da Padova per la prima volta trascritto e illustrato', *Rivista musicale italiana*, 20 (1913), 731–62.

BECK, JEAN BAPTISTE, *Die Melodien der Troubadours* (Strasburg, 1908).

BENT, MARGARET, '*Resfacta* and *Cantare Super Librum*', *JAMS* 36 (1983), 371–91.

BERNARD OF CLAIRVAUX, Sämtliche Werke, ed. Gerhard B. Winkler, iii (Innsbruck, 1992).

BERNHARD, CHRISTOPH, 'On the Art of Singing; or, Manier', *The Music Forum*, 3 (1973), 13–29.

BINKLEY, THOMAS, 'The Work is not the Performance', in Tess Knighton and David Fallows (eds.), *Companion to Medieval and Renaissance Music* (New York, 1992), 36–43.

BLACKBURN, BONNIE J., 'A Lost Guide to Tinctoris's Teachings Recovered', *Early Music History*, 1 (1981), 29–116.

——'On Compositional Process in the Fifteenth Century', *JAMS* 40 (1987), 210–84.

BONAVENTURA DA BRESCIA, *Regula musice plane* (facs. edn., Monuments of Music and Music Literature in Facsimile, 77; New York, 1975).

—— *Rules of Plain Music (Breviloquium Musicale)*, trans. Albert Seay (Colorado College Music Press Translations, 11; Colorado Springs, 1979).

BONCELLA, PAUL ANTHONY LUKE, 'Toward a New Recension of the Frankish-Gregorian *Antiphonale Missarum*', in *Revista de musicología*, 16 (1993), 2229–45.

BOWER, CALVIN M., 'Natural and Artificial Music: The Origins and Development of an Aesthetic Concept', *MD* 25 (1971), 17–33.

BROWN, HOWARD MAYER, *Embellishing Sixteenth-Century Music* (Early Music Series, 1; London, 1977).

—— 'Improvised Ornamentation in the Fifteenth-Century Chanson', *Quadrivium*, 12 (1971), 235–58.

BRUNNER, LANCE W., 'The Performance of Plainchant: Some Preliminary Observations of the New Era', *Early Music*, 10 (1982), 317–28.

BURSTYN, SHAI, 'The "Arabian Influence" Thesis Revisited', *Current Musicology*, 45–7 (1990), 119–46.

BURTIUS, NICOLAUS, *Florum libellus*, ed. Giuseppe Massera (Florence, 1975).

CACCINI, GIULIO, *Le Nuove Musiche, 1601*, ed. and trans. H. Wiley Hitchcock (Madison, Wis., 1970).

CALDWELL, JOHN, 'Plainsong and Polyphony, 1250–1550', in Thomas Forrest Kelly (ed.), *Plainsong in the Age of Polyphony* (Cambridge Studies in Performance Practice, 2; Cambridge, 1992), 6–31.

CARDINE, EUGÈNE, *Semiologia gregoriana* (Rome, 1968); French trans. as 'Sémiologie grégorienne', *EG* 11 (1970); Eng. trans. by Robert M. Fowels: *Gregorian Semiology* (Solesmes, 1982).

—— 'La Sémiologie grégorienne', in Johannes B. Göschl, *Semiologische Untersuchungen zum Phänomen der gregorianischen Liqueszenz: Der isolierte dreistufige Epiphonus praepunctis, ein Sonderproblem der Liqueszenzforschung*, 2 vols. (Forschungen zur älteren Musikgeschichte, 3; Vienna, 1980), i, pp. i–xxv.

COHEN, JUDITH, 'A Medieval Bulgarian Performance Style?', *International Society of Early Music Singers Newsletter*, 1 (1983), 6–8.

—— 'Oral Tradition as a Clue to Ancient Practice', *Continuo*, 6 (1983), 16.

CONNOLLY, THOMAS H., 'The *Graduale* of S. Cecilia in Trastevere and the Old Roman Tradition', *JAMS* 28 (1975), 413–58.

——'Jewish Influence on Early Christian Chant: A New Model', paper delivered at the annual meeting of the American Musicological Society, 7 November 1996.

CORBIN, SOLANGE, 'Neumatic Notation' (parts I–IV), *New Grove*, xiii. 128–54.

—— 'Note sur l'ornamentation dans le plain-chant grégorien', *International Musicological Society: Report of the Eighth Congress, New York 1961* (Kassel, 1961), i. 428–39.

—— *Die Neumen* (Pälaeographie der Musik, 1/3; Cologne, 1977).

COUSSEMAKER, EDMUND DE, *Scriptores de musica medii aevi*, 4 vols. (Paris, 1864; repr. Hildesheim, 1963).

CROCKER, RICHARD, AND HILEY, DAVID (eds.), *The Early Middle Ages to 1300* (New Oxford History of Music, rev. edn., ii; Oxford, 1990).

CSERBA, SIMON M. (ed.), *Hieronymus de Moravia, O.P.: Tractatus de musica* (Freiburger Studien zur Musikwissenschaft, 2; Regensburg, 1935).

DALGLISH, WILLIAM, 'The Origin of the Hocket', *JAMS* 31 (1978), 3–20.

VAN DIJK, S. J., 'Saint Bernard and the Instituta Patrum of Saint Gall', *MD* 4 (1950) 99–109.

DITTMER, LUTHER (trans.), *Anonymous IV* (Musical Theorists in Translation, 1; Brooklyn, 1959).

DUFAY, GUILLAUME, *Opera omnia*, ed. H. Besseler, 6 vols. (CMM 1; Rome, 1964).

DYER, JOSEPH, 'A Thirteenth-Century Choirmaster: The *Scientia Artis Musicae* of Elias Salomon', *MQ* 66 (1980), 83–111.

EVERIST, MARK, *French 13th-Century Polyphony in the British Library* (London, 1988).

FALLOWS, DAVID, 'Embellishment and Urtext in the Fifteenth-Century Song Repertories', *Basler Jahrbuch für historische Musikpraxis*, 14 (1990), 59–85.

FERAND, ERNST T., 'A History of Music Seen in the Light of Ornamentation', *International Musicological Society: Report of the Eighth Congress, New York 1961* (Kassel, 1961), i. 463–69.

—— 'The Howling in Seconds of the Lombards', *MQ* 25 (1939), 313–24.

—— *Die Improvisation in Beispielen aus neun Jahrhunderten abendländischer Musik* (Cologne, 1956).

—— *Die Improvisation in der Musik* (Zurich, 1938).

FISCHER, KURT VON, 'Die Rolle der Mehrstimmigkeit am Dome von Siena zu Beginn des 13. Jahrhunderts', *Archiv für Musikwissenschaft*, 18 (1961), 167–82.

FRANCO OF COLOGNE, *Ars cantus mensurabilis*, ed. Gilbert Reaney and André Gilles (CSM 18; American Institute of Musicology, 1974).

FREISTEDT, HEINRICH, *Die liqueszierenden Noten des Gregorianischen Chorals* (Veröffentlichungen der Gregorianischen Akademie zu Freiburg, Heft 14; Freiburg, 1929).

FROBENIUS, WOLF, *Johannes Boens Musica und seine Konsonanzenlehre* (Stuttgart, 1971).

FROGER, JACQUES, 'L'Épître de Notker sur les "lettres significatives" ', *EG* 5 (1962), 23–72.

—— 'Les Prétendus Quarts de ton dans le chant grégorien et les symboles du ms. H. 159 de Montpellier', *EG* 17 (1978), 145–79.

GERBERT, MARTIN, *De cantu et musica sacra a prima ecclesiae aetate usque ad praesens tempus*, 2 vols. (St Blasien, 1774; repr. Graz, 1968).

—— *Scriptores ecclesiastici de musica sacra potissimum*, 3 vols. (St Blasien, 1784; repr. Hildesheim, 1963).

GILLINGHAM, BRYAN, *The Polyphonic Sequences in Codex Wolfenbuettel* (Musicological Studies, 35; Brooklyn, 1982).

GMELCH, JOSEPH, *Die Viertelstonstufen im Messtonale von Montpellier* (Eichstätt, 1911).

GODT, IRVING, AND RIVERA, BENITO, 'The Vatican Organum Treatise–A Colour Reproduction, Transcription, and Translation', in *Gordon Athol Anderson: In Memoriam*, 2 vols. (Musicological Studies, 49; Henryville–Ottawa–Binningen, 1984), ii. 264–345.

GÖSCHL, JOHANNES B., *Semiologische Untersuchungen zum Phänomen der gregorianis-*

chen Liqueszenz: Der isolierte dreistufige Epiphonus praepunctis, ein Sonderproblem der Liqueszenzforschung, 2 vols. (Forschungen zur älteren Musikgeschichte, 3; Vienna, 1980).

GRIER, JAMES, 'Scribal Practices in the Aquitanian Versaria of the Twelfth Century: Towards a Typology of Error and Variant', *JAMS* 45 (1992), 373–427.

—— 'Transmission in the Aquitanian Versaria of the Eleventh and Twelfth Centuries' (Ph.D. diss., University of Toronto, 1985).

GUIDO OF AREZZO, *Micrologus*, ed. Joseph Smits van Waesberghe (CSM 4; American Institute of Musicology, 1955).

GUILIELMUS MONACHUS, *De preceptis artis musicae*, ed. Albert Seay (CSM 11; Rome, 1965).

GÜMPEL, KARL-WERNER, 'El canto melódico de Toledo: algunas reflexiones sobre su origen y estilo', *Recerca Musicológica*, 8 (1988), 25–45.

GÜNTHER, URSULA, FINSCHER, LUDWIG, AND DEAN, JEFFREY (eds.), *Modality in the Music of the Fourteenth and Fifteenth Centuries/Modalität in der Musik des 14. und 15. Jahrhunderts* (Neuhausen–Stuttgart, 1996).

HANDSCHIN, JACQUES, 'Eine alte Neumenschrift', *Acta musicologica*, 22 (1950), 69–97.

HARRÁN, DON, *In Defense of Music* (Lincoln, Nebr., 1989).

HARASZTI, ÉMILE, 'La Technique des improvisateurs de langue vulgaire et de latin du quattrocento', *Revue belge de musicologie*, 9 (1955), 12–31.

HARUTUNIAN, JOHN, 'A Comparison of the Oriscus in the Introits of the Manuscript Vatican Latin 5319 with its "Translations" ' in those of the Manuscript Archivio di San Pietro F.22' (MA thesis, University of Pennsylvania, 1976).

HAUG, ANDREAS, 'Zur Interpretation der Liqueszenzneumen', *Archiv für Musikwissenschaft*, 50 (1993), 85–100.

HERLINGER, JAN, 'Marchetto's Division of the Whole Tone', *JAMS* 24 (1981), 193–216.

—— Marchetto's Influence: The Manuscript Evidence', in André Barbera (ed.), *Music Theory and its Sources: Antiquity and the Middle Ages* (Notre Dame, 1990), 235–58.

—— (ed.), *The Lucidarium of Marchetto of Padua* (Chicago, 1985).

HESBERT, DOM R. J., 'L'Interprétation de l' "equaliter" dans les manuscrits sangalliens', *Revue grégorienne*, 18 (1933), 161–73.

HEYDEN, SEBALD, *De arte canendi* (Nuremberg, 1540; facs. edn. New York, 1969). Translation and transcription in Clement A. Miller, *De Arte Canendi* (American Institute of Musicology, 1972).

HILEY, DAVID, 'Notation', *New Grove*, xiii. 347.

—— 'Plica', *New Grove*, xv. 12.

—— 'The Plica and Liquescence', in *Gordon Athol Anderson: In Memoriam*, 2 vols. (Musicological Studies, 49; Henryville–Ottawa–Binningen, 1984), ii. 379–91.

—— *Western Plainchant: A Handbook* (Oxford, 1993).

HOURLIER, JACQUES, AND HUGLO, MICHEL, 'La Notation paléofranque', *EG* 2 (1957), 212–19.

Hucbald, Guido, and John on Music: Three Medieval Treatises, trans. Warren Babb, ed. Claude V. Palisca (New Haven, 1978).

HUCKE, HELMUT, 'Die Herkunft der Kirchentonarten und die fränkische Überlieferung des Gregorianischen Gesangs', in *Bericht über den Internationalen Musikwissenschaftlichen Kongress Berlin 1975* (Kassel, 1980), 257–60.

—— 'Karolingische Renaissance und Gregorianischer Gesang', *Musikforschung*, 28 (1975), 4–18.

—— 'Toward a New Historical View of Gregorian Chant', *JAMS* 33 (1980), 437–67.

HUGLO, MICHEL, 'Bilan de 50 années de recherches (1939–1989) sur les notations musicales de 850 à 1300', *Acta musicologica*, 62 (1990), 224–59.

—— 'Les Noms des neumes et leur origine', *EG* 1 (1954), 53–67.

—— 'Notated Performance Practices in Parisian Chant Manuscripts of the Thirteenth Century', in Thomas Forrest Kelly (ed.), *Plainsong in the Age of Polyphony* (Cambridge, 1992), 32–44.

—— (ed.), *Musicologie médiévale: notations et séquences* (Paris, 1987).

JACOBSTHAL, GUSTAV, *Die chromatische Alteration im liturgischen Gesang der abendländischen Kirche* (Berlin, 1897; repr. Hildesheim, 1970).

JACQUES DE LIÈGE, *Speculum musice*, ed. Roger Bragard, 7 vols. (CSM 3; American Institute of Musicology, 1955–72).

JAMES, BRUNO S., *The Letters of St. Bernard of Clairvaux* (London, 1953).

JEFFERY, PETER, *Re-Envisioning Past Musical Cultures: Ethnomusicology in the Study of Gregorian Chant* (Chicago, 1992).

JOHANNES AFFLIGEMENSIS, *De musica cum tonario*, ed. Joseph Smits van Waesberghe (CSM 1; Rome, 1950).

JOHANNES DE GARLANDIA, *Concerning Measured Music*, trans. Stanley H. Birnbaum (Colorado College Music Press Translations, 9; Colorado Springs, 1978).

—— *De mensurabili musica*, ed. Erich Reimer, 2 vols. (Wiesbaden, 1972).

JOHANNES DE GROCHEO, *Concerning Music (De musica)*, trans. Albert Seay (Colorado Springs, 1967, rev. edn. 1973).

JOHANNES DE MURIS, *Musica speculativa*, ed. Susan Fast (Musicological Studies, 61; Ottawa, 1994).

—— *Die* Musica speculativa *des Johannes de Muris*, ed. Christoph Falkenroth (Stuttgart, 1992).

JOHN OF SALISBURY, *Ioannis Saresberiensis Policraticus I–IV*, ed. K. S. B. Keats-Rohan (Corpus Christianorum Continuatio mediaeualis, 118; Turnhout, 1993).

KARP, THEODORE, *The Polyphony of Saint Martial and Santiago de Compostela*, 2 vols. (Oxford, 1992).

LEECH-WILKINSON, DANIEL, 'Written and Improvised Polyphony', in *Polyphonies de tradition orale: Actes du colloque de Royaumont–1990* (Paris, 1993), 171–82.

LEVY, KENNETH, 'Charlemagne's Archetype of Gregorian Chant', *JAMS* 40 (1987), 1–30.

—— 'Latin Chant outside the Roman Tradition', in *The Early Middle Ages to 1300* (New Oxford History of Music, rev. edn.; Oxford, 1990), 69–110.

—— 'On Gregorian Orality', *JAMS* 43 (1990), 185–227.

—— 'On the Origin of Neumes', *Early Music History*, 7 (1987), 59–90.

MACCLINTOCK, CAROL, *Readings in the History of Music in Performance* (Bloomington, Ind., 1979).

MACHAUT, GUILLAUME DE, *Messe de nostre Dame*, ed. Daniel Leech-Wilkinson (Oxford Choral Music; Oxford, 1990).

MCGEE, TIMOTHY J., 'Eastern Influences in Medieval European Dances', in R. Falck and T. Rice (eds.), *Cross-Cultural Perspectives on Music* (Toronto, 1982), 79–100.

MCGEE, TIMOTHY J., 'The Liturgical Origins and Early History of the *Quem Quaeritis* Dialogue' (Ph.D. diss., University of Pittsburgh, 1974).

—— *Medieval and Renaissance Music: A Performer's Guide* (Toronto, 1985).

—— 'Medieval Dances: Matching the Repertory with Grocheio's Descriptions', *Journal of Musicology*, 7 (1989), 498–517.

—— *Medieval Instrumental Dances* (Bloomington, Ind., 1989).

—— ' "Ornamental" Neumes and Early Notation', *Performance Practice Review*, 9 (1996), 39–65.

—— 'Ornamentation, National Styles, and the Faenza Codex', *Early Music New Zealand*, 3 (1987), 3–14.

—— (ed.), with Klausner, David N., and Rigg, A. G., *Singing Early Music: A Guide to the Pronunciation of European Languages in the Middle Ages and Renaissance* (Bloomington, Ind., 1996).

MARTINEZ-GÖLLNER, MARIE LOUISE, 'Marchettus of Padua and Chromaticism', in *L'Ars nova italiana del Trecento*, 3 (1969), 187–202.

MILLET, JEAN, *La Belle Methode ou L'Art de Bien Chanter* (1666; repr. New York, 1973).

MOCQUEREAU, ANDRÉ, *Le Nombre musical grégorien*, 2 vols. (Rome and Tournai, 1908, 1927).

—— 'La Tradition rythmique grégorienne à propos du *Quilisma*', *Rassegna gregoriana*, 5 (1920), 225.

MÜLLER, HANS, *Eine Abhandlung über Mensuralmusik in der Karlsruher Handschrift St. Peter pergamen. 29a* (Leipzig, 1886).

MÜLLER-HEUSER, FRANZ, *Vox Humana: Ein Beitrag zur Untersuchung der Stimmästhetik des Mittelalters* (Kölner Beiträge zur Musikforschung, 26; Regensburg, 1963).

ODINGTON, WALTER, *De speculatione musicae*, pt. VI, trans. Jay A. Huff (MSD 31; American Institute of Musicology, 1973).

—— *Summa de speculatione musicae*, ed. Frederick F. Hammond (CSM 14; American Institute of Musicology, 1970).

PAGE, CHRISTOPHER, 'Jerome of Moravia on the *rubeba* and *viella*', *Galpin Society Journal*, 32 (1979), 77–98.

—— 'Johannes de Grocheio on Secular Music: A Corrected Text and a New Translation', *Plainsong and Medieval Music*, 2 (1993), 17–41.

—— 'A Treatise on Musicians from ?*c*.1400: The *Tractatulus de differentiis et gradibus cantorum* by Arnulf de St Ghislain', *Journal of the Royal Musical Association*, 117 (1992), 1–21.

—— 'Le Troisième Accord pour vièle de Jérome de Moravie–jongleurs et "anciens Pères" de France', in Christian Meyer (ed.), *Jérome de Moravie: un théoricien de la musique dans le milieu intellecteul parisien du XIIIᵉ siècle* (Paris, 1992), 83–96.

—— *Voices and Instruments of the Middle ages: Instrumental Practice and Songs in France 1100–1300* (London, 1987).

—— (ed.), *The Summa Musice: A Thirteenth-Century Manual for Singers* (Cambridge, 1991).

Paléographie musicale (repr. Berne, 1971).

PETROVIC, ANKICA, 'Les Techniques du chant villageois dans les Alpes dinariques (Yougoslavie)', *Cahiers de musiques traditionnelles*, 4 (1991), 103–15.

PHILLIPS, NANCY C., '*Musica* et *Scolica Enchiriadis*: The Literary, Theoretical, and Musical Sources' (Ph.D. diss., New York University, 1984).

PIRROTTA, NINO, 'Music and Cultural Tendencies in Fifteenth-Century Italy', in *Music and Culture in Italy from the Middle Ages to the Baroque* (Cambridge, Mass., 1984), 80–112.

—— '*Musica de sono humano* and the Musical Poetics of Guido of Arezzo', in *Music and Culture in Italy from the Middle Ages to the Baroque* (Cambridge, Mass., 1984), 1–12.

PLANCHART, ALEJANDRO ENRIQUE, 'The Transmission of Medieval Chant', in Iain Fenlon (ed.), *Music in Medieval and Early Modern Europe: Patronage, Sources and Texts* (Cambridge, 1981), 347–63.

REANEY, GILBERT, 'Color', *MGG*, iii. 1566–78.

RECKOW, FRITZ, *Der Musiktraktat des Anonymus 4*, 2 vols. (Wiesbaden, 1967).

ROESNER, EDWARD, 'The Emergence of Musica Mensurabilis', in Eugene K. Wolf and Edward H. Roesner (eds.), *Studies in Musical Sources and Style: Essays in Honor of Jan LaRue* (Madison, Wis., 1990), 42–74.

—— 'The Performance of Parisian Organum', *Early Music*, 7 (1979), 174–89.

ROHLOFF, ERNST, *Die Quellenhandschriften zum Musiktraktat des Johannes de Grocheio* (Leipzig, [1972]).

SACHS, CURT, 'Primitive and Medieval Music: A Parallel', *JAMS* 13 (1960), 43–9.

SHILOAH, AMNON, 'La Voix et les techniques vocales chez les Arabes', *Cahiers de musiques traditionnelles*, 4 (1991), 85–101.

SIMMS, ROBERT, 'Avaz in the Recordings of Mohammad Reza Shajarian' (Ph.D. diss., University of Toronto, 1996).

SNYDER, JOHN, 'Non-diatonic Tones in Plainsong: Theinred of Dover versus Guido d'Arezzo', in Marc Honegger et Paul Prevost (eds.), *La Musique et le rite sacre et profane* (Actes du XIII\ :sup:`e` Congrès de la Société Internationale de Musicologie, Strasbourg, 29 août–3 septembre 1982; Strasbourg, 1986), ii. 49–67.

SOWA, HEINRICH (ed.), *Ein anonymer glossierter Mensuraltraktat 1279* (Kassel, 1930).

SPANKE, HANS G., *Raynauds Bibliographie des altfranzösischen Liedes, neu bearbeitet und ergänzt, erster Teil* (Leiden, 1955).

STÄBLEIN, BRUNO, *Schriftbild der einstimmigen Musik* (Musikgeschichte in Bildern, 3: Musik des Mittelalters und der Renaissance; 4; Leipzig, 1975).

STEGLICH, RUDOLF (ed.), *Die Quaestiones in Musica: Ein Choraltraktat des zentralen Mittelalters und ihr mutmasslicher Verfasser Rudolf von St. Trond (1070–1138)* (Leipzig, 1911; repr. 1970).

STRUNK, OLIVER (ed.), *Source Readings in Music History* (New York, 1950).

SUÑOL, DOM GRÉGOIRE M., OSB, *Introduction à la paléographie musicale grégorienne* (Tournai, 1935).

THORNTON, BARBARA, 'Vokale und Gesangstechnik: Das Stimmideal der Aquitanischen Polyphonie', *Basler Jahrbuch für historische Musikpraxis*, 4 (1980), 133–50.

TINCTORIS, JOHANNES, *The Art of Counterpoint (Liber de arte contrapuncti)*, trans. Albert Seay (MSD 3; American Institute of Musicology, 1961).

—— *Opera theoretica*, ii, ed. Albert Seay (CSM 22; American Institute of Musicology, 1975).

TREITLER, LEO, 'The Early History of Music Writing in the West', *JAMS* 35 (1982), 237–79.

—— 'Oral, Written, and Literate Process in the Transmission of Medieval Music', *Speculum*, 56 (1981), 471–91.

—— 'Reading and Singing: On the Genesis of Occidental Music-Writing', *Early Music History*, 4 (1984), 135–208.

—— 'The "Unwritten" and "Written Transmission" of Medieval Chant and the Start-up of Musical Notation', *Journal of Musicology*, 10 (1992), 131–91.

VAN DER WERF, HENDRIK, *The Chansons of the Troubadours and Trouvères* (Utrecht, 1972).

—— (ed.), *Trouvères-Melodien II* (Monumenta monodica medii aevi, 12; Kassel, 1979).

VAN DEUSEN, NANCY, 'Style, Nationality and the Sequence in the Middle Ages', *Journal of the Plainsong and Medieval Music Society*, 5 (1982), 44–55.

VIVELL, P. CÖLESTIN, *Commentarius anonymus in Micrologum Guidonis Aretini* (Vienna, 1917).

WAESBERGHE, JOSEPH SMITS VAN, 'The Musical Notation of Guido of Arezzo', *MD* 5 (1951), 15–63.

—— 'Singen und Dirigieren der mehrstimmigen Musik im Mittelalter,' *Dia-pason: Ausgewählte Aufsätze von Joseph Smits van Waesberghe* (Buren, 1976), 165–87.

—— 'Verklaring der lettertekens (Litterae significantivae) in het Gregoriaansche neumenschrift van Sint Gallen', *Musiekgeschiedenis der Middeleeuwen* (Tilburg, 1939–42), ii.

—— (ed.), *Expositiones in Micrologum Guidonis Aretini* (Amsterdam, 1957).

WALLNER, BERTHA (ed.), *Das Buxheimer Orgelbuch* (Das Erbe deutscher Musik, 37–9; Kassel, 1958–9).

WARREN, CHARLES W., 'Punctus Organi and Cantus Coronatus in the Music of Dufay', in Allan W. Atlas (ed.), *Dufay Quincentenary Conference* (Brooklyn, 1976), 128–43.

WIESLI, WALTER, *Das Quilisma im Codex 359 der Stiftsbibliothek St. Gallen, erhellt durch das Zeugnis der Codices Einsiedeln 121, Bamberg lit. 6, Laon 239 und Chartres 47: Eine paläographisch-semiologische Studie* (Bethlehem Immensee, 1966).

WOLF, JOHANNES, 'Ein Beitrag zur Diskantlehre des 14. Jahrhunderts', *Sammelbände der internationalen Musikgesellschaft*, 15 (1914), 504–34.

YUDKIN, JEREMY, *The Music Treatise of Anonymous IV: A New Translation* (MSD 41; Neuhausen-Stuttgart, 1985).

—— 'The Rhythm of Organum Purum', *Journal of Musicology*, 2 (1983), 355–76.

—— (ed.), *De musica mensurata, the Anonymous of St. Emmeram* (Bloomington, Ind., 1990).

ZIINO, AGOSTINO, 'Polifonia "arcaica" e "retrospettiva" in Italia centrale: nuove testimonianze', *Acta musicologica*, 50 (1978), 193–207.

—— 'Polifonia nella cattedrale di Lucca durante il XIII secolo', *Acta musicologica*, 47 (1975), 16–30.

Index